The Struggle for Rural Mexico

THE STRUGGLE FOR

RURAL MEXICO

Gustavo Esteva

with the collaboration of
David Barkin
Alejandro Betancourt
Oscar Colman
Andrés Lambert
Rosa Miriam Ribeiro
Javier Rodriguez

Bergin & Garvey Publishers, Inc.
Massachusetts

First Published in 1983 by
Bergin & Garvey Publishers, Inc.
670 Amherst Road
South Hadley, Massachusetts 01075

3456789   056   987654321

Printed in the United States of America

Library of Congress Cataloging in Publication Data

Esteva, Gustavo.
  The struggle for rural Mexico.

  Translation of: La batalla en el México rural.
  Bibliography: p.
  Includes index.
  1. Land reform—Mexico. 2. Peasantry—Mexico.
3. Mexico—Rural conditions. I. Title.
HD1333.M6E7713 1983   333.3'1'72   82-24447
ISBN 0-89789-025-6

Contents

Appendices

Note to the English Edition

From the date on which this book was circulated at the Fifth World Congress on Rural Sociology, I have received many suggestions to correct, enrich, and modify it. I must mention, very specially, the intelligent observations made by Steven E. Sanderson.

It must also be noted that during this period the rural situation in Mexico has undergone significant changes. The exceptional results of the 1981 harvest, associated with the implementation of the Mexican Food System (SAM), may be seen as a reversion of the trends observed during the previous decade.

After careful consideration I concluded that to introduce the changes that were being proposed or that I considered to be pertinent would mean writing a completely different book. If I did so, surely the value of this one—as introduction to a variety of subjects—would be lost: such subjects as rural Mexico, the recent debate over *campesino* economy, and alternatives for rural development under current perspectives, among others.

Therefore, for this edition I have limited myself to correcting some obvious mistakes in the first edition. Likewise, I have added two appendices: one is my interpretation of the recent evolution of events, particularly the SAM, and the other includes a short bibliography of English-language titles about Mexico.

ACKNOWLEDGMENTS

This book was first translated for English-speaking participants at the Fifth World Congress on Rural Sociology (held in Mexico City, August 1980), by a group of members of the Universidad Autónoma Metropolitana—Unidad Xochimilco, under the coordination of Carlos Rozo.

For the present English edition, coordinated by Leonor Corral, the translation was reviewed and revised by David Castledine, Linda Finegold, Leslie Geller, Maria Ortiz, and Georgeanne Weller, and was typewritten and proof-read by Clara Hurtado with the assistance of Dolores de Lozano.

—G.E.

"Don't beg for anything. Demand what's rightfully ours. What he should have given me but never did . . . Make him pay dearly, my son, for having forgotten us."

The road climbed up and sloped down: it climbs up or slopes down according to whether you are arriving or leaving. When you leave, it climbs up; when you arrive, it slopes down.

—Juan Rulfo
Pedro Paramo

Foreword

Dr. Rodolfo Stavenhagen, Chairman of the Organizing Committee for the Fifth World Congress on Rural Sociology, conceived the idea of preparing a book on rural Mexico as part of the preliminary activities for this event, which was to take place in Mexico City 7–12 August 1980. For the first time, the Congress was to be held in a Third-World country and, moreover, one with a long agrarian history. It was planned to allow for field trips to different parts of rural Mexico where diverse aspects of rural problems and modes of social organization of labor could be observed. It was thus deemed advantageous for the participants, especially those coming from other countries, to be handed a summary of Mexico's rural history and present situation.

Towards the middle of 1979 Dr. Stavenhagen invited me to coordinate this project. I accepted with a great deal of enthusiasm but not enough forethought. Soon the difficulties of the task became apparent. A comprehensive *objective* synthesis of rural Mexico based on rigorous studies can only be made if the necessary information is available, but in Mexico it is glaringly absent. For many reasons, discussion of this subject is always highly charged with ideology, which limits the possibility of a deep, scientific study of our own reality.

Getting information on the rural areas of Mexico often involves some kind of metaphysical search, something like looking for a non-existent black cat in a dark room. In spite of recent efforts and publications produced by the Secretaría de Programación y Presupuesto, it is important to recognize that information on the rural situation in Mexico is very inadequate. In fact, there is not one group of statistical data that can be fully relied on. At every step, sources contradict each other. Frequent changes in methodology and obvious errors make comparisons over time impossible. At present, the situation is even more serious. The second most recent census was taken in 1970; another was taken in 1980, and several sectorial censuses in 1981. Apparently the quality of the later information is better, but unfortunately it was not available at the time the English edition was being prepared. The 1970 census cannot be compared to previous ones, since for electoral reasons it was taken at a period in the agricultural year different from the others. Obviously, then, information obtained on rural production units and workers was distorted. Furthermore, the last direct research project, with back-up surveys, was also carried out more than ten years ago and was based on the census of 1960. This has been used up to now as the basis for many studies of rural conditions, although it is evident that this study, and the census on which it was based, cannot pretend to give a true picture of rural Mexico today, particularly in view of the profound changes that have taken place over the last decade.

In order to deal with these problems, a method was required that would reduce the weight of quantitative analysis. In addition to relying on more dependable statistics, an attempt was made to supply data on the present situation through averages from the last decade. Although averaging erroneous figures does not eliminate errors, we felt that in this way it would be possible to focus on structural and global aspects that would be more likely to correspond to reality. Greater weight was given to historical data. Although here, too, the picture was rather discouraging, some important work and sufficiently proven facts afford the researcher a certain amount of security with which to work. For the sake of brevity, sources and methods used have not been given for all figures quoted. Some of this information will be found in the appendices.

I have attempted to be brief, in view of the aims of the book, and any repetitions would seem to be out of place. They have been retained, however, because the book was written in what might be called a "spiral form"—that is, gradually going deeper into the main points. I hope in this way to facilitate comprehension, rather than to become tedious.

In order to get the task under way, a group of research workers devoted much of their time to the project. For several months we had weekly analysis and discussion meetings to clarify our ideas and solve some of the specific problems involved in the preparation of the book. Individual researchers wrote the first draft of certain chapters: Part One, Chapter 1, was done by Alejandro Betancourt; Andrés Lambert did the following three; in Part Two, Oscar Colman prepared the first two chapters, Rosa Miriam Ribeiro the third, and David Barkin the fourth. Alejandro Betancourt's help was decisive in gathering and processing the information, as was Javier Rodríguez's in completing the book, and Víctor Palacio's in revising it.

I was responsible for the general coordination of the project, for the complete formulation of some chapters, and for the integration and editing of the final draft of the text. However, I wish to emphasize that preparation of the book was made possible through the constant sharing and participation during our weekly meetings. At the same time I accept responsibility for the shortcomings, limitations, and inadequacies of my own work. I cherish the hope that this book will encourage other researchers to carry out further studies—more profound, more extensive, and more rigorous than this one—on conditions in rural Mexico. Working on this study has made me more aware than ever before of the seriousness of our lack of material on the subject.

Gustavo Esteva
Director, Fondo de Cultura Campesina A.C.
Mexico City

Introduction

The homeland of the Mexican people is extremely rich, but harsh.

Vast resources lie in the subsoil. Frequently these have been exploited with more voracity than judgment, but even today they remain inexhaustible and unexplored. A much larger population than the present one could find sustenance and room for development with such a variety of soils and climates. However, Mexico has been, and still is, a poverty-stricken, hungry nation.

Nature, generous in the distribution of wealth throughout this land, has shown itself unwilling to relinquish that wealth: reaching it has challenged the strength and imagination of Mexico's inhabitants. A difficult orography obstructs communication and the integration of the country, emphasizing all the more the imbalance of natural conditions. Of Mexico's few rivers, some tend to overflow their banks, and others are full only from time to time. Deserts and arid or semiarid areas occupy two-thirds of the land. An erratic climate characterizes most of the arable land. Thus, Mexicans have had to surmount great difficulties in order to conquer the natural wealth of their country and transform it into something capable of satisfying their needs. The very magnitude of such wealth in the soil and subsoil has also awakened the greed of Mexicans and foreigners who have disputed the right of the resident people to use the land for their own benefit.

The history of rural Mexico is one of constant violence. This history has been described as an eternal battle to overcome a hostile environment by adapting it to the needs of its inhabitants. And it has become an intense and permanent battle between those making this effort and others who dominate them.

Many Indian societies of Prehispanic Mexico had already reached the stage that analysts of human evolution call "high culture." As a result of the agricultural surplus already being produced, they developed more advanced political structures and many different crafts.

In this type of society, as is well known, man is not thought of as an island. Man is family, clan, tribe. The idea of loneliness as presently conceived of and felt in the Western World would perhaps have been horrifying and alien to the Aztecs, the most developed state in Prehispanic Mexico.

Agriculture was virtually the only basis for development in these societies. The Aztecs were basically *campesino*-soldiers until their migration stopped in 1325. During the next two centuries they became citizen-soldiers capable of exerting an aggressive despotism over other tribes and even over themselves. But they never ceased to be *campesinos:* their lives were inseparably related to agriculture.

At the beginning of the sixteenth century, during the first two decades of the Spanish Conquest, the conquerors were determined to destroy the close-knit social community of the Indians. Although this resulted in the Indians' loss of some of their customs and traditions, it also meant that the Indians acquired a common objective: to fight for the survival of their own communities. The Spaniards, concerned only with their own immediate interests and the demands of colonial government, not only took the agricultural surplus and available wealth but also took over the forces of production without providing for their replacement.

Historical research has convincingly shown the predatory nature of colonization. Estimates of the size of the Indian population at the time of the Spanish Conquest vary between 7 and 25 million. But whatever the figure, it dwindled to a little more than 1 million during the next century. Famine and plague partly explain this decrease, but the major cause was the systematic genocide of entire tribes as well as the irrational and inhumane exploitation and subjugation of the Indian population. Evidence of this is provided by the different methods of self-destruction adopted by Indian society in order to avoid this kind of aggression—measures such as birth control, systematic abortion, infanticide, and mass suicide.

The growing shortage of labor available to the Spaniards, who were already suffering from a scarcity of supplies, together with more and more persistent resistance from the Indian communities, forced the colonial administration to relent in its rule. Thus the structure of this period was shaped over a long period, defined by the coexistence of two apparently separate concerns. On the one side were the Indian communities, which had managed to maintain their own social and productive organization, while bound at the same time to the Spanish Crown through tribute exacted from them (initially through Aztec noblemen). On the other side were the Spaniards, later *criollos* and occasionally *mestizos,* who worked directly with the productive units, most of which were in the form of *haciendas.* These two systems had a common denominator: the agricultural worker.

The communities were self-sufficient; any surplus was paid as tribute. The provision of labor was a part of this tribute and, together with laborers from other places, formed the basis of the maintenance and development of Spanish exploitation. The actual conditions of the rural workers varied from one extreme, that of "slave," to the other, wage earner, with different kinds of serfdom in between. This wide range reflected the complex situation of a period in which Mexican society was gradually integrated into the world market, then in the process of formation. However, the dialectic between community and *hacienda* that characterized this development lasted beyond the colonial period and was permanently associated with the omnipresence of the church.

Again, unconfirmed figures estimate that half the population of five million, at the beginning of the nineteenth century, was Indian. A quarter of this was made up of *castas*—the result of the mixing of different ethnic groups. There were about one million *criollos*, seventy thousand white Europeans, and some six thousand black Africans.

In 1810, the year of independence, the Indian communities, in spite of foreign domination, had managed to safeguard for their own exploitation about 18 million hectares. Many of the workers on some ten thousand *ranchos* covering more than 70 million hectares maintained community organization among themselves. Approximately 100 million hectares were declared wasteland. The *peón* of the *hacienda*, who suffered the disadvantages of both "slave" and wage earner, was still struggling for survival and development within the social structure of his own community, which itself was in constant conflict.

In the fifty years following independence, the productive structure collapsed, and economic growth came to a halt. Commercial agriculture, controlled by Spaniards and *criollos*, entered a recession. For the recently emerging capitalists, the land was a source of rent or collateral, but rarely was investment for production made. Their business activities were centered on mining, commerce, speculation, and investment in nonproductive real estate, and generally took the form of commercial capital. During this period, the rural communities achieved a certain degree of autonomy, though there was neither stability nor development. There was no political power capable of controlling them effectively, although they constantly had to face plundering and expropriation. Many uprisings marked the constant struggle of these communities against the *hacienda*, which remained throughout the century the principal form of rural productive organization. However, these uprisings merely served, and then not always, to ensure the necessary production for their own needs and survival as social organizations.

From 1867 to 1876, during the period of the restoration of the republic, the conditions for a democratic-liberal organization of the Mexican people were established. Confiscation of the Catholic church's immense wealth and disregard for the system of collective property of

Indian communities were the results of a decision to open the way for small and medium-size agricultural holdings, a pattern modeled on that in use at the time in North America. The sudden intrusion on *campesino* lands of individuals and enterprises taking .over productive development, along the lines of the North American model, caused many revolts, which were severely suppressed.

Under Porfirio Díaz's dictatorship, access to the land was opened up for new farmers at the expense of the *campesinos*. *Ejidos* and communities continued to be disbanded, since they could be legally expropriated by simple administrative procedures. In order to take over uncultivated areas, *compañías deslindadoras* ("boundary-setting companies") were formed under new laws authorizing them. One of their tasks was to encourage the immigration of foreigners. From 1877 to 1910, these companies promoted the distribution of more than forty thousand title deeds, accounting for almost 40 million acres of land. Since the *hacendados* were able to participate in the definition of boundaries, those most affected were the communities and small holdings whose land was taken over together with uncultivated areas by these companies. In less than two decades (1876–1894), one-fifth of Mexican land fell into the hands of fifty owners and the number of *haciendas* was tripled.

By 1910, 12 million, out of a total population of 15 million, worked in agriculture. Some eight thousand *haciendas* belonging to an even smaller number of owners covered 113 million hectares. These *haciendas* employed about 4,500 administrators, 3,000 tenants, and 3 million *peones acasillados* and *peones aparceros*. There were 50,000 *rancheros* with 10 million hectares, and 110,000 smallholders with 1.4 million hectares. Some 150,000 Indian landholders occupied about 6 million hectares (12 million less than in 1810); these *comuneros,* together with their families, formed a population of approximately one million (50 percent of the nation's total Indian population). Half of the population dwelt in 57,000 villages, which were controlled by the *haciendas* and *ranchos*. The other half lived in 13,000 "free villages"; they were subjected to many varied forms of exploitation, such as seasonal work as *peones* in the *haciendas*. Thus, less than 1 percent of the population owned 90 percent of the land and more than 90 percent of the rural population was denied access to it.

In 1910 the impoverished *campesinos,* who a century before had made independence possible by seeking liberation, again looked for freedom; this led to a generalized popular insurrection, which toppled the dictatorship of Porfirio Díaz. They were the main initiators of a vast social movement which seemed to have arisen initially without them but in which the *campesino* armies were soon to become a dominant force. Their military hegemony, however, was not capable of turning into political power and withered away.

Between one and two million people died between 1910 and 1920; i.e. approximately 10 percent of the populaton (apparently no modern revolution, or for that matter any other, has had such a high death rate). The 1910 population and production growth rates were not equaled until 1920. Violence increased regional and sectional differences. The number of agricultural workers increased, but their production and income decreased. Petroleum and mineral production, in the hands of American and British interests, showed such rapid and sometimes spectacular increases that by 1920 these products figured among the principal exports. Industrial, business, and urban centers in general came through it all relatively strengthened. Per capita agricultural production increased in the north of the country, and in the northeast, where the largest *haciendas* under the Porfirian dictatorship had been located. However, in the rest of the country it decreased, especially in the central states, precisely where the *campesino* insurrection had been most intense and persistent. Although many *campesino* communities recovered their land, particularly in the State of Morelos, the overall concentration of agricultural property remained virtually unchanged.

The historical definition of modern Mexico, embodied in the Constitution of 1917, did include some of the main historical *campesino* demands, but the *campesinos* have been fighting ever since to have them satisfied in full. The history of rural Mexico in this century is largely one of confrontation between these historically based claims and privately owned commercial agriculture, which, in turn, is in permanent conflict with the *campesinos* over control of productive resources. Up until the 1930s, the model of Porfirian *haciendas* persisted, with changes of ownership and organization but no structural changes. From 1934 to 1940, under the Lázaro Cárdenas administration, more than 20 million hectares were redistributed among the *campesinos*—almost twice as many as during the preceding twenty years. Agricultural production increased at a rate of 5 percent per year and the *campesino ejidos*, who by 1940 occupied almost half of the land available for cultivation, went through a period of great innovation and unexpected growth. In this decade, privately owned commercial agriculture underwent advances and setbacks as a result of both the varying *campesino* strengths and the changes taking place in national and international policies. After World War II, an agricultural transformation, concentrated in specific areas, took place. This gave privately owned commercial agriculture a clear hegemony, fitting smoothly into the overall process of the internationalization of capital so characteristic of the last decades of world evolution, while the economy of the *campesino* declined. After a few years, more than half of all production and around 70 percent of agricultural and cattle-raising activities were concentrated on one-tenth of the agricultural and cattle-raising land. The rural population represented just over a third of the total population (as against 65 percent in 1940) and was declared the poorest sector of Mexican society.

After 1965, the rural crisis inherent in this process became more evident. In the 1970s, 25 million tons of grain had to be imported. In order to meet the demands of 1980, a quarter of all basic foodstuffs required had to be imported. And in spite of this, over half the population suffers from serious malnutrition. As the crisis increases, so does *campesino* mobilization, with the consequent growth of unrest in rural areas and continual clashes between antagonistic groups fighting for control of the resources of production. Not a day passes without casualities from these struggles.

This book will attempt to analyze the origin, content, and possible outcome of this story of extraordinary and constant violence.

PART ONE

THE FRAME FOR THE CONFLICT

This section deals with the context and background of the struggle for rural Mexico.

First, some international comparisons are necessary in order to situate the country within a world context and to highlight some of the inequalities.

The first chapter on rural production and population gives basic information on the rural scene. In particular it describes for whom the *campesinos* actually work, i.e., the final recipients of their production. Following this, information is given on what they do (the kind of crops they cultivate), and how they do it (what kind of resources they have available). The chapter concludes with a brief statistical account of their living conditions.

The next two chapters give some points of reference for understanding the struggle for rural Mexico. The threads of the struggle for control of resources (the social conflict) and of the struggle for transforming them (the technological struggle) have become inextricably interwoven in the web of history. However, for the sake of description and analysis, these have to be examined separately. Thus, the second chapter highlights the changes since the Mexican Agrarian Reform which have led to the present forms of land tenure in this country. The third chapter describes the so-called "Green Revolution" which has been associated with the technological development of the last four decades.

The fourth and last chapter describes government intervention in rural evolution. The governmental attitude, as an expression of the forces at play, provides a precise and necessary framework of the existing social dynamics in rural Mexico.

1

RURAL PRODUCTION AND RURAL DWELLERS

MEXICO: SOME INTERNATIONAL COMPARISONS

Indicator	In the world	In the Third World	In Latin America
Territorial extension	13	8	3
Length of coast lines	5	2	1
Population	12	7	2
Production and resources			
Gross National Product	17	4	3
Oil and gas reserves	4	2	1
Electricity	17	4	2
Mining (excluding oil)	21	4	2
Agriculture and cattle production	9	4	2
Fishing production	26	13	4
Industrial production			
Communication network			
Length of highways	18	4	3
Length of railway systems	14	3	3
Airports (passengers/km)	13	2	2
Licensed vehicles	14	3	3
Telephones	15	2	2
Radio receivers	8	2	2
Television receivers	13	1	1
Newspapers	7	4	2
Social indexes			
Per capita production	60	29	11
Population growth rate	4	8	3
Life expectancy at birth	43	16	10
Physicians per inhabitant	61	25	11
Hospital beds per inhabitant	176	147	41
Mortality rate	50	45	21

PRODUCTION AND WHERE IT GOES

Mexico is among the leading food-producing countries.
It is among the first fifteen in the world. In 1980
its production per capita was higher than the nutritional level generally considered as the minimum for
subsistence: 2,750 calories and 80 grms of protein
per person per day.

However, Mexico is not using this productive
capacity to feed her own people. In the same year,
1980, more than a quarter of basic food requirements had to be imported. Even this rate of importing did not assure the recommended minimum of calories and proteins for half the population. Almost
90% of the rural population suffers from a severe
deficiency of calories and protein; a quarter of
the entire Mexican population subsists on from 25%
to 40% below the recommended minimum levels. Some
rural areas are on the verge of starvation.

This evident contradiction between food production and consumption is a result of the way in which
productive resources are used and distributed.

   -Mexico exports a significant volume of food,
    some of high nutritional value. In economic
    terms, the value of sales to other countries
    represents from 10% to 15% of total agricul-
    tural and cattle raising production.

   -Food products for internal consumption are
    not evenly distributed. 3.5% of the popula-
    tion consumes more than 4,000 calories per
    person per day and another 16% between 3,000
    and 4,000. At the other extreme, a fifth of
    the population consumes daily less than 2,000
    calories per person and never eats meat, eggs
    or wheat bread. 40% of the population never
    drinks milk; 70% never eats fish.

Thus, about half the agricultural and cattle
production of Mexico goes to foreign consumers
or to a select minority of the population. The
other half feeds the rest of the population and
satisfies the industrial demand for raw materials.

Looked at from another point of view, agricultural and cattle raising production, apart from its
function of supplying foodstuffs in the way described
above, generates foreign exchange and finances urban
development. In spite of the increasing need for
importing food, the agricultural and cattle raising
commercial balance remains favorable. Likewise,
different economic mechanisms (commercial, financial
and fiscal) facilitate the transfer of rurally produced resources to other agents and sectors of the
economy.

Present day tendencies of agricultural and
cattle raising production in Mexico illustrate the
conflict between the revenue producing areas -aimed
at export or high-income levels- and those areas
whose production corresponds to the basic needs of
the people. This conflict has been present throughout the country's history.

- Three centuries of colonial exploitation meant
  that the needs of the majority of the people
  were neglected in favor of the demands made
  by the metropoli or the colonizers. Thus the
  system of internal production was severely
  upset, with the result that the Indian population had to face increasing difficulties
  for their own subsistence. Towards the end of
  this period, in 1786, the hunger suffered by
  the vast majority of the population became
  starvation; approximately one hundred thousand
  Mexicans died (out of a population of 6 million)
  and many of those who survived did so by eating
  weeds and roots. Alexander von Humboldt, visiting this country said: "Mexico is the land of
  inequality." The Bishop of Valladolid added to
  this observation by remarking that in Mexico
  there were only two groups: "those who have
  nothing and those who have everything." The
  first group encompassed five million Indians,
  mestizos and mulattos, and one million whites;
  the second group, 20 thousand Spaniards and
  10 thousand *criollos*.

- The War of Independence took many lives and
  reduced the value of agricultural production
  by half. During the first three or four decades of turbulent independence -between
  1821 and 1850 there were 50 different govern-

ments- agricultural activity was directed
towards local consumption, i.e. each region produced only according to its own
requirements, in conditions of extreme
poverty.

- After losing half of her territory and after
suffering two foreign invasions, Mexico tried
to organize herself into a liberal republic.
During the Restoration of the Republic, and
in the 30 years of dictatorship which followed
that attempt, local subsistence production was
again disrupted by the development of commercial exploitation directed towards domestic
or international markets.

- Throughout the present century, the conflict
between opposite tendencies of production has
been constantly felt. During the period of
great revolutionary activity, agricultural
production was again concentrated on local
and regional needs, while commercial production decreased. However, at the beginning of
the '30s the insufficiency of domestic food
production became even more dramatic and in
the following ten years, grain imports made
up between 10% and 15% of basic foodstuffs
while, at the same time, exports increased.
Between 1950 and 1965 when the profit criteria coincided to a certain extent with domestic priorities, self-sufficiency was rapidly achieved. There was even an excess of ex-
portable basic products though internally
the consumption of most of the population
was still below average. After 1965, however,
domestic needs were again relegated to a
lower priority in view of the Mexican economy's
growing relationship with a new international
division of labor. This division assigned
Mexico the task of exporting meat, fruit and
vegetables, while importing grains and internally consuming some processed food. This
last process shows the tendencies of production over the past few years until 1980.

CROPS

Mexican agriculture has historically been dedicated to, and still is associated with, the production of grains, regardless of new tendencies.

Precolonial Mexicans cultivated corn. They also produced beans, chile and squash, used cactus plants, and gathered cocoa and fruits. They raised turkeys and dogs for consumption, hunted and fished.

During the Colonial Period, the structure of production underwent crucial changes. Wheat was food mainly for the Spaniards, but only when they took over responsibility for its cultivation did it begin to cover vast areas, especially in the central regions of the country. Sugarcane, coffee, tobacco, cotton and other commercial products aimed at the metropolitan market were also developed. Products based on dyewoods came to occupy an important place among those sent to this market. Livestock increased notably and was used for transportation and agriculture, and to assist in mining activities, as well as for the rawhide and leather export trade. At the end of the Colonial Period, the outstanding areas of production were corn cultivation, in the hands of the Indians, more or less integrated sugar plantations, single crop plantations, and the large cattle *haciendas*. The stability of the agricultural and cattle *hacienda* depended largely on their ability to produce for the external market in times of plenty, while maintaining their self-sufficiency in times of crisis. During the first fifty years of Independence, commercially-based agriculture decreased and crops were directed at local and regional markets.

This situation changed drastically under the Porfirian dictatorship when the land of the *campesinos* passed into the hands of the *hacendados*. These then used the land to satisfy the needs of the domestic market by supplying corn, wheat, barley, sugarcane and other products. As the *hacendados* turned towards the external market, they concentrated on cattle and the production of coffee, rubber, *henequén* (Mexican agave) and sugarcane.

The first decades of the revolutionary period emphasized internal food needs while at the same time consistently developed crops for exports. These were cotton, fruit and market vegetables, coffee, tobacco, sugarcane, chick peas and cattle, products which came to hold an important place in exports during the second half of this century.

After 1950, there was spectacular progress in the production of grains for fodder and some oil seeds, as well as certain fruits and market vegetables; cattle and aviculture also flourished. Basic crops showed a significant increase at the end of the '50s and beginning of the '60s, and even though since 1965 this has not been the case, they still play an important role.

The structure of agricultural and cattle raising production in the last 20 years has been indicated in Table I, while Table II illustrates the production value of the ten main products in the past decade.

TABLE I

PRODUCTION STRUCTURE BY TYPE OF PRODUCT (1960-1980)

Item	Percentage of production value
Basic food products (corn, wheat, rice and beans)	26
Fruit and market vegetables	18
Oil seeds	6
Fooder	6
Agro-industrial produce	16
Other grains	0.5
Meat, milk and eggs	27.5
TOTAL	100.0

Source: Data taken from *Dirección General de Economía Agrícola, Secretaría de Agricultura y Recursos Hidráulicos.*

TABLE II

MAIN CROPS (1970-1980)

Product	Value (in millions of pesos)	Percentage of value of agricultural and cattle production
Corn	92 713	14.56
Feather cotton	26 000	6.03
Sugarcane	25 102	5.82
Wheat	23 231	5.39
Coffee	21 236	4.93
Sorghum	25 893	6.01
Oranges	16 632	3.86
Green alfalfa	20 818	4.83
Tomatoes	14 718	3.42
Beans	18 206	4.23
TOTAL	284 549	66.00

Source: Data taken from *Dirección General de Economía Agrícola, Secretaría de Agricultura y Recursos Hidráulicos.*

Up until the last century, almost a third of Mexican territory was covered by forests. During the present century this proportion has decreased to the point where forests cover only one fourth of the land. This trend continues as the result of the irrational exploitation of wooded areas as well as their destruction to obtain agricultural and grazing lands. Although the country has great quantities of high quality forestry resources, their exploitation has not yet become an important element in the overall production framework. At present, the value of silviculture production represents about 5% of the total agricultural and cattle production. Mexico has never been an important exporter of forest-based goods, apart from wood dyes during the Colonial Period. In fact, it must even import to cover its needs; 90% of its paper requirements, for instance are imported.

RESOURCES

It is estimated that Mexico has about 30 million
hectares of arable land, i.e. just under half
a hectare of land per person. But only 18 million
hectares are under cultivation: 9% of the national
territory. A quarter of them have irrigation systems, while the rest are at the mercy of uncertain
rainfall.

Improved seeds, fertilizers and other agroche-
mical inputs are used in less than 40% of the cultivated areas, but in more than 60% of the irrigated areas. Approximately 150,000 tractors with a
total of ten million horsepower are available, the
majority of these being concentrated in 10% of the
exploited areas. In half of these areas only animal
power is used.

A little more than a third of the national territory is covered by natural grassland, tropical
meadows, irrigated meadows and fodder crops. According to the 1970 adjusted census figures, the livestock population of the country consists of: 28 million cattle, 6 million horses, 11 million pigs, 8
million sheep, 9 million goats, 3 million mules, 3
million donkeys, 34 million egg-laying hens and
about 210 million chickens for consumption.

Cattle raising is mainly extensive and inefficient. The rate of cattle production, for instance,
is only about 13% or a third of that of developed
countries. On an average, milch cows produce around
500 liters per annum each, which is approximately
one tenth of the average yield in European countries.

Of the 196 million hectares which make up the
total of the national territory, 140 million are
"potentially exploitable." Half of this territory is
in hands of individuals, while the other half is in
hands of groups (ejidos or communities). The total
area "potentially exploitable" is distributed as
follows: 16% cultivation; 52% meadows and permanent
grass lands; 14% hills or woods, and 18% other lands.
The average size of the lands "potentially exploitable" is 134 acres; 0.5% of them have more than
5,000 acres and they occupy almost half of the terri-

tory, while 25% of the areas "potentially exploitable", have less than one hectare (with 0.1% of the
surface area), and 26% have from one to 5 hectares
(with 0.5% of the surface area).*

According to the 1970 census figures, in that
year there were 3'284,000 units of production in the
140 million hectares of land available for exploitation. This area was equally distributed between *ejidos* and privately exploited land; however, there
were 2 122,000 *ejidatarios*; 825,000 private properties of less than 5 hectares and 337,000 with more
than 5 hectares. In 1970, the investment per private
unit was 194,000 pesos and per *ejidal* unit, 32,000.00
pesos. The horsepower available on private property
was almost three times more than in *ejidal* lands.

RURAL POPULATION AND PRODUCERS

It has been estimated that about 40% of the population still lives in rural areas (villages of fewer
than 2,500 inhabitants). Distribution is almost e-
qual between men and women. The age hierarchy is as
indicated on Table III.

Using the system of land tenure, the rural population can be divided as follows:

- About two million heads of families have 95
  million hectares in about 25,000 *ejidos* or
  Indian communities, within the system of
  collective property, in which individual or
  collective use of the land prevails.

- About one million heads of families occupy
  83 million hectares under private ownership.

- Around half a million heads of families own
  almost 20 million hectares of national land
  under a system of individual ownership (as
  colonos, in 783 agricultural colonies covering 7.5 million hectares, or as *nacionaleros*, in more than 10 million unlegalized
  hectares of land).

*The evident bias of these data, derived from the
1970 census on which they are based, is that they
consider as "units of exploitation" both those in
the hands of individuals and those belonging to groups.

TABLE III

DISTRIBUTION OF RURAL POPULATION BY AGE, 1970

Age group	Percentage	
Up to 4 years	16.94	
From 5 to 9 years	16.01	
From 10 to 14 years	13.26	
Subtotal		46.21
From 15 to 19 years	10.49	
From 20 to 29 years	15.12	
From 30 to 39 years	10.59	
Subtotal		36.18
From 40 to 49 years	7.40	
From 50 to 74 years	8.94	
Over 75 years	1.24	
Subtotal		17.58
TOTAL		100.00

Source: Data taken from the *Manual de Estadísticas Básicas Sociodemográficas* of the *Secretaría de Programación y Presupuesto*.

An estimate based on the 1960 census and on a direct study classified producers according to their income. This study showed that 3.5% of the units of production produced 54% of the total value of the agricultural product and owned about 70% of irrigated areas and of capital. This group absorbs two thirds of the total of the country's current input. Another 13% of exploited land provides a quarter of the value of production. In each of the units which make up this group a *campesino* family can find work and

subsistence. And finally, a fifth of the value of
production is provided by 83.5% of the exploited
lands (50% of them provide only 3% of the total value). Under these conditions, a family has to obtain
a great part of its income elsewhere in order to
subsist.

According to another analytical estimate, 3% of
the producers operate as owners of capital; 10% is
made up of agricultural workers (either as permanent
wage-earners or as migrant workers); another 10% is
made up of *campesinos* devoted exclusively to work
their land, and the remaining 77% are peasants who,
besides working their small holdings, give their
services as *jornaleros* in other agricultural concerns
or in other activities which provide them with some
additional income.

Average living conditions among the rural population have, among others, the following characteristics:

Literacy: 68%
Average schooling: 1.3 years
Life expectancy at birth: 45 years
Mortality rate: 9 per 1,000 inhabitants
Infant mortality rate: 74 per 1,000 live births
Daily consumption of calories: 2,100
Daily consumption of proteins: 62 grams
Income per capita: 162 dollars per annum
Family size: 6 members
Type of dwelling: 91% of families live in their
                  own house (with one or two
                  rooms)
Physicians per 1,000 inhabitants: 0.3
Availability of drinking water: 60% of the
                  villages
Availability of electrical energy: 76% of the
                  villages, where more than 6
                  million *campesinos* have no
                  electricity.

These figures are averages and obviously do not
show the great inequalities. Apart from the relative
lag of the rural population compared to the urban
one, it is important to keep in mind the differences
which exist among the inhabitants in rural areas.
These differences certainly exist between the rural
populations in the Northern and Central areas and in

the South; between Indian and non-Indian; between
those working on basic crops and those working on
commercial crops; among those on the high plateau,
in the fertile valleys, in tropical areas, dry areas,
those in the mountains and those on the coast; between those who enjoy relative peace and tranquility
and those who live in a climate of constant violence.
A substantial group of Mexicans live under conditions which no one in his right mind could describe
without indignation. Many tend to see these groups
as some kind of dead weight, alien to the modern
and go-ahead Mexico to be seen in cities. For others,
far from being a burden, they are an explanation,
a humiliating explanation for the country's moder-
nity.

2

THE MEXICAN AGRARIAN REFORM: AN UNFULFILLED DREAM, A CONTINUING NIGHTMARE, AN INCIPIENT PROJECT

There must be hundreds of definitions of agrarian reform, enough to fill an encyclopedia. Some people even claim that the agrarian reform has produced specialized literature rather than anything else. However, academic arguments on this subject no longer have any place.

In spite of all the technical and theoretical arguments which touch on the subject, there is wide agreement about the political nature of the processes of agrarian reform. It comes down to a political argument which reflects a social struggle for the control of productive resources. There are different explicit goals, different ways of seeing the process, and different procedures with varying characteristics. But above all, it is the historical context within which it developed that varies. Nevertheless, it is always a political process, whose origin, evolution and consequences depend on the correlation of the social forces involved.

Seen from this point of view, a large number of agrarian reforms have taken place in Mexico: each of them for a specific reason, with its own specific impact and its stages of conception, development, climax and death. Some of them have satisfactorily fulfilled their historical function. Nevertheless, and in contrast to what has happened in other countries, where long periods of stability have resulted after these political and social upheavals, in Mexico all of them have been inconclusive. Within each "final result" of one of these upheavals, the basis for the next conflict has always been present, tearing apart the apparent "consolidation." The reason for this is because not one of them has succeeded in resolving an ever present basic contradiction: the nature, social or private, of control of the country's productive resources.

It has been observed that in one dimension of
the problem, there has been an almost linear advancement in the agrarian evolution of Mexico, which peak-
ed in 1917 and 1938: this dimension refers to total
control over the national territory as an expression
of popular and national will, which rescued the original ownership of the land in the name of the nation. In this century Mexico finally succeeded in
taking over control, in modern terms, of its own
territory. She had to do this by building on the remains of the theocratic state of the first Mexicans,
on the inheritance of a colonial government (born
from an absolute monarchy, in the process of constituting a national state) and on the teachings in a
democratic-liberal tradition which eventually cost
the country half of its territory.

Yet this advance has not paralleled the development of another open-ended dimension of the problem:
the nature of the specific control over resources.
On the one hand, it has always been maintained, with
great vitality and vigour, that social control of
resources, together with their autonomous and democratic exploitation, should be in the hands of their
historical usufructuaries, the *campesinos*. But this
drive has never been able to defeat, on a stable
and permanent basis those wanting to achieve private
control over productive resources.

The *campesinos*' revolutionary force, shown in
the first decades of the history of agrarian reform
of this century, may be described in terms of an
unfulfilled liberal-anarchist dream. The anti-agrarian answer to the *campesinos*' struggle eventually
became the kind of agrarian developmentalism which
turned out to be a continuing nightmare: the effective and constant predominance of the forces that
support it has lost weight and scope every time an
attempt has been made to give the final blow and
get the job done, i.e., completely exclude peasants from production. Within the violent and conflic-
tive context which has characterized the whole
process, a solid attempt to give a modern social
form to the *campesino* quest has slowly begun to
emerge as a project proposing the last and final
phase: the social reform. Such an endeavour attempts to base itself on the present production
regime as the formula to solve its immediate contradictions, although it has set itself targets
and concepts that go well beyond this.

THE PAST

The instabilities and upheavals experienced in the history of rural Mexico result from the latent and silent, or explosive and uncontrolled nature of a struggle whose evolution has been associated with the fate and conflicts of four main groups: *campesino* communities (Indian and non-Indian); market-oriented producers; small independent producers; and agricultural workers. Obviously each one of these groups has adopted different structures and ways of behavior -according to its historical, economic and social context.

During the entire Colonial Period, some of the precolonial communities, succeeded in preserving life styles and forms of organizing production that became their principal basis for survival. Even though their techniques and internal forms of organization showed unusual stability, the communities themselves were forced into constant transformation in order to adapt to a variety of outside pressures.

The control over the Indian population set the bases for the commercial exploitation of the land, oriented towards the metropolitan market and that of the new urban settlements undergoing an accelerated expansion (vis à vis the pace of the time). After experimenting with a great variety of forms of domination, rural colonial exploitation adopted *haciendas* as the predominant form of organization. Along with this a certain number of small independent producers emerged, who were never totally successful either productively or as a social group. These groups, however, fulfilled several social and economic functions within their context. Both of these forms of productive organization used agricultural workers in different ways: as "slaves", if the term is accepted, less and less throughout the period; "*peones acasillados*" (paid or unpaid); and "free" temporary or permanent workers, who one way or another were part of the tribute the communities paid to the *haciendas*.

The dynamics of the relationship between these various components tended to be resolved at a regional or local level and at the heart of the productive units. The Indian groups concentrated their efforts on their own communities and ethnic groups.

Colonial power successively or simultaneously exercised over them both centrifugal and centripetal
pressure that sometimes brought about their dispersal
and sometimes their cohesion. The *hacendados* lacked
authentic rural roots, since their principal interests lay in the *metropoli* or in the cities of New
Spain. The contradictions between *criollos* and
Spaniards in rural environments were in general an
extension of those of the urban world.

During the stagnation or recession of commercial
agriculture in the first fifty years of Independence,
some *haciendas* succeeded in consolidating themselves
as integrated productive structures. But the majority
of them tended to continue operating as commercial
enterprises -with great heterogeneity regarding the
forms of domination practiced. Communities tended to
remain committed to resistance and to progress in local or regional spheres. During this period, even
though the small independent producers barely survived, it is very likely that their numbers increased.
However, this period was characterized by the break-
down of rural productive mechanisms and a weakening
of the different forms of social organization of
rural life. This, in spite of the fact that the overall situation was geared towards the development of
local or regional production for self-consumption.

In the second half of the XIX century the communities underwent an acute process of decline, mainly due to the increased pressure exerted upon them
by the *haciendas*, as these progressively took on
their own commercial features. Communities lost importance as productive organizations when their relationship with the land, which had previously enabled them to survive, was weakened or destroyed.
Apart from those which succeeded in retaining or
reconquering their land, especially in the South and
Southeast of Mexico, the communities ceased to exist
as productive structures, even though they retained
different functions associated with the survival of
the population. The strengthening of the *haciendas*
went along with the development of small independent
producers (*rancheros*, small landowners, tenants) who,
at the beginning of the century, numbered approximately half a million. Although they tended to associate
their interests with those of the *haciendas*, very
often they were closer to the *campesinos* than to the
hacendados in the concrete organization of their

lives. As far as the *hacendados* were concerned, they were directly linked to the structure of urban power, and in continuous interaction with it, as their own interests became more diversified.

THE REVOLUTION ERUPTS

In 1910, when revolutionary violence broke out, a small nucleus of *hacendados* -less than 1% of the population- owned 97% of the land. The rural population had no land and worked as *peones acasillados*, laborers or 'slaves.' The agricultural, cattle raising and the agroindustrial *haciendas* were extensive rural corporations: one *hacienda* had seven million hectares under the control of one owner. The *hacendados*, both Mexican and foreign, lived luxuriously in provincial capitals, in Mexico City, in the United States or in Europe. Their administrators, foremen and accountants were in charge of the management of the *haciendas*. Labor supply in the *haciendas* increased more on the basis of *pegujal* than that of wages. The *pegujal* was a piece of land "granted" to the worker by the *hacendado*. It guaranteed enough food for the family's subsistence. The worker very seldom received his wage, since this returned to the hands of the *hacendado* through the *tienda de raya*. The "free" laborers, nevertheless -who did not have a home, a piece of land to cultivate, or a permanent job- already represented an increasing number among the rural population. They were the first, along with the "slaves", who enlisted in the revolutionary army, attracted by Emiliano Zapata's slogan of "*Tierra y Libertad*" (land and freedom). They were also fertile soil for the anarchist ideals which prevailed among the radical ideologies of that time, especially in the labor movement.

During the first years of revolutionary action, the historical content of the land workers' claims reinforced the unity of their action. Indians, *peones acasillados*, many small landowners, and agricultural workers from many different backgrounds, joined forces in the fight to recover the land. Nevertheless, these claims did not always include the elimination of the *hacienda* as a form of productive organization. For example, in Emiliano Zapata's "*Plan de Ayala*", the most important agrarian document of the Mexican Revolution, a proposal was made for the ex-

propriation, after compensation, of only <u>one</u> <u>third</u>
of the *latifundios*, as well as the return <u>of</u> *ejidos*
and communal lands. Apart from tactical considerations which might have influenced such a definition
of the Plan's goals it must be pointed out that the
campesinos were more concerned with recovering lands
which had been taken from the *ejidos* and the communities, than with the elimination of the *hacienda*
system.

In 1917, after seven years of revolutionary
struggle and violent disputes among the different
political factions, with between one and two million
casualties and many *haciendas* destroyed or abandoned,
the backbone of the Porfirian system of oppression
and exploitation finally gave way and in its place
the new Mexican State began to emerge.

The 1917 Constitution expressed the country's
new economic and socio-political aspirations, combining the liberalness of Juárez's 1857 Constitution
with the new social orientation of the State. It was
hoped through this new State to safeguard the people's rights and to ensure the construction of a
more just society by means of free education, labor
protection and agrarian reform. The latter was explicitly based on the principle of sovereignty, as
provided for in the 27the Article of the Constitution: "the ownership of land and water within the
limits of national territory, belong first and
foremost to the nation, which has had and has the
right to transmit this control to individuals in the
form of private property... the nation will have at
any time the right to impose on private property any
measures dictated by public interest, as well as to
regulate the utilization of natural resources that
can be appropriated in order to assure an equitable
distribution of wealth and the conservation of these
resources."

The Constitutional Congress had a large *campe-*
sino component: only two years before, the leaders
of the two largest revolutionary *campesino* armies
had symbolically occupied the presidential chair,
even if it were just to go back immediately to the
rural areas they controlled. In the following years
the Federal Government's power was progressively
consolidated despite constant competition with regional and local powers. This integration of the

federal power was always defined in agrarian terms:
the agreement between new and old *latifundistas*, who
were waiting for a chance to return and the agrarian
forces of the Revolution.

... AND STAGNATES

The *hacendados* were unable to oppose the revolution
with any unified power. They were able to survive
thanks to their ability to adapt to the new conditions by taking advantage of all contradictions and
difficulties among different revolutionary groups.
Thus, they were quickly able to form organic links
with the new power structure, while the *campesinos*
were unable to control the process for which they
had fought. From 1916 to 1920 "legalizations" were
issued for 334 *ejidos*, with a total surface area of
382,000 hectares. The 77,000 *ejidatarios* who benefited from this measure received less than five hectares each. The situation regarding land under "provisional ownership" was under heated discussion.
This involved between three to four million hectares
which had been occupied directly by the *campesinos*.
In order to appreciate the full meaning of these
figures better, it should be kept in mind that the
"*hacienda* system" covered some 113 million hectares.

From 1920 on, less emphasis was placed on the
radical agrarian reform proposed in the 27th Article
of the Constitution, and more on the development of
small or medium landholdings, under different forms
of ownership. Thus the question of the elimination
of the "*hacienda* system" was avoided through the
liberal clauses in the Constitution. In the areas
controlled by Zapata as well as in different regions of the country where radical groups were still
claiming land, real and profound changes in the
productive organization took place. Yet this was by
no means the general situation which was characterized by systematic blocking of *campesino* initiative.
In this way, along with the *ejidos*, which were
inevitably revived by local or regional *campesino*
power, the "*hacienda* system" persisted and small
holdings developed, both of which were more in line
with predominant interests of the groups which gradually took over complete power.

In fact, the purpose of returning the *ejidos*
was not only to make the *campesinos* exchange their
guns for plows. It was also to have the *ejido* fulfill a necessary function creating conditions for
the *campesinos* to complement their wage. The *ejido*
was intended to have a transitory nature; i.e. it
would be a type of nursery to breed farmers for
small or medium land holdings, who would then follow
the traditional capitalist mode of agricultural
development. Thus the trend to divide up the *ejido*,
which in turn accelerated its process of extinction,
was evident in the very first land legalization
processes.

During this period, the *campesinos* lacked any
kind of organization which would have enabled them
to give coherence and clarity to their specific
interests. But above all they lacked organizations
which would have made the other social classes take
heed of those interests. An example of the fundamental weakness of these organizations, which supposedly
represented the *campesinos*' interests at this time,
was the *Partido Nacional Agrarista*. It neither rose
to support direct opposition to the *hacendados*, nor
was it the *campesinos* who organized it. It was the
first political organization which explicitly and
vigorously advocated the need to continue agrarian
reform after the fighting during the Revolution came
to an end. Around 1924, it was the party with the
greatest political power. It was unable, however, to
draw up any concrete proposals: it relegated the
central problem of productive organization to a
second level and lacked specific proposals for implementing the 27th Article of the Constitution it
supposedly defended. It is not strange, therefore,
that the party gradually disappeared as a political
organization within a few years, as its leaders were
absorbed into government service. Something similar
happened to the *Confederación Nacional Agraria* which
in 1923 had broken away from the *Partido Nacional
Agrarista*. It too tended to follow the official
line. In 1924 the *Confederación Nacional Agraria*
proposed the voluntary break-up and redistribution
of the *haciendas* which, as was to be expected, came
to nothing.

In this context the *hacendados* were able to
successfully devise ways of controlling their properties. Often they achieved this by sharing them

with the revolutionary leaders. At the same time, the number of small independent producers rapidly increased. Some of them simply reassumed the functions they had had before the Revolution and after the liberal reform of the *República Restaurada*. Others emerged from the agrarian redistribution itself, as a direct consequence of the *pegujal*, and yet others came from the urban post-revolutionary world. All of them received varying kinds of support from the different governments which thus tried to avoid a radical confrontation with the *haciendas*.

Right up to 1934, agrarian reform was characterized by the restitution of lands to communities deprived of them by Porfirio Díaz. It was also characterized by the creation of new centers of population. Both these courses of action involved the expropriation of lands from some *haciendas*, thus reducing them to the constitutionally stipulated limits, i.e., 100 irrigated hectares or its equivalent in land under seasonal use. The legislating body exempted the agro-industrial units from expropriation and tried to regulate the administration of production on the lands given to the *campesinos*.

Both administrative measures and the legal declarations of this period highlighted two opposing concepts of the objectives of agrarian reform and of the social and economic functions of the centers of population. One point of view which saw the State as responsible for promoting social justice through the distribution of public wealth, simply tried to endow the *campesino* with some means of subsistence. The other point of view saw agrarian reform, under either *ejidal* or communal form, as the basis for supporting a collective system of land ownership and exploitation. Under this system agricultural and livestock technology could be developed; consequently it provided more rational and promising methods of production than the smallholding system of exploitation. The latter system had very little influence over agrarian reform during this period even though the *Comisión Nacional Agraria* issued a circular in 1920 which set out these concepts. This happened because the agrarian course of action at this time was more in line with the first *Ley de Ejidos* in 1920. This law established that all the lands given to a rural community -i.e. those given to *ejidos*- should be

divided into individual plots of land, the size of
which should be sufficient "to produce for those
working them twice the amount of the average local
wage." (This minimum was defined a little later as
plots of land varying from three to five irrigated
hectares or its equivalent on other types of land.)
Only forests, pasture grounds and water were to be
exploited collectively. In keeping with this, it was
established in 1927 that smallholdings could be as
much as fifty times the size of the individual *ejidal* plot of land. In 1925, along the same lines,
the *Ley de Riegos* directly promoted the formation
of a "rural middle class" as the strategic key to
the establishment of new irrigated areas and more
highly developed agriculture. The *Ley del Patrimo-
nio Parcelario Ejidal* in the same year, was created
to "protect" the *ejidatarios* by providing them with
individual title deeds, which could not be sold,
mortgaged or seized. This meant the definitive break
ing up of *ejidos* into plots.

Between 1917 and 1934, about 11 million hectares were divided into 6 thousand *ejidos* among nearly a million *campesinos*, giving them about 10 hectares each. Starting in the '20s the *Comisiones Nacionales de Irrigaciones y Caminos*, the *Banco Nacional de Crédito Agrícola* and four other regional *ejidal* banks, as well as a strong drive for rural education, resulted in active rural development.

Throughout this period, the *hacendados* were
losing effective political power. In 1931 they were
even denied the right to ask for legal protection
with regard to land expropriation. This fact, together with renewed *campesino* pressure, probably
explains the terms of the *Código Agrario*, which in
1934 tried to clarify the confusion created by the
proliferation of agrarian laws. The *Código* placed
a ceiling of fifty irrigated hectares or its equivalent on land under seasonal use as the maximum
surface of private property that cannot be distributed under the agrarian reform. This measure made land
available to *peones acasillados*, *peones aparceros*
and tenants previously excluded from land redistribution. The Code concentrated on the restitution of
ejidos to be assigned in the form of individual
plots of land, with a minimum surface area of four
irrigated hectares or its equivalent on land under
seasonal use. (This distinction between irrigated

and land under seasonal use was the most precise definition arrived at with regard to the quality of land
subject to agrarian reform).

It is evident that during this period the *campesinos*, apparent winners of the Revolution, did not
succeed in satisfying their aspirations. Most of
them had remained without access to the land and
those who had it, did not have the economic resources
for its adequate exploitation. In spite of this, or
probably because of this, at the end of the 1920s,
the faction that had succeeded in acquiring hegemony
within this revolutionary government decided that
the agrarian period of the Mexican Revolution had
come to an end, and that it was necessary to open up
the way for conventional modernization by stimulating small private properties. The anarchist ideal of
the *campesinos* fulfilling their aspirations by land
recovery and a return to their community organizations,
was strongly opposed by a model of agrarian development which came closer to the capitalist trends
observable in the rest of the economy. In order to
give coherence to such modernizing efforts, the dominant faction deemed it necessary to bring together
all the revolutionary groups which still maintained
their spheres of power, under one umbrella organization which was to be the *Partido Nacional Revolucionario*.

One of the *campesinos*' answers to the anti-
agrarian winds of the time took the form of a messi-
anic movement, the "*Cristero*" Movement. Its nature
and the alliances it established, which were paradoxically also anti-agrarian, meant that conflicts
with the Federal Power were reinforced, thus provok-
ing severe repression. Other movements, however, had
developed at the same time. Their strength at regional levels was felt on different occasions, and in
1926 they brought about the creation of the *Liga Nacional Campesina* which grouped together organizations from
15 states and claimed to represent 400 thousand *campesinos*. This League proposed a radical confrontation
with the *latifundistas*. It also tried to get involved in the laborers' struggle and looked for ways of
socializing the land and the means of production.
When invited to join the *Partido Nacional Revolucionario*, this coalition split and lost strength as an
independent group at the beginning of the '30s. How-

ever, the leaders of the League were the same *campe-sinos* that rallied and tried to redirect the country's social process by supporting Lázaro Cárdenas for President.

THE REVOLUTION MOVES INTO ACTION AGAIN...

Between 1934 and 1940, Lázaro Cárdenas' government redistributed 20 million hectares among 11,000 *eji-dos*, thus benefiting three quarters of a million *campesinos*, who received an average of 25.8 hectares each. In six years almost twice as much land was redistributed as compared to the immediately preceding period which was three times as long.

Under Cárdenas, the *ejido* became the pillar of the national agricultural economy, i.e. it occupied half the cultivated land. A decisive step forward in this new direction was taken in 1935, with the expropriation of the large agro-industrial enterprises, safeguarded until   then by a fear of affecting production. These enterprises were handed over as co-operative *ejidos* to the workers and *peones* who had practically turned them into fighting unions after demanding their expropriation by government.

The fact that the Cárdenas administration distributed many more hectares than all the previous revolutionary governments obviously reflected on the awakening of old agrarian revolutionary principles. During this period the strength of an increasing number of small independent producers began to be felt and most of the *hacendados* were either eliminated or forced to adopt defensive attitudes. All this was possible and even reinforced because of the support Cárdenas gave to the *campesino* movement and, above all, to the organization of production on a collective basis. In order to ensure greater organic integration of the social basis which could bring about agrarian redistribution, a Presidential decree in 1935, created the *Confederación Nacional Campesina*. During the following three years important movements took place. This even included the delivery of arms to the *campesinos* in order to defend redistributed lands. It also led to a Constitutional Congress of the Confederation, which was attended by many *campesino* organizations from throughout the

country. The agrarian redistribution itself,
a vigorous step towards the collective organization
of production, together with large supporting programs, were put into practice by means of a clear
understanding between *campesino* organizations and
federal political goodwill. In this way they were
successfully able to face opposing interests, i.e.
the ancient Porfirian *latifundistas*, new privately-
owned commercial agriculture, local and regional
structures of economic and political power, and
important national and international economic interests.

...AND FLOUNDERS ONCE MORE

The internal and external forces at the end of the
'30s and the beginning of the '40s brought about
the conditions which led to the checking of this
trend in the Mexican agrarian process. This happened
before there was time to consolidate the process or
to create a strong basis for its total development.
After 1937, the year of the most intense land redistribution (more than five million hectares)
Cárdenas administration began to decelerate the
pace of redistribution. In 1938, a government agency
was created to take care of the problems of small
landholders, the *Oficina de la Pequeña Propiedad*.
Although this agency was closed in 1940 because of
the conflicts it had generated, its actions were
significant, although quantitatively modest. In two
years it had taken 45,000 hectares from *campesinos*
and given them back to their previous owners.

    In order to understand the following period, it
would be helpful to glance at the balance of agrarian reform of the revolutionary governments up to
1940. For a quarter of a century, 1.7 million *ejidatarios* had received nearly 30 million hectares, i.e.
15% of the total national territory and 23% of the
total surveyed area. However, only a quarter of these
lands were suitable for agriculture and less than
5% irrigated; almost half were pasture land and a
fifth, forest. The surface area per person
increased in inverse proportion to its quality:
from 2.5 hectares in 1919 to almost 40 hectares in
1940; the average for this period was 17.5 hectares.
The total number of *ejidatarios* occupied more than

half of the agricultural land of the country, even though their lands were in general simply subsistence plots.

Small private properties showed spectacular increases in the 1930s, i.e. the number of holdings of less than five hectares was increased by 61% and their surface area by 136%. In 1940 there were almost one million rural land holdings along these lines, which accounted for one third of the total number of holdings in the country. Nevertheless, they occupied less than 1% of land covered by the survey (while the *ejidatarios* with 56.8% of land holdings occupied 22.4% of the total area). Private holdings from five to one thousand hectares (*ranchos*) represented one tenth of the holdings and 15% of the surface area (with an average of 69.8 hectares per holding). Finally, there were 9,697 holdings with more than 1,000 hectares; 1,472 with more than 10,000 hectares, and 301 of more than 40,000 hectares. These *haciendas* represented 0.3% of the holdings but owned more than 60% of the available land. The 300 owners of more than 40,000 hectares occupied nearly 32 million hectares, that is a quarter of the areas covered by the 1940 survey, and one sixth of the national territory.

In the 1930s, the number of private holdings of more than 1,000 hectares decreased by 27.6% and their total area by 22.6%; those of more than 10 thousand hectares decreased by 18.8% and their total area by 21.2%. As is obvious, *ejidos* and small properties were formed at the expense of the *haciendas*.

It is useful to take into account the geographical distribution of the large holdings. Half of the holdings with over 1,000 hectares were located in the Northern region and 17% in the Northern Pacific region. Also 61% of the holdings with more than ten thousand hectares were located in the North. There were none in Zapata's state: Morelos. Also in the North there was a concentration of *ranchos* (from one to five thousand hectares). A large number of these were also found in the Gulf states (16.1%) and in the Northern Pacific region (11.2%). As far as the *ejidos* were concerned, almost 40% were located in the central areas (where there were almost no holdings with more than 40 thousand hectares and few over 1,000 hectares) and just 20% in the North.

In 1940, the population of the *ejidos* was only 25% of the total population, one third that of villages with less than 10,000 inhabitants and 40% that of villages with less than two thousand five hundred inhabitants. In each *ejido* there was an average of 109 *ejidatarios*. In five states (Yucatán, Mexico, Morelos, Campeche and Nayarit) the population of the *ejidos* represented more than 40% of the total in the State.

In 1910, 0.2% of the active rural population owned 87% of the occupied property (60% of the total territory). In 1940, 0.3 of the owners had 61.9% of the areas covered by the survey (42% of the total). In 1910 the areas controlled by 8,431 *haciendas* (in the hands of a smaller number of owners) consisted of 113 million hectares. In 1940, there were 9,697 holdings with more than one thousand hectares which occupied nearly 80 million hectares.

In 1910 there were 48,633 *ranchos* that occupied 9.7 million hectares: an average of 199.4 hectares per *rancho*. In 1940, there were 280,639 *ranchos* (holdings from 1 to 5 thousand hectares) that occupied 19.7 million hectares with an average of 69.8 hectares per *rancho*.

In 1910 there were 109,378 small landowners. They occupied 1.4 million hectares, i.e. an average of 12.8 hectares. In the same year there were just over three million *peones acasillados, peones aparceros* and tenant farmers.

In 1940, 1.7 million *ejidatarios* had 30 million hectares (17.5 hectares per plot of land) while 928,593 private *minifundistas* had one million hectares (properties with less than five hectares).

In 1910, 91.3% of the active rural population lacked access to the land; by 1940, less than a third of the population found itself in that position. Even though half of the active agricultural population, 1.9 million people, was made up of agricultural *jornaleros*, many of them (about 700 thousand) *ejidatarios* or private *minifundistas* complemented their income by selling their labor.

This was the structure of land tenure when Cárdenas handed over the Presidency of the Republic to
Manuel Avila Camacho. Although it was by no means
clear that the efficiency of *ejidal* production was
inferior to that of private production, the fire
was rekindled once again.

Calles' comments on the agrarian reform as expressed ten years before, became current again:
"If we want to be honest with ourselves, we, the
children of the Revolution, have the obligation to
confess that agrarianism, in the way we have understood and practiced it up until now, has been a failure. The happiness of countrymen does not lie in a
plot of land, if they do not have the necessary
skills or tools to cultivate it. In this way, we are
only leading them towards disaster by creating false
hopes and encouraging their sloth... Until now we
have been handing out land left, right and center,
and all we have succeeded in producing is a horrifying commitment for the nation. We have to put a
stop to our failures. Each of the State governments
must set a limit within which those who still have
the right to ask for land, do so; but once the limit
is reached, not a word more should be said about the
matter. Then everyone must be assured of guarantees
in order to stimulate private investment and public
credit."

Calles' goals, interrupted by Cárdenas' agrarian system, began to take shape after 1940. In Avila Camacho's administration, land redistribution
slowly came to a halt. During the six years of his
government, the total of land distributed was the
same that Cárdenas had redistributed in only one
year: 1937 (about five million hectares). At the
same time collectivization, associated then with
campesino movement, was substituted for support to
small private holdings and in particular to modern
marketable agriculture.

Thus, while *ejidos* and communities began a
period of increasing deterioration -with few exceptions in time and space- *latifundios* or agribusiness were devoted to bringing about the "Mexican agricultural miracle." The 1940's saw the
dawn of vigorous infrastructure development. Much
of this was concentrated in the North of the Republic, precisely in the areas where large holdings,

haciendas and *ranchos* were found. In irrigation
projects, for example, more than 60% of public investment between 1940 and 1970 was channelled into the
North and North Pacific zones. This meant that only
in three States, where 20% of holdings with over
1,000 hectares were located but which had only 9%
of the *ejidos* and 6% of the *ejidatarios*, received
40% of the investments for irrigation purposes. This,
added to large programs of promotion (described in
the following two chapters) meant that these commercial farmers flourished in the '50s. Their links
with large urban capital grew and they developed
within the legal framework of the small private
holdings and the livestock *latifundios* (permitted as
a result of vague laws) or within the illegal system
of open or apparently open *latifundios* and the leasing of plots of land. These farmers acted politically through the *Confederación Nacional de la Pequeña
Propiedad* (incorporated into the popular sector of
the *Partido Revolucionario Institucional* the new
name for the old *Partido Nacional Revolucionario*),
or through employer organizations, formally excluded from political activity, but quite effective
pressure groups.

Both administrations, Miguel Alemán's (1946-52)
and Ruiz Cortines' (1952-58) redistributed about 3
million hectares, the equivalent of what Cárdenas
distributed in 1938, when he had already decelerat-
ed the pace.

Between 1940 and 1970 the country underwent a
demographic and economic transformation which quad-
rupled the population and inverted the rural-urban
integration balance: 65% of the total rural population in 1940 was already urban in 1970. The agrarian reform during this period was predominantly
conservative. This political bent supported small
and medium agricultural holdings based on the 1946
Constitutional reform, which once again extended to
100 hectares the maximum area of private property
that cannot be distributed under the agrarian reform. Government encouragement resulted in the
creation of private technological agricultural enterprises; the opening up of new irrigated lands
placed mainly in private hands, the construction of
infrastructure for communications and services,
scientific research on grains, the ample use of
credit for private activity, the individualization

of *ejidal* production and the dispersion of cooper-
ativist *ejidos*. In fact, since the idea was to bring
about a revolution in the productive apparatus in
order to raise productivity and achieve rapid growth
of production, the agrarian process had to be frozen
and not encouraged. Even though redistribution continued throughout these thirty years, important
changes did not take place with regard to the structure of land tenure. The 19 million hectares which
were redistributed throughout this period was land
of poorer quality and less extensive than that of
previous periods (the average plot of land was 36.1
hectares per *ejidatario*). Besides, this amount was
in some respects just an illusion, i.e. the redistribution stated in presidential resolutions and
statistically registered did not match the land actually handed over. At the beginning of 1970, there
were nearly 30 million hectares of land "redistributed" only on paper, because the presidential resolutions were still pending execution. It was possible
for this process to develop because of the decisive
participation of one element of the local and regional power structure which had begun to prosper since
the beginning of the Cárdenas period: the *cacique*.
The agrarian movement did in fact manage to bring
about the destruction of the old productive units
associated with the Porfirian *haciendas*. However, it
rarely succeded in providing alternatives by means
of the collective organization of the *campesinos*
which could substitute for these old units. Federal
support for this was necessarily limited, even in
Cárdenas' time, and it could not help the *campesinos'* economic limitations, or their lack of resources
that would enable them to adequately exploit the
lands given to them.

    Under these conditions, the *caciques* strengthened
their position in the rural communities as a cohesive
element for the production process but without organizing it. Their origin was varied, they could be an
ex - *latifundista*, a local merchant, an agrarian leader who led the fight for redistribution, a government
agent who took part in the agrarian process or in a
subsequent activity, etc. Little by little the *cacique* acquired specific functions, as an intermediary
between the *campesinos* on the one hand and the "national society" on the other. Some authors have
identified them as political intermediaries whose
function is to manipulate and control the *campesino*

groups, on behalf of federal or state power. For
others, the political function of the *cacique* has
been founded on a strictly economic basis as a supplement and as a condition for its performance. This
last option seems to come closest to reality. In
some cases their political functions work two ways:
the *cacique* acts as the *campesinos'* spokesman with
the authorities -in order to get public support- and
he also represents political authority to the *campesino* group. But both types of participation are
based on a strictly economic function which he tries
to foster. It is a function of accumulation based on
appropriation of the *campesinos'* economic surplus,
through specific mechanisms, clearly different from
those of the industrial proletariat. The *cacique*
structure of local or regional power acquired increasing importance, along with other political
forces on the national scene. During the Second
World War the forces which, since the end of the
last decade, had begun to worry about the trends of
the Cárdenas administration, organized themselves
more firmly. By 1934 U.S. interest in the patterns
of development of Mexican agriculture was already
clear. Accelerated industrialization appeared to be
vital for big cities, and in order to achieve this
it was necessary to rely on resources which only the
agricultural sector could provide. The intensive
accumulation that this process demanded -together
with a process of concentration of wealth- could not
be achieved if the popular movements of the previous
decade were allowed to continue. In order to put a
stop to them, it was first necessary to weaken the
coalition between *campesinos* and workers, which had
made them possible, and secondly it was necessary to
gain control over their oganizations. Control of
workers' organizations was based on the continuous
granting of economic advantages to the groups best
organized. This made it possible to offer constant
improvement in real income for those groups, while
at the same time it worsened their position in the
overall scheme of distribution of the social product. As far as the *campesinos* were concerned, in
order to put a drastic end to agrarian trends, it
was deemed necessary to support the forces that
opposed these tendencies, in addition to using mechanisms of manipulation and repression.

The so-called agrarian developmentalism which
characterized the post-war period was thus initiated.

The constitutional reforms of 1947 worked as an efficient means of blocking *campesino* demands for
land and created a climate of "confidence" and security with regard to land tenure. This, in turn,
stimulated private investment in agriculture. The
old agricultural interests of the Northeast of the
Republic -where the biggest *haciendas* in the country
were found before the Revolution- succeeded in
attracting most public resources for agricultural
and livestock improvement, in the so-called "Green
Revolution" (see next chapter). This group, in fact,
succeeded in directly influencing the overall political orientation of agrarian development. It also
assigned to high productivity areas the task of
supplying food and raw materials to the whole of the
population, while at the same time employing along
with industry and services the *campesino* labor
force which would thus be forced to leave rural communities. The *campesinos* themselves would have the
job of providing resources for financing industrialization, feeding themselves during the process and
constituting the reserve labor required by urban
development.

The co-relation of forces that favored this
process was expressed through the intervention of
the *cacique* on a local or regional level. The *Confederación Nacional Campesina* tended to function
in this period as a negotiating body. On the one
hand, it provided an outlet for the most intense
campesino pressures and on the other, it acted as
an instrument of control by undermining the coherence and strength of the *campesino* struggle.

In order to overcome these factors, various
attempts were made to form independent *campesino* organizations. During the post-war years, one sector
of the worker organizations, which had been the van-
guard during Cárdenas' government, separated from
the other organizations. First, an abortive attempt
was made to create an *Alianza Obrero Campesina*.
This was followed by the creation of the *Unión General de Obreros y Campesinos de México*. This Union
slowly began to lose its different labor groups, but
for several years it was viewed as a highly combative *campesino* organization, which by the end of the
1950s had achieved some resounding successes. In
the 1960s, in the heat of the *Movimiento de Liberación*

Nacional -associated with the political effervescence of the Cuban Revolution- the *Central Campesina Independiente* emerged. For several years, this organization vigorously supported agrarian claims, especially in the Northeast of the Republic.

By 1965, the crisis of the rural development model became apparent and the *campesinos* found themselves facing an extremely adverse coalition of forces. Their efforts to promote their own demands were disjointed: small uprisings, hunger marches and guerrilla movements with different goals and characteristics. Neither the *Confederación Nacional Campesina* nor the *Central Campesina Independiente* seemed capable of joining together and properly channelling their interests. This meant that rural tensions increased daily and were expressed in the proliferation of *campesino* movements. The economic and productive dynamism lost on an overall scale, was concentrated in areas where agri-business could exercise stricter control over operations and through which commercial agriculture could be more easily introduced into the international economy. Thus, by the early 1970s, the situation had become very explosive and the characteristic polarization of rural Mexico, seen throughout history, now concentrated social contradictions in the form of participation in production.

THE '70S: THE MORE THINGS CHANGE, THE MORE THEY REMAIN THE SAME

In 1970 the issue was not <u>only</u> that of land tenure. At that time, more than ever, the real issues were: control of productive resources, the actual planning of production, the general thrust of efforts, and the real benefits derived from the process.

Above all, the general thrust of productive efforts was being questioned. In accordance with the theory of comparative advantages it was necessary for production to remain conditioned by supply and demand, and for the strict criterion of profitability to predominate over improvement plans and efforts to increase productivity. This position was promoted not only for one type of crop but for an entire spectrum of products. Opposing this view was the argument favoring self-sufficiency in national food production. The former advocated continued reliance on modern agri-business for production, while the latter advocated dependence on *campesino* involvement in basic production, which would imply a drastic change in policies.

Increasing *campesino* pressure, as well as the repercussions of the world food crisis which came to a head in 1972, were decisive elements in adopting the self-sufficiency model. This model was also intended as a way of giving specific attention to *campesino* demands. An important part of public resources went to rural zones; the guaranteed prices of basic products were increased, and efforts were made to organize producers. In terms of agrarian reform, an effort was made to clear up the backlog of land expropriations which had already been resolved but which had not yet been executed. Some major decisions were made on the redistribution of a few large *latifundios*, which until then had not been affected by the whole process.

The encouragement given to the collectivization process during this phase took on different characteristics than during the Cárdenas period. The idea was no longer to stimulate an autonomous process of control and action on landholding by the *campesinos*, but to subject all the productive structures so far developed to a specific kind of rationality -that of the overall applicability of the system. The so-called agrarian development of the previous 40 years had in fact resulted in the proliferation of productively active elements which took on the status of "small independent producers." They fitted into different land tenure systems such as small holdings, *ejidos*, *comunas*, *colonias* that appeared to devote their efforts to working their plots on an individual or family basis. In fact, however, the weakening of the *campesino* productive organization, based on collective effort, had "individualized" exploitation in order to subject them more easily to the control of the re-established *latifundios* or commercial agri-business. The kind of control, habitually exercised through the power of the *caciques*, the leasing of plots and other illegal procedures had not, strictly speaking, given rise to a new organization of produc-

tion. Instead of the large agricultural holdings of
the pre-revolutionary period, business organizations
that controlled the productive processes from the
outside, had emerged. Thus, production was being
conditioned and determined by powers not directly
involved in their operation. The logic of these
operations also demanded that *campesino* labor retain
the conditions for its own self-renewal, in productive units that remained outside the direct control
of the dynamic agri-business system, even though
they were under the control of many different types
of commercial agents. As is obvious, this process,
partially affected by international forces, had
deepened the rural economic and productive crisis.
This, in turn, accelerated rural migration and weakened, on a national scale, efforts being made towards social and political organization.

The year 1975 saw the beginning of a great effort made towards collectivization in the hope of
finding an answer to these problems. Part of this
effort was aimed at the historical *campesino* initiative of direct participation, which managed to
take advantage of these efforts to forward its own
development goals. Yet most of these efforts served
merely as another form of *campesino* control. As one
researcher has pointed out, this effort towards
collectivization structured from the outside, constituted a mechanism of formally presenting as *campesino* initiatives, decisions which had actually
been taken behind their backs by superior outside
forces. Technical agencies held power, without responsibility, while *campesinos* had responsibility
without power. Both the effort towards collectivization and land redistribution were subjected to
plans for increased production without concrete
changes in the socio-economic structure ever
really being intended.

The first half of the decade witnessed impressive *campesino* mobilization, similar to that of the
'30s. There were, however, significant differences.
For thirty years *campesino* organizations had gradually been weakened and had lost their cohesiveness.
Campesinos were therefore skeptical when presented
once again with the opportunity to mobilize their
forces without being subjected to repression. The
political leaders were equally dubious and seemed

worried that the assemblage they were promoting might
get out of hand if it gained any real autonomy. In
many ways the *campesinos* were being shuffled like a
pack of cards, while at the same time their real
attempts to rally were being eliminated or blocked.
Attempts at restructuring *campesino* organizations
suffered the same fate: there were agreements imposed
from above which never got down to the movement's
grass roots. Thus the *Pacto de Ocampo*, a pact signed
by the principal *campesino* organizations of the
country in order to unify their plan of action, had
only short-term effects and was soon reduced to nothing. The same thing happened with the *Congreso Permanente Agrario* formed shortly before the *Pacto*. Many
factors prevented the *campesinos* from effectively
taking over the process of change which seemed to be
underway. Among these factors was the very speed with
which events occurred; the ways in which improvement
programs were implemented (blockading any effective
campesino participation); the institutional and socio-
political inertia resulting from forty years of so-
called agrarian development; the magnitude of the
political and economic pressures of multinational
agro-industry; the short-sighted and aggressive behavior of interests affected by the winds of change;
unrealistic anti-capitalist agrarian rhetoric,
divorced from reality; the gulf between the true
campesino organizations -at both local and regional
levels- and their formal organizations. Consequently,
the *campesinos* were unable to prevent this process of
change or to refocus it according to previous tendencies. In 1976, the interests of large agri-business-
es exercised decisive pressure on the authorities,
within the politically dangerous context of a currency devaluation which had been decided upon during
the period of transfer of power from one government
to the next. The pretext used was that "unexpected"
attention had been paid to an old *campesino* agrarian
dispute. This took place at the very heart of the
nation's agro-commercial system (in Sonora), ten
days before the transfer of government.

In the following years the crisis worsened. The
food shortage increased notably. Inflation adversely
affected rural income and unemployment increased. On
both local and regional levels, "solutions by force"
were increasingly substituted for economic policies.
Once again, the specific importance, the capacity for
negotiation, and leeway for maneuvering large nation-

al *campesino* organization were limited. Once more
they became elements of control over popular mobilization. The *cacique* power structure gained new
strength -subdued, yet more and more firmly linked
to the interests of national and international
capital whose hegemony over the land became increasingly obvious.

The rural problem continued at the forefront.
While hopes for real land redistribution tended to
fall by the wayside, together with historical claims
by the *campesinos* and their organizations, at the
same time the ineffectiveness of "solutions" attempted throughout the century was being acknowledged. It
seemed inevitable that a balance would have to come
about, and it did.

A survey of the structure of landholding throughout the country revealed the following statistics:
25,000 *ejidos* and communities with 95 million hectares, and a collective system of land tenure; one
million small holders, with 83 million hectares; 784
agrarian colonies with 7.5 million hectares, receiv-
ing private profits from federal property; 300
thousand *nacionaleros* with 5 million hectares of
non-legalized federal lands.

Apart from the unbalanced economic structure of
the producers under the different tenure systems,
the survey also revealed a tremendous backlog in
agrarian reform. It was considered vital that this
be "completed" as soon as possible. The situation
was described by the present President of the Republic, in his Third Annual Address to the Nation, in
the following terms: "Six million hectares which
have already been decreed upon still have to be
handed over to the *ejidatarios*." Five million hectares of federal lands "are still occupied by *nacionaleros* who do not have legal ownership nor right
to the occupied lands.   In the lands occupied by
'colonies,' 4.5 million hectares have still to be
investigated." With regard to *ejidos* and communities, "it has been estimated that the right to use
19 million hectares has not yet been legalized."
In effect, said the President "60 years after the
beginning of agrarian reform, 56% of the surface
area of national territory still has to be regulariz-
ed. There is also an enormous backlog of judicial
decisions waiting to be enforced: 1,400 presidential

resolutions regarding land appropriations which have
not been put into effect; 8,650 unresolved *amparos*;
31,900 applications for extension or creation of new
ejidal centers from 1.5 million applicants; and
12,400 expropriation claims of *ejido* lands."

   This prodded the authorities into a commitment
to clear up the agrarian backlog by 1982 at the
latest. There are doubts about the feasibility of
attaining this goal, not so much due to administrative problems, but because of the practical impossibility of solving many of the pending problems
under current legislative stipulations. Whether or
not this backlog is cleared up, nobody seems very
confident that this breakthrough will provide the
"solution" to the nation's agrarian problems.

DID THE ANARCHIST-LIBERAL REFORM FADE AWAY?

At the beginning of this chapter, the dialectics of
the two opposing forces which characterized the
agrarian picture of the XIX century were described.
On the one hand there was the force of the *campesinos*,
based on their traditional communities, and on the
other, the colonial powers which gradually took on
the capitalist guise of domination. In the second
half of the XIX century, the *campesino* drive towards
community organization seemed to lose ground and
almost disappeared under the liberal regime. Instead
of leading to a "Smallscale Producers Republic,"
this situation led to a capitalist system of land
concentration which rapidly deprived the *campesinos*
of their rights to the land.

   The 1910 revolutionary upheaval was an attempt
at re-establishing the drive towards community organization. This idea was to revive the *ejido* and to
reclaim communal title deeds recognized by the
Spanish Crown, but not by the liberal regime; however, these attempts tended to become anarchist in
nature. This was not only because anarchist points
of view were prevalent among the forerunners of the
Revolution, but also because of the real, historical
tendency of the *campesino* movement, whose aspirations
seemed to be concentrated on and formulated at a
strictly local level.

The Revolution also gave rise to the possibility of *campesinos* taking over liberal forms of rural
organization of production for individual or family
modes of land use of the *ejidos* or of the private
land holdings, depending on the economic and political trends that prevailed at the time.

There were thus two forces and two ways of
interpreting the world operating at the same time,
and they either converged or diverged according to
the circumstances.

When examining these questions, it is important
to remember that in December, 1914, for a whole
month, the two largest *campesino* armies (Villa's and
Zapata's) occupied Mexico City and became the dominant
faction of the revolutionary movement. "But the *campesinos* who, at the crest of the revolutionary wave,
had conquered the capital of the country, did not
know what to do with it. They wanted the land, and
while they could redistribute it by force, what they
now needed, in order to assure legal possession,
was a government which would sanction redistribution. But the *campesinos* did not have a program,
or a political party, or even people to form a
government. They were unable to constitute the dominant class." They had occupied the capital city, but
"since they could not do anything useful with it,
and in fact the city represented a danger to their
cohesion and strength, they abandoned it, to continue their fight in the rural areas." (1) It was
the beginning of their downfall, which ended with
Villa's military defeat at the hands of Obregón, the
assassination of Zapata and the gradual dying out of
the *campesino* war.

The *campesinos* were unable to take over power
after their triumphant revolution, even though they
had had the leading role. However, their very existence and their capacity for bringing about large
scale social mobilization had a decisive and permanent mark on the modern Mexican State. The statement
that Mexico's was the first social revolution of the

---

(1) Adolfo Gilly "La Revolución Mexicana: ruptura
y continuidad," in INVESTIGACION ECONOMICA,
Vol. XXXVI, No. 4, October-December, 1977,
p. 172.

century and not the last of the bourgeoise, is not
just an offhand expression. It involved all the
potential and all the limitations of the country's
evolution at the time. It was the first chronolo-
gically, but it happened at a less favorable economic
and geo-political time. Slow progress on a zigzagging
path toward achieving its goals seems the price Mexico would have to pay for these changes.

Those who legally took over power lacked the
dominant structure of inner strength. The land-own-
ing oligarchy had been disbanded by the Revolution,
but was always ready to fight for its privileges by
allying itself with whatever groups were rising to
power. In order to block these efforts, government
needed to find popular support among rural and urban
workers. As society advanced along the paths of
a capitalist economy, new classes and new power
groups were born. Economic automatism and the penetration of foreign capital encouraged both the State
and its public power away from the national and
social objectives which had been the very basis for
its constitutional existence. Social movements and the
nationalistic attitudes of large groups, for their
part, led them to confrontations with the economic
and political centers of society's dominating powers,
on both national and international levels. Room for
maneuvering in this situation was very limited, like
walking down a narrow precipitous path: the limits
could not be overstepped without serious consequences. To do so would jeopardize the overall
stability of Mexican society. Neither faction was
totally able to impose itself on the other, even
though one party progressively accumulated privileges and the other only resentment for its misery
and oppression.

In this way, the Mexican State, whose federal
power has been and still is, the basis for the development of private enterprise, has been constantly
forced to establish social or nationalistic goals in
the face of opposition by dominant economic and
political interests. Yet it has been unable to stop
a growing imbalance in the redistribution of the
social product.

As far as agrarian reform goes, this kind of
evolution as reflected through the different phases
described in this chapter, has tended (in spite of

fluctuations) to show a predominantly liberal concep-
tualization of the economy and of politics, a tendency which now seems to have led us to a dead end. The
framework for agrarian reform adopted in the last
century has tended to reflect the historical capitalist model followed by the industrially advanced
nations: it tried to create the conditions necessary
for bringing together family and individual concerns,
where "the best," the "most diligent" were capable
of contributing to a modern agricultural organization
under "reasonably" egalitarian terms. This model was
adopted to a certain extent by the *campesinos* as
their own goal during this century. In spite of the
social nature of the struggle for the land and the
strength of the *campesinos'* communal organizations,
their internal dynamics and pressure from the outside tended to promote individual use of the land,
whatever tenure system was in effect.

Nevertheless, progressive merging of individual
landholdings became impossible. Since agrarian redistribution was never completed, expansion of the
"best" at the expense of the rest, meant here in
classical terms the restoration of the *latifundio*
against which the fight still continued. Both
sectors, those who still did not have access to land
and who comprised an increasing number in spite of
continuous redistribution, and those who were about
to lose their land because of other economic forces
on the rise, efficiently blocked any attempt to give
the tenure regime the necessary legal structure to
back up an economic concentration of this process.
Capitalist expansion, consequently, had to adopt an
illegal form of development, linked to that of the
cacique power structure. "Entrepreneurial *neolatifundismo*" was the result. This constituted a "natural"
product of the liberal model which was systematically
encouraged, and which adopted the commercial, industrial or financial apparatus of the times. With
the exception of livestock, where the vagueness of
Law afforded legal protection for those who in fact
were outlaws invading *ejidal* or communal lands, the
"managerial *neolatifundio*" generally did not have
legal access to land tenure. Even so, their development constituted an authentic disruption of
legal order and provided a constant source of instability and conflict, and their presence meant a total
negation of the driving force behind the Mexican
Revolution, since they could only survive and expand

through authoritarian practices and in a climate of
endless violence.

Under these conditions, a collective, democratic organization for land exploitation not only became a part of important historical developments
by taking up once again the oldest and most valid of
campesino goals, but also emerged as the most suitable legal and institutional path to a gradual coalition of landholdings under a liberal model. It was
the only feasible and lasting form of modern productive organization, with real possibilities for development within the constitutional framework. However, this formula too was doomed to fall. On the
one hand, the very fact that it was an effective
substitute for the clustering of holdings organized by the "managerial *neolatifundio*" meant that it
represented a real threat to them. Consequently they
fought against it by every means in their power, and
they had many. On the other hand, democratic and
collective organization of production appeared as
the ever present thorn in the side of a capitalist
society. According to the system's logic its development was unacceptable be it through real mechanisms
of economic functioning, the inevitability of capitalist expansion, or the ideological apparatus and
superstructural organization; this collective formula had to be eliminated like any other foreign
body. Although it seemed impossible to erradicate it
totally, it was feasible to inhibit its development.
Furthermore, it was also possible to transform it
into yet another instrument of domination by making
its operation more functional according to the
requirements of the system.

During recent decades these contradictions
have taken on new meaning. Under the logic of modern
capitalist operation in the countryside, land ownership or usufruct of the land loses importance vis à
vis resource control. For a long time now, capitalist agricultural development has not been seen as
an expansion of agriculture and livestock raising,
but instead has been reduced to a mere link in the
urban agroindustrial chain, within the framework
of the concentration and internationalization of
capital. In this new context, where capital is more
interested in control of rather than ownership or
occupation of the land, agrarian reform has to be
rapidly completed in order to stabilize and broaden

its scope of activity without the risks and uncertainties associated with the conflicts of an incom-
plete and unstable process. But this movement also
means not recognizing agrarian reform, because this
very "compliance" implies not getting at the ultimate implications of the original historical driving force of the process. Rather it is taking away
from the *campesinos* any possibility of control over
productive resources. In this way, capital is the
controlling force, regardless of the tenure system
and the modalities that may eventually be adopted.
These contradictions are represented in different
ways among the *campesinos*. This process for them
means obtaining "all the land and soon" as Narciso
Bassols used to say at the end of the '30s. At the
same time, they have to deny the existence of
agrarian reform, that is, retread much of the path
already walked, knowing that the original anarchist-
liberal process has led them to a dead end and that
ownership of the land is not a guarantee for effective control over it. Taking over the land today
means assuring a material basis for a liberating
process, one which will go beyond historical claims
formulated, to a large extent, in the sense of
going back to communal structures of the past. What
is necessary today, on the contrary, is to leave
behind the anarchist principle in order to encourage
present-day communities to participate effectively
so that in the future there will be coalitions and
solidarity whereby land ownership will mean freedom.

    Within this set of contradictions there is no
clear way out of the impasse where Mexico's agrarian
situation finds itself at the beginning of the
1980's. Furthermore, it cannot be divorced from the
profound crisis or rural conditions in the country.
There is no agreement between social classes, nor
is there social agreement which can, in similar
terms, define the meaning of either compliance with
or denial of agrarian reform. But the matter tends
to be aired at a superstructural level, in increasingly ideological and sterile terms. There is no
scarcity of propositions which try to turn back the
clock of history and suggest initiating the now
classical process of a progressive affiliation of
individual plots. They propose to "liberate" the
ejidatarios and *comuneros* from their ties and allow
them to rent or mortgage their landholdings legally;

thus, together with the lands of the small property
owners, a whole area of available land would be
formed, where the most "able" would come together
in efficient economic units. Since this would require constitutional changes, which are difficult
to envisage in the near future, different formulae
have been suggested which would allow this process
to advance, even if only in a transitory way. With
a measure of this type, the dream of creating a
Republic of Small Producers, such as the one contem-
plated by the liberals of the last century, the
campesino would be able to escape from his prison
(a plot of land) in favor of earning a wage. Other
groups, with well-founded distrust of these *haciendas* without *hacendados*, insist on efforts towards
compulsive collectivization. They have not been able to
perceive that this, as the '70s experience clearly
proved, would place producers within the logic of
the system, disguised as a self-managing and democratic form, but this form only covers up what is
really a structure of unfair and inefficient domination. As was already pointed out, the collective
regime in the *ejido* and in the communities or the
cooperatives of small producers is inevitably transformed when promoted from above and from outside,
into a mechanism which gives power but not responsibility to the technical organisms -public or pri-
vate- and responsibility without power to the *campesinos*. Whatever the true or imagined subtleties
are, the fact is that these formulae are swamped
in unresolvable contradictions and vicious circles.
They are unable to offer real and concrete answers
to current agrarian questions without radically
tearing apart the very conception and interests
which gave rise to them. Meanwhile, the *campesinos*
-suffering from the steady deterioration of their
living and productive conditions -have been re-
building their local and regional organizations and
are making serious efforts to become articulated on
a national level. Both workers and *campesinos* are
assuming again their modes of alliance of the '30s,
whose rupture conditioned the subsequent chain of
events. Together with other elements, this has
brought about a modification in the political
co-relation of forces, under somewhat less adverse
conditions for the *campesinos*. In immediate terms,
this has sharpened tensions in addition to local
and regional conflicts, intensified by critical
circumstances, and has heightened the tendency to

look for violent solutions. At the same time, however, the conditions for a new political route for the problem are being created via a process which gives coherence and organic form, on a national level, to the distorted *campesino* claims. This process is already pointing, with increasing clarity, towards projects which propose overcoming, once and for all, the anarchist-liberal ideas of the *campesinos* shared during the first decades of the century. As will be seen in the last chapter of this book, they are getting ready for a final phase of the agrarian reform that may occur as the all-encompassing synthesis of the long historical road they have traveled, and a feasible and better future.

3

MEXICO:
BIRTH PLACE AND BURIAL GROUND
OF THE GREEN REVOLUTION

Certain spectacular achievements in Mexican agriculture during the 1950s aroused the attention of
the international community for some time. The "Mexican agricultural miracle" was spoken of, and the
experiment began to be used as an example in many
other countries. Later, the phenomenon spread, and
when the ·same exceptional results were obtained in
other regions of the world, it merited a special
title: The Green Revolution.

    As time went by, the optimistic tone of the
first commentaries became somewhat modified. The
subject was no longer the center of discussions on
rural development in backward countries and it
disappeared from the front pages of newspapers. After
some time, when it came up again, it was under awk-
ward conditions: on the defendant's stand. Today it
is a subject of intense controversy.

    It would be impossible to describe the present
state of rural Mexico without reference to these
facts. For better or for worse, the phenomenon known
as the "Green Revolution" corresponds to deep transformations in the Mexican rural world and is an
essential background material for the present situation.

AN UNEXPECTED MOVE FORWARD

The Mexican agricultural achievements between 1950
and 1970 were truly spectacular. They can be summarized as follows:

<u>Corn</u>. Production increased more than 250 per cent; average yields grew from 300 to 1,300 kg. per hectare.

<u>Wheat</u>. Production grew from 300,000 tons to 2.6 million, that is an eightfold increase; yield per hectare multiplied by four from 750 to 3,200 kg.

<u>Beans</u>. Production rose from 530,000 to 925,000 tons.

<u>Sorghum</u>. Production increased 14 times, from 200,000 to 2.7 million tons.

<u>Soybean</u>. From an insignificant level, production rose to 250,000 tons (today it amounts to several million).

Few countries, in fact, have been able to match a sustained growth of 7% in agricultural production, as was the case of Mexico during the 1950s. It was, to all intents and purposes, an authentic agricultural revolution.

A few years ago, Edwin J. Wellhausen, one of the most prominent participants in the experiment, pointed out that the progress of the Green Revolution "was achieved, to a great extent, through a combination of three technological factors: 1) the development of new varieties of plants of high yield, ample adaptability, sensitivity to fertilizers and resistance to diseases; 2) the development of improved 'packages' of agricultural practices that included better use of soil, adequate fertilization and more effective control of weeds and insects, all of which enabled the improved varieties to fully reach their high yield potential; 3) a favorable ratio between the cost of fertilizers and other investments with respect to the price the producer obtained for his produce." (1) To what degree was the revolution in effect due to technological advances? What was the relative importance of the elements involved? What are the economic and social consequences of this kind of progress?

Researchers and institutions all over the world have recently been asking themselves these questions.

---

(1) Edwin J. Wellhausen, "La agricultura en México, in CIENCIA Y DESARROLLO, Vol. I, NO. 13, March-April 1977, p. 40.

This international debate encouraged the United Nations Research Institute for Social Development
(UNRISD) to sponsor extensive and profound research
into the matter, to provide and answer to some of
these questions. A substantial portion of the study
and its report referred to Mexico. (2) A great deal
of specialized literature on the subject has been
produced, although the discussion has now cooled down.
Advocates of the idea are not as enthusiastic as
during the first years, and critics have let up on
their initial virulence. Things have returned to
normal.

    All of this suggests it would be wiser not to
deal here with an evaluation of the phenomenon. But
some of the basic reports on this experiment, which
have already left deep marks on rural Mexico, have
to be included. It is particularly important to
find answers to the question of whether the present
crisis can be understood as a necessary consequence
of that experiment or whether, as Wellhausen puts
it, what Mexico now needs is simply a new agricultural revolution, having successfully completed the
first one.

THE UNFOLDING OF THE EXPLOIT

In 1941, in the middle of World War II, the Rockefeller Foundation along with the U.S. Government showed
great interest in fostering advanced technical agricultural development in Mexico. General Manuel Avila
Camacho's government, for its part, was subjected to
intense pressure over agricultural development because, among other things, of a growing shortage of
food supplies.

    In 1943, an agreement between the Mexican Govern-
ment and the Rockefeller Foundation was signed. This
agreement resulted in the creation of an *Oficina de
Estudios Especiales* within the *Secretaría de Agri-*

---

(2) Cynthia Hewitt de Alcántara, LA MODERNIZACION DE
LA AGRICULTURA MEXICANA, 1940-1970. Siglo XXI Editores, México, 1978, and Global II Project on Social
and Economic Implications of the Introduction of New
Varieties of Foodgrains, Geneva UNDP/UNRISD, 1974.

cultura. It was semi-autonomous, financed mainly by
the Rockefeller Foundation and exclusively responsible for hiring its own scientific personnel. The
program had the double objective of pursuing scientific and technological improvements in the production of basic foodstuffs and training young
Mexicans in research work. The first of these specific objectives gave priority to "improvements in
the utilization of the soil; introduction, selection
or cultivation of better adapted, high yield and
quality varieties of plants; to the most efficient
methods of fighting diseases and pests, and to the
introduction of the best quality breeds of domestic
animals and poultry." Research also gave priority to
the maximization of yields per unit of land cultivated, and to the monetary income of farmers. The
program as a whole was aimed at fostering the development of Mexican agriculture, in order to ensure an
adequate supply of foodstuffs to the cities.

With time, the contents and objectives of the
project have come to be considered as having only
a technological orientation. It is essential, however, to bear in mind other elements which have become blurred over the years.

The initiative of the Rockefeller Foundation
resulted from Vice-president Henry Wallace's active
intervention; he in turn had been convinced by
Josephus Daniels, U.S. Ambassador to Mexico, when
both attended Manuel Avila Camacho's inaugural cere-
mony. It was not an isolated issue linked to technological preoccupations or the production of foodstuffs, but can be traced to the formulation of one
of the best studies made on the situation of rural
Mexico. The project was completed under the direction of Nathan L. Wetten who, in the preface to his
book, commented on the general context within which
the analysis had taken place: "I had the opportunity
of undertaking wide study (on Mexico) in 1942, when
I was elected by the State Department and the Foreign Agricultural Affairs Office of the United
States, as one of three rural sociologists to study
and report on social conditions and agricultural
development in Latin America. This book is the outcome of that experience. Between 1942 and 1945, I
worked as a rural sociologist attached to the U.S.
Embassy in Mexico, and in this capacity had the
opportunity to travel all over the country, visiting

all the States of the Republic and interviewing people of all classes and social conditions... Today,
it is particularly important that the United States
and Mexico understand each other. Mexico is the gate-
way to Latin America and her relations with the
United States are carefully observed by the rest of
the Latin American countries."(3)

The research program financed by the Rockefeller Foundation was thus clearly in keeping with the
context of Mexico-US relations, and within this
context, the problem of land tenure constituted the
central issue.

In 1910, foreigners held a quarter of the national territory: around 50 million hectares. Twenty
years later, during which a U.S. invasion of Mexico
had taken place and countless diplomatic difficulties had arisen, 32 million hectares were still in
the hands of foreigners, that is to say, one fifth
of all private estates and one sixth of the total
area of the Republic. More than half this amount
belonged to U.S. citizens and was concentrated in
the Northern states, the North Pacific and Gulf
regions. The redistribution of land between 1910
and 1940 took place mainly in the central states,
thus severely affecting those of Spanish descent
whose properties were located in that area, but
left the greater part of the North American properties untouched.

Substantial differences of opinion about the
concept   of   private property, were at the root of
the well-known 1920's controversy between the U.S.
and Mexican Governments. "My Government -said the
U.S. Secretary of State to the Mexican Minister of
Foreign Affairs in 1926- cannot agree with the fundamental concept that the Mexican Government evidently maintains... of a right granted only for the
use of property and to enjoy the usufruct thereof,
but which can be suspended or denied by regulations
affecting the future duration of that right, or
impose conditions on the future possibility of

_____

(3) Nathan L. Wetten, "México Rural," in PROBLEMAS
AGRICOLAS E INDUSTRIALES DE MEXICO, Vol. V, No. 2,
México, 1953, p. 13.

possessing the property." For Americans, the Mexican
doctrine attacked "the roots of private ownership
rights, which are the basis for all civilized societies." (4) Beyond doctrinary or historical aspects
the American attitude was influenced by the fact
that their country was an exporter of capital, in
full commercial expansion: they wanted to protect
U.S. citizens risking their capital in foreign countries. "If all our investments abroad were to change
from the status of property duly acquired, with
guarantees of permanence, to that of temporary concessions, with guarantees requiring renewal from
time to time, by means of contracts in whose wording
we could not intervene, we would be placed in an unprecedented situation. Our commercial relations, not
only with Mexico but with all of Latin America, depend on mutual trust." (5)   According to President
Coolidge, "the person and property of a citizen are
part of the nation's general domain, even though the
citizen is in a foreign country."(6)   From the Mexican point of view, the matter involved nothing less
than asserting the nation's sovereignty over its
territory in terms of the 27th Article of the Constitution: "If private ownership rights over portions
of national territory are not derived from the aggregate rights of the nation as a whole, then all those
nations who open their doors to foreigners will one
day witness how some of those portions acquired by
foreigners become subject to foreign laws outside the
sovereignty of the nation and destroy that sovereignty." (7).

Already at stake was the oil question which
would be defined in the following decade. During the

---

(4) Note from the U.S. Secretary of State to the Mexican Minister of Foreign Affairs, July 31, 1926. PRESS
BULLETIN, State Department, November 23, 1926, p. 2.
(5) Departamento de Comercio, Oficina de Comercio Interior y Exterior, No. 45, PRESS BULLETIN, October 7,
1918, Circular de la División Latinoamericana. Published in DOCUMENTOS RELATIVOS AL INTENTO DEL GOBIERNO ME-
XICANO DE CONFISCAR LAS PROPIEDADES PETROLERAS DE LOS
EXTRANJEROS, recopilados por la Asociación de Produc-
tores de Petróleo de México, February 1919, p. 50.
(6) United States Daily, April 26, 1927, p. 2, column 2.
(7) BOLETIN de la Secretaría de Gobernación, El Artículo 27 de la Constitución Federal, México, September,
1922, p. 2.

1920's, the solution to the controversy was found
through acceptance of Mexico's argument, under the
condition that she, in turn, would accept the transformation of simple dominion into perpetual concession. With land owners having to accept the transformation of their title deeds into concessions,
the basis was laid for the claim that brought about
the 1938 oil expropriation.

U.S. interest in rural Mexico, shown by Henry
Wallace, Josephus Daniels and the Rockefeller Foundation, cannot be understood merely within the limited scope of technical cooperation. Apart from the
global context of World War II, and the hemispheric
and trade relations between Mexico and the U.S., the
main thorn in their affairs was the extensive rural
properties of U.S. citizens in Mexico, concentrated
in the Northern states and the North Pacific area.

The research program of the *Oficina de Estudios
Especiales* gave priority to corn and wheat, particularly the latter. Their progress paralleled that of
expanding agriculture and cattle-raising in the
North and Northwest regions of the Republic. They
were, in fact, self-stimulating processes: the research work contributed genetic material, and the
cultivation techniques would yield their full potential in the areas where important irrigation
works were being constructed. Furthermore, both
processes related to a specific type of farmer: the
largest, "most linked to trade and best able to obtain fertilizers and make other investments." As
Wellhausen points out, "up to 1968, the agricultural
revolution in Mexico moved forward under its own
steam, without need of any great effort to assist the
farmers technically." (8)   Actually, the support
needed was not so much technological as economic:
other mechanisms of strategic importance such as
credit and marketing were added to the results of
research and infrastructural works. The "favorable
relationship of fertilizer costs and other investments, with respect to the price received by the
producer" was not the result of natural market conditions, but the outcome of an explicit decision
taken by the authorities, which resorted to increas-

(8) Wellhausen, OP. CIT., p. 43

ing subsidies, both to lower the farmers' costs of
production and to raise incomes by means of guaranteed prices above those of the market. It was the
relatively slow dynamics of the process, and not
the limitations of the diffusion system, which were
responsible for the delay of more than 15 years in
the publication of experimental results.

Because of its very inertia, the program concentrated more and more on the irrigated areas of
the Northwest and began to develop side effects on
the spatial distribution of production. The yield
increased in areas which could apply the new technology, whose water requirements reduced its
application to irrigated areas, so that regions of
seasonal production, which traditionally had
generated the greatest proportion of wheat produced
in the country, were no longer cultivated. In fact,
research related to seasonal production was explicitly excluded from the program and put in the hands
of the *Instituto de Investigaciones Agrícolas*,
created in 1947 by a group of Mexican researchers
committed to the principles of agrarianism and
concerned with giving a clear social orientation
to their work. The idea was to continue the work
initiated many years before.

The efforts of the *Oficina de Estudios Especiales* in the field of corn produced important advances as well. Nonetheless, the cost of the production structure limited massive incorporation of new
technology to areas of irrigated commercial agriculture, where wheat, cotton, safflower or soybean
offered better economic results.

In areas with seasonal rains, lack of water
and the limited resources of producers prevented
spread of the new technology. Thus, wheat became the
main crop during the first years of the Green Revolution.

In 1961, the *Oficina de Estudios Especiales*
merged with the *Instituto de Investigaciones Agrícolas* to form the *Instituto Nacional de Investigaciones Agrícolas* (INIA). The office's regional facilities, created in part with the support of the
powerful Northwestern credit unions, became the
patrimony of the INIA. With the new administrative
arrangements, the Rockefeller Foundation began to

reduce its financial contributions, a gap which was not compensated for by government funds. As a result, during the 1960s, the program's budget was substantially reduced, notwithstanding an extension in its scope and responsibility for crops and regions.

Following the disappearance of the *Oficina de Estudios Especiales*, the Rockefeller Foundation directed most of its efforts towards the export of its scientific achievements, particularly those of genetic material. This was done through the *Centro Internacional de Mejoramiento del Maíz y el Trigo* (CIMMYT). From 1960 onwards, and more specifically since 1968, when the Institute acquired experimental facilities of its own, it began to spread the results generated by the project to other Third World countries.

During the sixteen years of the program's existence, approximately 750 Mexican researchers participating in field work and laboratories received intensive training. Some of them were later incorporated into the *Secretaría de Agricultura*'s promotion program, and the rest continued to be assigned to INIA or the graduate program at the Chapingo Agricultural School.

THE CHICKEN AND THE EGG

As often happens in the field of social sciences, the discussion over the Green Revolution has centered on one interpretation of the consequences and casual connection of the phenomena. The sort of evaluation applied depends on the order of the factors. The creators and advocators of the Green Revolution violently reject the view that an increase in inequality is due to the process of technological progress itself. They acknowledge, however, that "not every farmer is benefited to the same extent by technological improvements -and that, as was expected, the new technology seemed to prosper better in those areas where production risks were lower and profit expectations higher." When they observed that the impact of the agricultural revolution came to an end by the late '60s, they believed it might have been due to the fact that "there is almost no one left to utilize the technological package under the conditions it is now being offered." Their diagnosis led to the suggestion to develop "special technological packages" suited to seasonally cultivated areas, and reorienting the technical assistance program, "in order to bring them to the level of the farmers and see that a higher proportion of them rapidly adapt to this advantageous technology." (9)

How valid is the criticism that technological progress is associated with the social effects of the process into which it is inserted? "The work of the scientists has been good -said Andrew Pearse, manager of the UNRISD project for evaluating the Green Revolution- but it cannot be expected -he warned- that technological changes in the methods of production be neutral." On the contrary "it is probable that they are as much a dynamic force of social and political change as they are economic." It is necessary to ask, then, about the degree to which technological innovations "contributed to the development of Mexican economy and society." (10)

"Electronic computers are reactionary," stated a radical economist in Mexico some years ago. "Not all of them," answered another, equally radical. Under present conditions, discussion around the alleged neutrality of technological progress is useless. It is neutral neither in origin nor in goals or effects. "A chip off the old block" as the popular saying goes. In fact, "it was to be expected," as Wellhausen stressed, that the benefits of the Green Revolution would be concentrated, and thus increase existing inequalities: the benefits arose from the structure of inequality as its direct and linear expression, not as its negation. The UNRISD study, as well as other projects, have highlighted the adverse social implications of the Green Revolution and questioned its economic contributions. The causal connections have been identified between this technological experience and subsequent problems in the society involved. But this is not enough. Something besides perception of an error is needed to correct it. It will inevitably be repeated, even though it takes on different forms, as long as its causes are not determined and overcome. In order not to repeat the unwanted effects of the Green Revolution, both under its conventional patterns or under revised forms which

---

(9) ˉIbidem.
(10) Cynthia Hewitt, OP. CIT., p. 9

have carried it to seasonal rain areas, it is necessary to inquire about the origins of the phenomenon.
It is not possible to dissociate the scientific and
technological research program and its results from
the development model under which it is operating,
from its implicit hypothesis and the social and political context from which it emerged. In order to
encompass these aspects, other elements have to be
introduced into the analysis.

THE UPS AND DOWNS OF A REACTION

On February 5, 1938, at twelve o'clock, General Lázaro Cárdenas inaugurated the *ejidal* sugar mill
"Emiliano Zapata" in Zacatepec. In his notes, General Cárdenas wrote: "a modern mill, planned by the
present administration with social purposes to improve the *ejidatarios'* economic conditions... It
will be managed under a cooperative system formed
by *ejidatarios* and factory workers." (11)

   After a few weeks, on March 10th, Lázaro Cárdenas and Francisco J. Mújica returned from a visit
to the sugar mill. They stopped at a fruit garden in
Palmira and talked for over an hour. There, under a
tree which still bears the mark made on it by General Cárdenas, he entrusted to Mújica the task of
preparing an address to the nation. On March 18th,
General Cárdenas made it public: the oil industry
expropriation thus came into effect, despite the
defiance of private foreign companies, who had rejected a Supreme Court ruling ordering the fulfill-
ment of the workers' demands. "While fascism was
gaining momentum, our country opened the door to
the world of the future. And it was done within our
legal system and with the backing of workers' organizations. The Constitution blended with a class
struggle to give the nation a new historical sense.
The social conquests of workers -persecuted in Germany, harassed in Italy, humiliated in Japan- became
a national response in Mexico. The expropriation was
not only an act of dignity, it was also an opening

_____
(11) Lázaro Cárdenas, OBRAS, No. 1 Apuntes 1913-1940,
Nueva Biblioteca Mexicana de la UNAM, No. 28, UNAM.
Dirección General de Publicaciones, México, 1972, p. 23

to the world of tomorrow." (12)

The anecdotal situation which associates the
emergence of modern cooperative agroindustry, in
the hands of the working people, with the oil expropriation is neither casual nor irrelevant. In 1938,
the Cárdenas administration culminated, historically, in a double-edged action: the <u>radical</u> rescue of
the nation's rights over its territory and the <u>radi-
cal</u> allocation of the exercise of those rights to
the rightful historical owners. The class alliances
which permitted the Cárdenas agrarian reform and the
expropriation of the oil industry, found their
roots, destiny and historical meaning in this cooperative organization which was capable of excluding
exploitation from the relationship between producers. All of this meant placing the country at the
treshold of the future, beyond immediate reality.

A reaction to an act of such magnitude was
inevitable. The newly opened roads represented a
concrete threat to those interests which have
historically disputed the Mexican peoples' right
to the use of their own territory and the fruit of
their own efforts. Agrarian reform has always been
a rural project (of the working class too, in its
widest sense), which the power structure has always
resisted: sometimes blockading it and on other occasions directing it against its original goals.
Amid great difficulties, after being postponed for
more than a quarter of a century, the project finally seemed able to hold its course in history in the
1930s. It was losing anarchist and village ballast,
characteristic of its formative period, in a colo-
nialized society. Instead it showed strength as a
radical promise when the historical claim for the
land, combined with social and political organization, openly opposed capital. It was essential for
the power structures to come up with their own
opposing project, while at the same time stripping
all anarchist elements from the liberal dream they
had embarked on during the 1920s.

---

(12) Gastón García Cantú, "Los idos de marzo", in
SIEMPRE, No. 1397, April 2, 1980, p. 23

The terms of the global model are widely known. The modernization of the country, planned in the midst of a world war, was naturally linked to the industrialization process. To support the model it was necessary to intensify capital accumulation in the agricultural sector, which had to perform several functions: supply, foodstuffs and raw materials to society as a whole; generate foreign exchange and other resources to finance industrial development in urban areas; contribute with the labor force required in the process and ensure the livelihood of a "surplus" population, i.e. people who could not be easily absorbed in the course of industrialization. Assuming that the rural economy would be incapable of fulfilling the task, enclaves of high productivity needed to be created in rural areas, in charge of a group of "progressive farmers." If the adequate technological innovations were available, the required foodstuffs would be produced in these enclaves, and the rural labor force, inevitably expelled from deteriorated holdings, would be absorbed with support from the industrial and commercial sectors. At the time, possibly no one had given this conceptual form to the model. It was not, and never had been, some sort of Machiavellian conspiracy thought up inside or outside the country. It was, in fact, the resultant processes of economic logic, set in concrete political history; its present form is an analytical product and it is irrelevant whether somebody had thought of it or not in terms of this final version, which works necessarily as a description *a posteriori* of what has already occurred.

The model worked splendidly in its destructive dimension: the rural economy at first became stagnant, and then showed outright deterioration as dependence on commercial agriculture increased. Today's crisis, which began in 1965 according to some analysts, has above all, hit corn producers: the *campesinos*. In its constructive dimension, the results of the model were notable in many aspects: a high growth rate of production; a conspicuous increase in productivity -which for certain products and at certain periods came to be the highest in the world-; the emergence and development of a select group of prosperous modern farmers... This promising movement seemed to be completely separate from the negative effects. It was not clear how it drew strength from the same process. This only be-

came clear with an analysis of the model's limits
and failures: its inability to produce enough food
for the population, to absorb the labor force expelled from the *campesino* sector and to create authentic rural development, as well as its exact role in
the present crisis.

This kind of evolution was in fact, to be expected. The logic of subsidies cannot defeat the
logic of the economy. Areas of high productivity,
conceived for basic production, were committed to
the program only in the first stages, under artificial conditions of economic and commercial protection and during periods of coinciding social priorities and profit criteria.

When the economy became exposed to the forces
of international markets, and the logic of economic
functioning imposed itself on commercial producers,
diverting them from social priorities, the latter
were hopelessly abandoned. The leader of the Northwestern vegetable producers sees it clearly in these
terms: why, he has asked, should farmers give up a
profit of one hundred thousand pesos per hectare with
the production of tomatoes, in order to turn to the
cultivation of corn yielding a profit of only ten
thousand pesos? The logic of his behavior and that
of the market coincide. It cannot be any other way.

It is thus a question of the protagonists of
production. Who, why and under what conditions will
they take care of the tasks of production? What
should the fate of the nation's resources be in regard to priority aspects of foodstuffs supply and
the development of cattle raising? The definition of
a development model and its technological requirements depends on the answer to these questions. In
1940, they had a precise answer: it was vital to
rescue those *hacendados* that had been able to survive thirty years of agrarian process, forget "*ejidal* rhetoric" -as Calles suggested in 1930- and
entrust the productive tasks of the agricultural
sector to a group of "modern farmers" aided by
support mechanisms of the State.

In Nathan L. Wetten's study made for the U.S.
State Department, it is pointed out that in 1940,
two thirds of the properties of over one thousand
hectares in size "were found in regions too dry for

non-irrigated crops to prosper without considerable
risk." 61 per cent of all properties with an area
of over 10,000 hectares were also located in those
Northern regions. (13) The redistribution of land
did not seem reversible, but it was still possible
to place the responsibility of production on those
rural producers whose land, located in semi-arid
zones, had been spared from the effects of the
agrarian winds of change, and thus could be turned
into irrigated lands. Most investments between 1940
and 1970, as has already been pointed out, were
channeled into these regions. It is interesting to
see who received these benefits. "Whereas more than
200,000 of the irrigated hectares opened up during Cárdenas administration were given to rural
workers, those entering production after 1940 (approximately 1.8 million hectares until 1963), were
in general sold as private property to relatives of
politicians and important businessmen... many of
whom were already landowners." (14) During this
period, the state of Sinaloa received the lion's
share of investments for irrigated lands: 22.2 per
cent of the national total. When Wetten critically
evaluates the Cárdenas redistribution of land, he
mentions the organizing of small gangs of bandits
in Southern Sinaloa, which killed 600 or 700 *ejidatarios* and as many non-*ejidatarios* over a period of
four years. What originated conflicts in this area
was the question of whether certain properties were
liable to expropriation or not. Large tracts of
land had been informally divided by the owners
among their descendants. These took possession of
their plots without officially having made any
change of property in the public records office.
Although the descendant claimed to be a small land-
holder, the government, without any further investigation, and merely basing its information on that
of the records office, began to open cases of expropriation against the large holdings. The new
owner, after having strongly protested, fled to the
sierras and organized groups to oppose the appplica-
tion of the reform. It has been said that they took
pleasure in killing agrarian leaders whenever the
occasion arose. The *ejidatarios* found themselves

---

(13) Wetten, OP. CIT., p. 134
(14) Cynthia Hewitt, OP. CIT., p. 134

plowing the land with a rifle over their shoulders.
A *Banco Ejidal* employee was shot in the arm when
returning from collecting payments on credits granted to *ejidatarios*. In many places personal security
was so precarious that *ejidos* were abandoned, and
those who claimed to be the owners, took over the
land. Recently, a presidential agreement returned
the land of the abandoned *ejidos* to the alleged
former owners." (15)

As Wellhausen has correctly stressed, one agricultural "revolution" has come to an end, and Mexico
needs to start another. The first has responded to
questions formulated in a context dominated by
"progressive farmers" whom it served. However, as
Wellhausen says, these no longer exist. There are
only a few of them and in fact, fewer and fewer as
time goes by. That is the logic of their existence
and functioning: the logic of concentration. If a
"technological package for seasonally cultivated
lands" forms part of the new agricultural "revolution," and is aimed at these farmers, it is possible
that they will not be found. To define them, as Wellhausen does, by their location in good, seasonally
cultivated lands (the area in which the "technological package" can be effective), is an obsolete answer.
In any case, the present question would remain: what
is to be done with those *campesinos* that the new
revolution would displace or marginate? In what way
could commercial farmers be induced to produce
according to social priorities, detached from the
logic of profits? Is there a *campesino* or *campesinis-
ta* option to today's rural development? Would the
new agricultural revolution have a renewed agrarian
component? Mexico has entered the 1980s in the midst
of the debate around these questions.

---

(15) Wetten, OP.CIT., p. 116.

4

THE STATE AND THE COUNTRYSIDE:
THE STORY OF
A CONFLICTIVE RELATIONSHIP

The Agrarian Reform and the Green Revolution were
not only different projects; they were in direct
opposition to each other. Since the second movement
was capable of revitalizing the first which never
got too far, in retrospect some people are of the
opinion that in fact this was only one project,
which took different forms according to circumstances. From this point of view, those involved
were forced to follow the whims of the power structures, which were always able to turn to advantage
everything they touched. Facts, however, reveal in
agrarian reform a deeply rooted force of great historical significance coming from the *campesinos* that
has been unable to impose itself upon all other
social forces. Thus any progress the project makes
appears to be a concession by the power structures
as a result of strong rural pressure; setbacks and
changes -which have gone so far as to deny land
redistribution- would be manifestations of the weaknesses and deficiencies of this drive.

What part have the Mexican State and federal
power played in this process? How could the same
State, without any significant structural changes
and under conditions of exceptional stability within
the Latin American countries, simultaneously or successively undertake projects leading in opposing
directions?

A STORMY ROMANCE

On September 24, 1913, in a famous speech delivered
in Hermosillo, Sonora, the leader of the Constitutionalist Army, Venustiano Carranza, the father

of the Constitution, stated: "The Mexican people
must understand that once the armed struggle is
over... the formidable, majestic social struggle,
the class struggle, must begin." Four years later,
when the *Pacto Constitucional* was signed, Mexican
society felt that it would be politically able to
handle its class conflicts. Soon, however, it was
seen that this was not to be the case, as Carranza's
violent death proved.

On January 6, 1915, Venustiano Carranza tried to
take over the Zapatistas' banner with a radical a-
grarian law. The concessional character of that decree could not have been clearer. The intellectual
author, Luis Cabrera, noted as early as 1912: "The
rural population needs to complement its wages. If
they had *ejidos*, they would devote their energies to
harvesting them for half the year for their own benefit.
Without them, they are forced to live for six months
off their daily wages and the other six to take up
their rifles as Zapatistas." The decree (among other
limitations) demanded that villages prove their need
for land as well as their previous right to them,
while, at the same time, it gave *hacendados* the
chance to oppose agrarian action by resorting to
court action.

Carranza seemed conscious of the balance of
forces around him. On one side were the large Mexican and foreign interests, involved mainly with the
haciendas, oil production and mining, while on the
other side were the vigorous *campesino* armies. In
1914, he organized a convention to outline, in con-
ciliatory terms, the program for a new government.
The conference, however, quickly became radicalized:
the combined pressures of Zapatistas and Villistas
imposed a program which demanded the immediate return of *ejidos* to the people and the definitive
breaking of *latifundios*.

Although the convention did not recognize his
authority because of his views on agrarian matters,
Carranza took advantage of the conventionists' inca-
pacity to establish a structure and maintain political power, and regained control of the movement. In
his *Plan de Veracruz*, he announced, among other
things, his decision to pass agrarian laws "to favor
the formation of small holdings, by dissolving *latifundios* and restoring to the villages the land which

had unjustly been taken away from them." This
policy of concessions and equilibrium together with
Obregón's military actions which defeated Villa,
enabled Carranza to increase his control over the
country. However, to ensure that control would not
be lost again, and in answer to pressure from all
sides, and possibly because he was also concerned
about the social reforms being put into practice by
some of the leaders of the movement, Carranza con-
vened a Congress whose main task would be the draft-
ing of a new Constitution.

But the draft of the Constitution was negotiated in the midst of revolutionary effervescence, under the shadow of the real economic powers -whose
influence remained almost untouched- and in a very
short two month period. So once again it was presented in concessionary terms. The Constitution basically
brought together the *Programa de Reformas Sociales*
which had been formulated by the great *campesino*
armies of Villa and Zapata. However, neither the
Constitution nor the government which stemmed from
it, presided over by Carranza, could satisfy the
campesinos' concrete claims. Neither in form nor in
essence did it fit into the real world.

"Zapatism did not question the State nor did it
propose any kind of alternative. Through its rejection of all bourgeois factions and in its desire for
total autonomy, it placed itself outside the State.
Its form of organization did not derive from the
latter but from other roots. And if those who are
outside the State decide to take up arms, they auto-
matically place themselves against the State." (1)

In fact, the constitutionalist regime found a
many-faceted and insurmountable challenge in the
Zapatista movement: government was impossible without it or against it. And it could not govern with
it unless it denied its own existence. Zapatismo,
furthermore, was quite decided on doing without the
State. The movement not only had a program but also
an autonomous organization: that of the villages.
In the course of the Revolution, it had found "an
organizational form independent from the State and
its political fractions, specially tailored for the

_____

(1) Adolfo Gilly, "La guerra de clases en la Revolución Mexicana", in INTERPRETACIONES DE LA REVOLUCION
MEXICANA, UNAM-Nueva Imagen, México, 1979, p. 23.

campesinos, anchored in their own tradition, open to alliance with the industrial working class (even though this may never actually take place)." (2) Negotiations were impossible. The State, in the process of defining its nature through the Constitution could not accept at its core a force of such dimensions which was trying to detach itself from the State's zone of influence, even though it was not attempting to substitute it. And it was impossible to channel this contradiction through a political process, because the Zapatista's demands could not be reduced to the *Pacto Constitucional*. It was tearing apart -unknowingly perhaps- the framework of the relations of production within which it was constructed. It was necessary, again, to resort to force. On April 10, 1919, Zapata was assassinated in Chinameca. Nevertheless, *al caer Zapata en acción desleal, mataron a un hombre pero no a su ideal.**

Zapatismo in effect, did not die with Zapata, and the governing group that tried to build up federal power after the Revolution, remained opposed to it. The ardous search for stability led them, time and again, to make concessions to all other groups, without ever assuming the rural project as their own. As the centralized structure of federal power continued, on a national level, the solution to the question of land on a local level was defined not by politics but by force. Violence continued, while men from the state of Sonora -fundamentally opposed to Zapatismo-, began a progressive consolidation of the sort of economic and social structures which could support the exercise of power at national levels. By the end of the decade, it seemed as though the time had arrived to give political expression to the domination scheme through the establishment of the *Partido Nacional Revolucionario*. This wise decision initiated the Mexican State's "policy of the masses" which would place it irrevocably in a modern context. In this way, the State was able not only to bring together the different factions involved and give organic national direction to those local and regional powers which still remained, but was also able to create suitable conditions for promoting

---

(2) OP. CIT., p. 33

*   (Translator's note) When Zapata fell in a disloyal act, a man was killed but not his ideal.

social consensus which tends to operate as pre-condi-
tion for the effective functioning of modern capitalist societies.

The political stance of the new context made
President Calles, from Sonora, feel obliged to recognize the end of agrarianism. It seemed that the
illusion of the *campesino* community had to be done
away with in order to enter openly into the conventional transformation of capitalist production in
agriculture. It was a somewhat precipitous decision,
however. Zapatismo had become a concrete material
force, capable of exerting effective pressure on the
political system, in spite of its ideological confu-
sions, its lack of organic articulation and the
constant division amongst its leaders and *caudillos*.
It was impossible to eliminate Zapatismo at one
stroke, much less destroy people's expectations al-
together, since these had been maintained by partial
concessions granted from time to time to *campesinos*
throughout the Republic. The dormant restlessness of
the rural population was abruptly awakened by actions
such as that of Calles. They were on the move again.

At the beginning of the 1930s, a double force
rose against the landholding bourgeosie which, during
the previous decade, had recovered: on the one hand,
a new dynamics of the *campesino* which grouped together Calles' anti-agrarian policies, and on the
other, the industrial and commercial structures of
economic power advancing at the same pace as capitalist expansion. The effects of the Great Depression
and the commotion prior to World War II were also
being felt throughout the country. Within this context, the workers were beginning to make their presence felt through organizations which they had been
forming. The power conflicts which were still alive
between different political groups were reactivated
and the country trembled to its foundations. In
order to direct such diversity of contradictions in
political terms, the Cardenista administration adopted a radical framework for action. This included the
Plan Sexenal of 1934, as well as the launching of an open
and consistent policy of the masses, which turned
popular mobilization into the key for transforming
government action.

The process through which the *Confederación
Nacional Campesina* came into being has already been

mentioned. Between 1935 and 1938 the Zapatista flag
continued to fly at regional levels. The accelerated
redistribution of land, an attempt to create collective organizations, and the ability once more to
oppose landowners' aggressions through the use of
arms supplied by government, together with many other
factors, stimulated the *campesinos'* political participation, which seemed to be of a much higher level
than during the Revolutionary uprising. In Zapatismo
there existed the germ for development of the *campesino*-worker alliance embodied in the figure of the
campesino-proletariat working in the sugar fields and
modern sugar mills of Morelos." (3) The establishment
of the Emiliano Zapata cooperative sugar mill, on
February 10, 1938, culminated this period and symbolically took up once more the historic line of this
alliance. It had ceased to be a germinative element
and had become a concrete possibility even though it
was not, as yet, a tangible reality.

All this was too much. And too soon. Internal
and external pressures radically changed the possibilities and the direction of events. The Cardenista
administration -within the constitutional framework
and because of the dynamics of forces outside its con-
trol- strengthened the economic structures capable of
blockading the political option it had open through
popular mobilization. These forces were willing to
stop short, before it was too late. They had already
managed to do so during the first ten years of revolutionary actions, when foreign military intervention was only symptomatic of that decision and of the
power behind it. Now, the same international conditions which had previously reduced the risks of oil
expropriation or the creation of worker-*campesino* organizations and federal power, which played a strategic role in the mobilization and organization of the
workers, were now operating as a restraint. The internal dynamics of these organizations, which had been
encouraged and reactivated by Cardenista fire, were
unable to express themselves fully in a context which
conspired to extinguish or repress them. Federal power
could not and did not want to deny the nature of the
State system merely in order to follow the impulse of
an impetuous popular trend which it had itself pro-

---

(3) Ibidem.

moted as a survival weapon but that now tended to
destroy it.

   The military turbulence of the first decade of
the Mexican Revolution was followed by twenty
years of political turmoil. The social content of
the 1917 Constitution was defined as a result of
this turmoil. The worker-*campesino* project which had
emerged in embryonic form during the revolutionary
upheaval and had taken on new life in the following
years, was not adopted by the State since the dominating structure denied the very essence of the project. At first the federal power of the State had
accomodated different revolutionary factions. These
were still trying in the 1920s to free themselves
from control. Their contradictions disarmed the
State and blocked the construction of a truly national project: the creation of a State party. In
the 1930s, federal power had been invigorated by the
very dynamism of the social forces which had originally given strength to the Revolution. However,
when these forces gained momentum, and wanted to go
further, federal power found itself tied to forces
opposing the project. In the face of the increasingly insistent and specific demands of the latter, it
became necessary to subordinate the former, i.e., it
became necessary to open up possibilities for those
forces which were in keeping with the established
social order, for those forces that could develop
within the State. At the same time all opposing
forces had to be removed from the heart of federal
power. Above all, Zapatismo had to be extinguished,
especially since it was now adding to the strength
of its historic significance a realization of its
potential as a modern social movement, as it savor-
ed the sweetness of its alliance with other social
classes. It was necessary to exclude the *campesinos*
from the project: they had no place in it. Now, the
question was not one of getting rid of a burden
from the past, but one of preventing an option that
was beginning to appear for the future. For the next
forty years, the Mexican State, through the strength
of its federal power, dedicated its efforts to precisely that task. This was achieved by carefully
dismembering the alliances that had been formed
during the previous period and encouraging the formation of others more in line with State projects.

In 1935, Ramón Beteta voiced an attitude prevalent among Cardenistas by suggesting that Mexico
was capable of shaping her own destiny: "By observ-
ing the effects of the capitalist world's last crisis, we believe that we can reap the benefits of
the industrial age without having to suffer the negative consequences... We have dreamed of a Mexico
made up of *ejidos* and small industrial communities,
with electric power, health institutions, where
goods are produced to satisfy the population's needs,
where machinery is employed to alleviate men from
hard labor, and not for so-called overproduction."
A few years later, Ramón Beteta became one of the
main designers of a radically different model.

The griddle was too hot for pancakes. The same
Cardenista drive intensified pressure for rapid industrialization. The World War opened extraordinary
opportunities for industrial entrepreneurs, especially among the younger generation who found no difficulty in combining their interests with those of
their more traditional colleagues. A decrease in the
supply of industrial products because of the war was
moving in the same direction. The landowners seemed
relieved that the emphasis of the development model
was no longer on agrarian transformation. They knew
they could link their enterprises to the new industrial structure. The workers, for their part, could
not but observe with interest the prospect of constant increases in the number of jobs. The *campesinos* were the only group that did not have a place
at the banquet of the industrial revolution. When
President Avila Camacho was sworn in, he announced
a new project and warned that in order for it to be
put into practice, the country would rely mostly on
"the vital energy of private enterprise." The agricultural sector did not form part of this promised
destiny. Its task was to create the "basis for
achieving industrial greatness;" in order to do
that "protection for agricultural private property
would be increased, not only to defend those already
existing, but also to form   new private properties
in vast uncultivated regions."

A MARRIAGE OF CONVENIENCE

To exclude the *campesinos* does not mean doing without them. It is to let them make their strategic con-

tribution to the project -subordinating their own
revindications and not enjoying its results- with
the sole expectation of later becoming a part of it,
as soon as they cease to be what they are.

The model of industrial urban development adopted in Mexico during the last decades fell within the
context of delayed capitalism subordinated to the
capitalist system of the United States. This model
assigned three specific functions to agricultural and
cattle-raising activities:

- The provision of foodstuffs and raw materials at
low and stable prices for the domestic market in
order to facilitate urban wage control. (4)

-----

(4) The wage question implies a serious contradiction
in the application of the model. On the one hand, it
is essential to keep them low and stable to foster
capital accumulation in the industrial sector, which
is the key to the model. On the other hand, the new
class alliance on which it is based, finds a fundamental component among the "organized" workers. This
contradiction has demanded since the 1940s, special
efforts producing every uneven results. Up until 1970,
it was possible to grant real income improvements to
the most advanced sectors of the working class, even
though their share of the social product decreased,
while the share of other workers, the campesinos and
the ever-increasing number of marginal population in
the cities, was considerably reduced. In order to
make this pattern of evolution possible, the State
proceeded first to break up the alliance established
in the 1930s between the worker and campesino organizations. After that, the links and mechanisms of
ideological and political control of federal power
were strengthened over those worker organizations
that could become part of the impious alliance. The
efforts of the independent unions movement were thus
obstructed or repressed in their search for support
from the rising middle classes, into which the workers of the organized sector were rapidly being incorporated. The massive repression of a long range
independent worker movement, which in 1958 posed a
serious threat to the global model, was as unorganiz-
ed as it was violent. During the seventies, in view
of the exhaustion of the model, it became necessary

-The generation of foreign exchange through a favorable agricultural balance of trade, and the contribution of resources through commercial, financial
and fiscal transfers in order to support the process
of industrial accumulation and the financing of
development.

-The partial covering of the cost of reproducing the
labor force required in rural areas of high productivity or in urban services, as well as the supply of
labor force in permanent demand for the industrial
and commercial development in the cities.

At the beginning of the 1940s, the first of
these functions was of decisive importance. The
increasing food deficit and the high rate of inflation caused severe upheavals. Though imports were
available to meet the most immediate needs the problem had to be tackled at its roots. The problem was
not the stagnation of agricultural and livestock activities, whose yearly production growth rate was
more than five per cent between 1935 and 1942. The
problem arose from the fast growth in urban demand,
which in turn was related to industrialization and
to rural production (being withheld as a result of
the change in distribution) as well as to the vora-
cious appropriation of surplus generated in the
agricultural sector in accordance with the new model.
The task was entrusted, basically, to the "progres-

---

to resort to external borrowing and to deficit financing of public expenditure to meet the increasing
demands of conflicting groups. The political concessions granted during the first years of the decade,
had been more rhetorical than real, but effective in
many ways. However, they led to the 1976 crisis,
after which a deterioration in income extended also
to those who, until then, had enjoyed constant improvements, thus bringing them down to the 1940 level. In the struggle that developed during the 1970s
over the use of oil revenues, among other things,
the set of alliances backing the model were being
rearranged.
For an analysis of this process during the last
decade, see Carlos Tello, LA POLITICA ECONOMICA EN
MEXICO, Siglo XXI Editores, México, 1979, and "La
disputa por la Nación," in NEXOS, No. 24, December
1979, as well as David Barkin and Gustavo Esteva,
INFLACION Y DEMOCRACIA: EL CASO DE MEXICO, Siglo XXI
Editores, México, 1979.

sive farmers" of the North, i.e. large capitalist
enclaves. As has been previously indicated, the technology of the Green Revolution was only one component
of the development programs, which were based on
irrigation projects.

Only seven per cent of all arable land in Mexico can produce satisfactory results without irrigation under existing technology. That is why hydraulic works have always played a strategic role in
agricultural development, even in Aztec times. At
the turn of the century it was estimated that only
70,000 hectares were under irrigation and even these
used relatively small-scale and scattered systems.
The 1917 Constitution placed great responsibility
for this task on the revolutionary governments, in
terms of the 27th Article of the Constitution. In
1921, the *Dirección de Irrigación* was created for
that purpose, and in 1924 it became the *Departamento de Reglamentación e Irrigación*. Two years later,
as part of a policy designed to support medium-sized
private farms, Calles founded the *Comisión Nacional
de Irrigación*, which had an allocation amounting to
4.4 per cent of the federal budget for two years.
During the Cardenista administration this amount
rose to 7.8 per cent for the construction of
200,000 irrigated hectares and the rehabilitation of
a similar number of hectares which were given to
ejidatarios and small private landowners.

The new model promoted irrigation works from
1940 onwards. Between 1941 and 1946 they absorbed
15 per cent of all public investments -a sum equivalent to more than 90% of the total resources allo-
cated to agricultural development. In 1946 the *Secretaría de Recursos Hidráulicos* took the place of
the old *Comisión Nacional de Irrigación* and was
charged with this huge task. By 1940 there were
310,000 hectares in the officially irrigated districts. This figure represented one third of all
irrigated land. Ten years later, public works had
expanded to an area of 859,000 hectares, almost
half the national total. These figures showed a
twofold increase by 1960, and reached, in the '70s
the sum of 3 million hectares in officially irrigated districts, and around 5 million including
non-public irrigated lands. Whereas in 1940, land
irrigated from public investment funds did not

reach 5 per cent of the total land under cultivation, the proportion in the seventies had risen to
two fifths of the total.

The distribution of irrigated land followed the
concentration pattern indicated by the model. As
shown earlier, investments were channeled mainly into
the Northern and North Pacific States, where Sinaloa, Sonora and Tamaulipas absorbed more than 40 per
cent of the investments made between 1941 and 1970.
However, at present, less than one per cent of
current producers own 20 per cent of all irrigated
land. Concentration has tended to operate through
control mechanisms (such as the illegal leasing of
plots), rather than through direct ownership.

During the 1950s the privileged areas were thus
able to satisfy their food requirements, and since
then have been used to fulfill the second function
assigned to them: that of the generation of foreign
exchange through exports. Meanwhile, the *campesino*
economy was slowly dying, paying the costs of survival and providing temporary labor for domestic
zones and those of the Southern United States. Migration to urban areas increased rapidly, surpassing industrial requirements which had originated
the so-called phenomenon of marginal populations in
the cities.

The model demanded an improved national land
communications system, and as a result the network
has grown from 10 thousand km to 200 thousand in the
last forty years. In keeping with global conceptions,
although not in keeping with the real priorities of
Mexican society, emphasis was placed on road transportation because a substantial increase was expected in the number of motor vehicles (from 150 thousand in 1940 to over 4 million in 1980), while rail-
road transportation became stagnant.

It is also necessary to include in the overall
perspective, public investment in electrification,
which showed an extraordinary increase, although it
only reached the rural sector in the last decade;
and investment in educational and health services,
which should also be included, although it should be
pointed out that the gap in this area is widening.

Credit funds directed to agricultural production have represented a very substantial part of the
official budget for the agricultural sector. In
spite of this, however, producers' access to public
financing has always been very limited, especially
in the case of seasonal lands, since the *ejidatarios*
and small property owners are unable to adjust to
the profit and guarantee criteria through which
official agricultural banking operates. These producers have been caught in a vicious circle because
of their deficient accumulation which prevents them
from being able to comply with the requirements. They
thus continue to resort to non-institutional sources
(*caciques* and money lenders) that only lessen the
possibility of accumulation. The relative scarcity of
operating credit further limits the options open to
these producers.

In areas of commercial agriculture, farmers have
had relatively easy access to credit both from public and private sources. During the last forty
years, private credit to this group grew at annual
rates of above ten per cent. This can be explained in
part by the creation of a trust fund to guarantee and
foster agricultural projects called *Fondo de Garantía
y Fomento de la Agricultura*. This organization provided private banks with federal funds at low interest rates.

Market intervention aimed at regulating them has
been one of the essential components of official
policy to promote agriculture and cattle-raising.

During the last two years of the Cardenista administration, a committee to regulate the markets
for basic goods, the *Comité Regulador de los Mercados
de Subsistencia* fulfilled a strategic function in the
protection of small rural producers and consumers.

A good part of its actions were undertaken
through worker and *campesino* organizations, which
directly operated union stores and other facilities
with open support from the government. At the end of
Cárdenas' presidential term, the *Comité* came to be
one of the central points under attack by the private
sector, which accused it of unfair competition
with traders.

Avila Camacho disbanded the *Comité*. Although inflationary pressure and other factors forced its reappearance under different guises between 1940 and 1970, it operated basically as a subsidy mechanism for urban consumers (within the policy of low incomes) and as a decisive backing to large commercial farmers. In the 1950s the guaranteed prices offered to producers of basic goods -above those of the domestic and foreign markets- ensured crop profitability. In theory they were fixed in terms of the small producers' needs ("It constitutes the minimum wage of the rural workers," said President López Mateos in 1964), but they rarely reached the *campesinos*, who were forced to sell their crops to middlemen who in turn, together with the large farmers, took advantage of the subsidy included in the official system. In 1963, when export surpluses of basic foodstuffs were beginning to appear and signals from the U.S. market induced a different product orientation, guaranteed prices were frozen and began to function as ceiling prices for the exclusive protection of urban consumers.

In the seventies, when the self-sufficiency objective was adopted as a result of the grave situation of the increasing food production deficit, guaranteed prices rose and efforts were made to have these reach the *campesinos*. These efforts were interrupted by the 1976 crisis, and their effects were neither deep nor lasting, because they were not integrated with other elements of official policy towards the rural sector.

The *Compañía Nacional de Subsistencias Populares* (*CONASUPO*), the institution at present in charge of this specific task, as well as other institutions that preceded it, has fulfilled functions of utmost importance in relation to the rural sector throughout this period: the export of surpluses and import of complementary production, the setting and administration of guaranteed prices, the operation of the greater part of the storage systems, the wholesale and retail distribution of basic products and other CONASUPO activities as key elements in the general strategy. Furthermore, the institution's flexibility, which allows for easy modifications of the aims of its operations, have turned it into an indicator of the trends in the co-relation of forces, since it

can readily respond to the pressure of different social groups, to take care of their various demands.

The supply of fertilizer became a fundamental
variable of the model as the Green Revolution proceeded. In the sixties, the industry was nationalized.
Since then it has operated as a government monopoly,
and production of nitrated and phosphated products
increased over 20 times during the last two decades.
The greater part has been directed to irrigated commercial fields because of the technical argument
that it is in these areas that it can be most ad-
vantageously utilized. By the end of the 1960s, for
instance, four States with 42 per cent of the country's irrigated lands absorbed 54 per cent of all
fertilizers. Increasing subsidies to this operation
have constituted additional backing for this group.

Government exercises little control over the
insecticide market. It only intervenes in the production of certain raw materials of petrochemical
origin, and in the production of three products representing 15 per cent of total consumption. A few
multinational companies hold almost absolute control
over this market.

The production of improved seeds has been a
matter of constant conflict during the last decades.
Several institutions created at different times have
constantly fought, first with large private producers,
and later with certain international companies, the
multiplication of genetic material produced within
the framework of the Green Revolution. These institutions were the Comisión Nacional del Maíz created in
1947, the Comisión para el Incremento y Distribución
de Semillas Mejoradas, founded some time later, and
the Productora Nacional de Semillas, formed in 1961.
Official production, however, has not been able to
meet, to any significant extent, national needs for
seeds, except in the case of wheat. Operations have
been concentrated, naturally, in regions of commercial agriculture.

The task of agricultural expansion has traditionally been neglected by government, which lacks an adequate number of qualified technicians and effective
methods. The chronic   scarcity of funds and the
bureaucratization of these activities have been determining factors for qualified agronomists preferring

to work directly with large farmers or independently, under conditions that reduce their efficiency.

In the 1940s, a special official aid program enabled Mexico to be, at the beginning of the following decade, the Latin American country with greatest agricultural mechanization. Between 1940 and 1950, as a result of substantial imports, the value of agricultural machinery in the hands of large producers showed a five-fold increase, whereas that of the *ejidatarios* doubled and smallholdings increased two and a half times in this respect.

During the sixties, when irrigation, improved seeds, fertilizers, guaranteed prices and mechanization fostered large commercial agriculture, government began to limit imports in order to favor national production of agricultural equipment which since then has produced over 5,000 tractors a year.

Mexico has since lost her position in Latin America in terms of mechanization. At the same time she has a high proportion of under-utilized equipment, as a result of both maintenance and operational problems (which reflect the compulsive pattern in the introduction of the process), and of its irrational concentration in a few over-mechanized areas.

Throughout this period, a variety of institutions were created by Government, specializing in the regulation of specific markets (sugar, coffee, tobacco, *henequen*) and in agroindustrial operations. In some cases official agencies have acquired a monopoly status, over both domestic and foreign markets, as well as with regard to industrial or commercial activities. They have generally adopted current forms of relations with agricultural producers, drawing them in form only, or in fact, into the company's operations. In many cases, they have formed a link between national and foreign industries that perform the final processing and the distribution of agricultural and livestock produce.

DIVORCE ON GROUNDS OF INCOMPATIBILITY

Thus, in summary, it is clear that government actions in many ways have conflicted with the *campesinos'* interests. And this is the group which had constituted the main force in the Revolution, from which the modern Mexican State emerged and which continues to be the social group with the highest numerical weight in the whole social conglomerate. This conflict is one of the central concerns of federal power, and the dialectics of its relations with the *campesinos* has become the key to the overall political framework of subsequent administrations.

From the federal power's point of view, the problem may be defined as the need to maintain the *campesinos* close enough to prevent them from becoming an independent and opposing force that might weaken the State, but at the same time conveniently distant in order to avoid being forced to yield to their historical demands, which are in opposition to the general aims of government's present course. From the *campesinos'* point of view the problem has similar characteristics. Since the central question concerning land tenure lies in the hands of federal power, as well as access to credit, inputs, marketing, guarantee prices and all other support services needed for their survival and development, the *campesinos* cannot take their independence to the point of a radical political rupture with the authorities: those who do, find themselves immediately exposed to the loss of official backing and to political repression and are also defenseless in the face of exploitation. Moving too close to federal power, on the contrary, would mean delaying indefinitely their claims and being caught up in a bureaucratic tangle from which only marginal and passing concessions can be obtained and where only a few -those who integrate to the power structure- are in a position to benefit.

This situation explains, in part, the evolution of rural organizations during this period. The *Confederación Nacional Campesina (CNC)*, a national rural workers' organization, lost, in the 1940s along with its allies in the workers sector, its

capacity for mobilization. Since then, it has operated as an agent and control organism, dedicated to
defending the most urgent *campesino* demands and to
keeping them at a prudent distance from federal power.
Because of this, it has been, and continues to be the
principal *campesino* organization in the country,
although its militance is as weak as its real political and social capacity to negotiate. It has maintained a state of latency; there is no political organization capable of mobilizing a greater number of
people than the CNC, but that capacity is only used
occasionally, mainly in the regional context and in
general terms, to respond to initiatives of federal
power.

In recent decades, some independent organizations have played a relevant role in the mobilization of *campesinos*: the *Unión General de Obreros y
Campesinos de México* (UGOCM), during the fifties
and the sixties; the *Central Campesina Independiente* (CCI), in the fifties and sixties; movements led
by people like Jaramillo, Lucio Cabañas and Genaro
Vázquez in the sixties; the *Consejo Agrarista Mexicano* (CAM), the *Movimiento de los Cuatrocientos
Pueblos*, the *Consejo Nacional Cardenista*, the *Movimiento Nacional Plan de Ayala* and others in the
seventies.

After short periods of great influence, none of
these movements has gone very far. The UGOCM led to
great mobilization by the end of the 1950s. It had
wide national scope in spite of the fact that it was
concentrated in the Northwest of the nation. After
having obtained the redistribution of some large
estates, some of them from foreign owners, the UGOCM
began to be assimilated into the official apparatus.
After the death of its leader, Jacinto López, it
began to disintegrate and to lose importance at a
national level, being influential only in some regions. Something similar happened with the CCI,
which fought important battles in the seventies within the context of a national liberation movement
called the *Movimiento de Liberación Nacional,* but
since its incorporation into an agreement known as
the *Pacto de Ocampo* headed by the CNC and promoted
by government at the beginning of the seventies, it
has been converted into an auxiliary agency in the
CNC line. The Jaramillo movement has played a mini-

mal role since the death of its leader; those of Lucio Cabañas and Genaro Vázquez ended in guerrilla movements of limited scope and were extinguished together with them. The CAM has played an ambivalent role of agitation and only at a local level.

Under these conditions, the *campesinos* have had to reconstruct their organizations on a local and regional basis, utilizing their communal traditions and fighting experience to give modern political significance, based on solidarity, to their social structures. Thus, a myriad of independent and extremely combative organizations were born in *ejidos* and villages. Many of them have taken the form of politically oriented social movements, more than formal political organizations. Frequently *campesinos* who are members of these organizations, become militants in other *campesino* organizations or political parties in order to make their demands felt. These organizations have gradually been adjusting their efforts in order to express their goals through more general movements. Since August 8, 1979, for example, when they gathered independently to commemorate Emiliano Zapata's centennial, an important group of them formed a coordinating organization, called *Coordinadora Nacional Plan de Ayala*. During the first six months it organized two important conferences called *Encuentros de Organizaciones Campesinas Independientes*, which were attended by *campesinos* and their representatives from many different parts of the Republic.

The *Consejo Supremo de Pueblos Indígenas* is worth a special mention. Created by the initiative of the CNC and the Government at the beginning of the seventies with relatively little representation at the initiation, it established in its structure the organizing principles of the Indian peoples. In this way, it has gained growing autonomy from governmental powers, making progress in the independent representation of the six million Indian *campesinos* it comprises.

In this context, it has been especially difficult for the authorities to bring the present plan to its ultimate consequences. In the first half of the 1970s, the *campesino* movement led by the State and its policy of limited concessions acted as a channel for many *campesino* demands and encouraged

their expectations for change. In the second half
of the decade, it became necessary to frustrate
those expectations and give warning that the agrarian redistribution would come to an end soon. This
occurred within the context of a serious rural crisis, when latent *campesino* restlessness became more
aroused as a result of local conditions and the
movements and organizations these conditions
generated, which fit quite naturally into those of
national scope. Rural violence has thus increased
to levels that were unknown some decades ago. Local
repression by authorities, in the midst of conflicts
between federal public officials and those at the
State and municipal level, compounded the direct
action of the *guardias blancas* or private police of
large landowners, *caciques*, cattlemen and other
agents, as well as that of the *campesinos* themselves.
These acts, that have awakened general concern, reflect the end of political negotiation formulae
within a project that explicitly exclude *campesinos*
who do not accept their outcast, partly because of a
lack of real options.

The overall logic of national and international
economic and social pressure is forcing the Mexican
State to establish more and more precisely the terms
of its radical divorce from the *campesinos*, whose
demands are considered incompatible with those of
the adopted development model. But at the same time,
it appears incapable of overcoming present difficulties or of getting out of the blind alley in which
it finds itself. In practice, it has been impossible
for the economy as a whole to absorb in other agricultural, industrial and service occupations, the
campesino labor force that the process continues to
displace. According to the conventional patterns of
the model, it is not feasible to overcome the present productive crisis when the food deficit has reach
ed dangerous levels and the traditional contribution
of the sector in the generation of foreign exchange
is fading. Though the government could adapt itself
to these new circumstances, redirecting its efforts
to give firm support to the *campesino* economy, it
faces difficulties in attempting to achieve this,
for it is tied to alliances made since the 1940s
aimed at accomplishing current goals. Only effective reconstitution of these alliances, which
would appear to be beset with difficulties and limitations, could avoid a radical divorce between

Government and *campesinos* -and strictly speaking,
between the State and the *campesinos*- that neither
side seems capable of surviving unharmed.

PART TWO

THE PROTAGONISTS

The main protagonists of rural Mexico will be introduced in this part of the book.

Brief reference is made in the first chapter to
the economic context within which they function. Basically it offers a theoretical and analytical framework
for a better understanding of the synchronic
background of subsequent chapters. The protagonists
found at the different levels of multilinear development associated with the various "phases" and modes of
productive behavior, will then be introduced. This
framework follows the central underlying tendencies
which govern the behavior of the different protagonists.
It traces at both national and international levels the
determining factors to which they are subjected and to
which they react according to their previous historical
burden.

The protagonists described in the second and third
chapters have been grouped according to how they
identify with capital or work. This classification was
chosen in preference to one concentrating on productive
units or communities, life-styles, or family and
individual patterns — the assumption being that the
fundamental homogenization of the protagonists stems
from their social relations of production and from
their position in the productive process. Therefore
this kind of approach considers these relations as
determining factors in the general behavior of those
productive agents who obviously retain the heterogeneity
derived from ethnic characteristics, regions, income
level, degree of development of productive forces,
etc. Limited space has restricted the description of
these factors to a minimum.

In the fourth chapter, an attempt is made to remedy, in part, the limitations of having adopted a typological approach, through the overall presentation of the protagonists' characteristics by crops and regions.

1

THE ECONOMIC CONTEXT:
THE GLOBAL LOGIC OF
HOW AGENTS FUNCTION

The most important protagonist in rural Mexico is
neither Mexican nor to be found in Mexico. Although
this statement still causes horrified reactions, it
is actually, a simple statement of fact: agribusiness exists as a global reality, structuring
world domination and controlling food production. One
hundred large multinational corporations already control more than half the international exchange of
food and will soon control half of its production.
Five of them handle 85% of the world's grain exchange.
Cultivation itself has lost importance within their
operations; it constitutes only 15% of the aggregate
value of the food industry in the United States, but
this cultivation is determined and controlled by the
overall operation. The existence of "these huge
systems for transforming agricultural products represents, without doubt, the multinationalization of
production, the multinationalization of capital and
its system of know-how, culminating with the multinationalization of commercialization circuits. This
last element, obviously, completes the structure of
domination and control." (1)

This comment could be applied to almost every
country in the peripheral areas, due to the very
globality of its nature. However, in Mexico it is of
special importance and takes strange shades of
meaning. A variety of factors, some as obvious as the
proximity of the United States, have accelerated the
process of the country's insertion into the new international division of labor fostered by multinational
capital. The internal structure of production and the

---

(1) Enrique Ruiz García, "El Agribusiness, el mayor ne-
gocio del siglo," in CRITICA POLITICA, No. 3, April
15-30, 1980, p. 41.

organization of labor are determined by the actions
and economic logic of multinational corporations and
through the commercial and financial relations of
Mexican producers with them abroad. This interplay
of relations includes, of course, the periodic
hiring of a substantial portion of the Mexican rural
labor force in the fields of the Southern United
States, a phenomenon that plays a decisive role in the
general functioning of the rural sector in Mexico.

The presence of national and multinational capital in rural Mexico is part of a completely generalized reality. It is not always, however, an obvious
one. At the level of apparent phenomena and description — the elements which usually generate "posi-
tivistic knowledge" — the protagonists of production
often seem alien to this prevailing reality, the
quality of which is a consequence of analytical treatment and theoretical elaboration. These methodological
tools, make up the core of this book and should
therefore, be explicitly stated here, even if only
briefly and partially, in order to assert the criteria
which led to the specific order of data in this section.

THE GENERAL FRAMEWORK

The productive structure of modern Mexican agrarian
history has been molded in terms of the functional
modalities of capital which have given rise to con-
current lines of development in the rural sector.
Capital has subordinated the productive practices of
rural Mexico and has inserted them into its own logic. However, the importance of this role can only
be understood by looking at how capital has interacted
with the conditions which have arisen within Mexican
society since the Revolution. The fact that capital
has had to adapt to these conditions has meant that
concrete courses of action have been defined for its
diverse modi operandi.

As indicated before, an explicit Constitutional
provision made land the exclusive patrimony of the Nation, so that it can, if it is so decided, be given
in usufruct to individuals thereby establishing it as
private property. By so doing, however, it vetoes
the participation of mercantile groups in the direct

exploitation of the land. This legal measure and the socio-political context associated to it, has forced capital to look for atypical ways of generalizing its social relations and mechanisms of accumulation. Within this general framework, the different ways capital operates (industrial, commercial and financial) have given way to "models for the organization of production" which can be classified according to the general guidelines imposed on the productive structure of the sector; the importance of the characteristic ways capital operates within the overall organization of the agrarian system; and the kind of social relations between the agrarian protagonists, differentiated by their line of production.

Taking this as a basis, three evolutionary phases can be distinguished in the history of the capitalist development of the Mexican agricultural sector throughout this century: the mercantile capitalist phase, the period of agrarian developmentalism, and the agroindustrial multinationalization stage, together with the expansion of extensive livestock practices.

The mercantile phase is characterized by production governed by external demands and by the central presence of commercial capital. It is noticeable in the strong dependence of the Northwestern horticultural and fruit production and on the North and Northeastern cattle-raising activities upon North American market requirements. It reinforces the nation's long tradition of agricultural export.

The agrarian developmetalist phase, guided by federal power, falls within the industrialization project through which the functions of the agricultural and cattle-raising sectors were redefined. Modernization attempts were channelled through activities related to the Green Revolution (technological innovation, financing and infrastructure); and to the quantitative and qualitative expansion of public enterprises in the processes of commercialization and transformation of certain basic foodstuffs and traditional products.

The rural agroindustrial multinationalization stage is characterized by a reorientation of produc-

tive activity towards the demands of a concentrated
internal market, with its new diversified consumer
patterns from which the bulk of the population is
excluded. (2)   This re-orientation is encouraged
and guided by the overwhelming presence of multinational agroindustries. This stage responds to the
worldwide social reality of the institutionaliza-
tion of hunger due to reorganization of eating
habits and the concentration of productive efforts
on social groups that consume more than 3,500 calories, that is, the process of waste.

The protagonists in each stage of development
are revealed indiscriminately against the synchronic
background of the following chapters, in the same
way as the phases represented here as a linear process coexist within the present reality of rural
Mexico. In fact, not only has real evolution been
multilinear, but with the appearance of a new
phase or stage it revitalizes previous phases without eliminating them. For example the current
importance of agroindustrial multinationalization
does not mean that the agro-exporter's role is
eliminated from one of the sectors of rural economy.
This fulfills another aspect of the process of
insertion of the Mexican economy as both buyer and
seller into the world food system.

These "phases" -which can also be seen as
current modes of differing importance within the
totality- can be described in the following terms:

a) The Agrocommercial Operation

The process of capitalist articulation within
the Mexican agricultural and cattle-raising sector,
its expansion in dynamic sense, and its integration
into the framework of the new international division

---

(2) This is not an absolute exclusion. The "hungry
sector" of the population -that which consumes less
than 2,750 calories and 80 grams of protein per
person per day- increases its consumption of non-nu-
tritious "food" as their diet deteriorates. In Mexico basic consumption for the bulk of the population
has deteriorated over the last twenty years, but
consumption of soft drinks, refined flour and sugar
products has shown spectacular increases.

of labor are all related to the increasing control
of multinational agribusiness over market mechanisms. It has used this control to integrate local
and regional producers gradually into its mercantile
sphere. Throughout this process, productive specialization patterns have been imposed on the rural
sector, thus leading the way to a relationship of
dependence on agribusiness as the principal, or
sole buyer.

The position of agribusiness within the market
has enabled it to impose mechanisms for price determination according to the following factors:
quality of the product (classification, type, standarization); volume of demand; storage and transportation capacity; sales contracts; financing of
production; technical assistance and allocation of
industrial inputs and technical equipment.

This mode of commercial operation encouraged a
differentiation between producers within the agribusiness sphere of influence, thus reinforcing the
capitalist orientation of small private producers.
Stimulated by such encouragement, they attempted to
extend their control to other small properties or
over the ejidos by means of direct coercion, legal
land disputes or the illegal leasing of plots.

b) Agrarian Developmentalism

The industrialization project gave the Mexican
Government a strategic role in the process of "productive modernization." Its support of technological
innovation, through the Green Revolution, encouraged
agricultural forms of organization which emphasized
the differentiation of producers and the diversification of their behavior in relation to the market.
Thus, credit has been used as an active tool in technological expansion and has been a key element in the
implementation of projects related to the sowing of
hybrid seeds, mechanization, fertilization, fumigation,
irrigation, etc. Through these measures — complemented
by the construction of public and industrial services,
technical assistance, education and agrarian service
activities and price-regulating mechanisms — it has
been possible to expand the context of "modern" com-
mercially based agriculture, so closely linked to multi
national agribusiness operations and its local partners.

Government action has likewise been aimed at
generating a new dynamic process based on both
basic and traditional crops. It has actively intervened in the commercialization process by regulating the basic grains market through producer and
consumer price systems, and by advocating the
establishment of norms for the classification and
standarization of products. A system of public
ownership was initiated for the primary processing
of traditional crops (sugar, coffee, sisal, cocoa,
etc.) which centralized demand. An increasing
number of direct producers were thus won over. In
many cases Government offered marketing and price
guarantees which encouraged reproduction and made
the capitalist organization of production profitable.

c) Agroindustrial Multinationalization

Multinational agroindustries injected a new
dynamic relation into Mexican rural production in
keeping with the world-wide tendency initiated in
the 1960s and intensified during the 1970s. It
integrated the agricultural and cattle-raising
economy into the new international model of production organization, which spreads international
patterns of consumption throughout domestic markets.
It also subordinated the national economy to metropolitan reproduction, thus transforming it into a
buyer of agricultural inputs of imported industrial
origin (machines and equipment, fertilizers, insecticides, management technology, packing systems,
etc.). In this way, traditional and especially basic
crops have been displaced by others or made so much
less profit-producing that the land is abandoned.
The food deficit is thus increased and can only be
covered through imports. This completes the internationalization cycle.

Multinational agroindustry placed itself in
productive areas where it was able to use its technological advantages to impose those new patterns of
production which were actively related to the process
of technological innovation. Producers had to act
according to capitalistic logic as far as crops were
concerned, in order to adapt to the new kind of demands being made by multinational agroindustry. This
means applying a new kind of rationality to the
future and use of land, which resulted in the displa-
cement of basic crops.

Multinational agroindustry has also generated
a dynamic process integrating and subordinating
agricultural production and industrial transformation and processing. By placing itself at strategic
points in the agroindustrial chain, it is able to
apply a model of accumulation based on the absorption of increasing aggregate value rates throughout
the productive phases. It has established a production, financing and food consumption system
through multiple regulating mechanisms of subordination of these sectors. The distribution of resources,
production and productivity levels, technological
allotment and the final orientation of production
within this system are directly determined by the
overall strategy of accumulation.

The system imposed by multinational agroindustry -and also by national agroindustry, which now
functions according to the same logic- comprises, in
synthesis, the following elements: "a) the quantity,
quality and type of inputs (land, work, credit,
fertilizers, insecticides, machinery and equipment,
technical assistance, research and systems of agricultural administration); b) the price of these inputs (including salaries and services); c) the productive processes in agriculture; d) the market
processes (export of agricultural products, payment
to producers, prices for market services, transportation, packing and storage, distribution to wholesale
merchants, retail merchants and consumers, and the
destination of export articles); e) the earnings on
capital investments and on the use of agricultural
technology, as well as the way these are distributed
among the recipients." (3)

MODELS OF PRODUCTION ORGANIZATION

The overwhelming presence of capital expressed
through the diversity of "operational forms" has been
responsible for organizing rural economic practices.
The simultaneous or successive use of commercial,
industrial or financial modes of operation led to a
variety of different relations with direct producers

---

(3) Ernest Feder, EL IMPERIALISMO FRESA, Editorial
Campesina, México, 1977, pp. 18-19.

which are redefined by the type of production and
its final destination.

The different manifestations of capital in the
Mexican agricultural sector indicate how, historically, this has "penetrated" the rural sector, that
is to say, how it has propagated capitalist social
regulations of production. They also indicate the
true models of organization of the different protagonists in relation to the productive process, and
reflect their interaction. The important role of a
specific "operational form" of capital within the pro
ductive system permits the differentiation between
the relative position of agrarian protagonists and
their degree of association with the dynamics generated by it.

The implantation of capitalism in rural Mexico
under these generalized historical terms does not
imply the exclusion of specific forms of capitalist
accumulation (local, regional, sectorial, etc.). The
fact is, however, that it absorbs these specific
forms of agricultural and cattle-raising development
into its sphere of influence, thus subordinating
them to its own accumulation model, and accelerating
the internationalization process through the four
models of organization associated with it for the
last two decades.

a) The "Commercial Agriculture" Model

"Commercially-based agriculture" was one of the
first models or patterns to be introduced into the
country. Its direct ties to crops destined to satisfy the demands of the U.S. market, indicate the
intention to convert Mexican agrarian land into the
hinterland of the western U.S. markets.

Agribusiness functions as a trigger for this
system of interrelations and as the focal point of
the productive activities of thousands of national
producers. Agribusiness regulates prices and
production through the control of market mechanisms
and the presentation, packaging and transportation
of products.

Sensitizing the Mexican economy to the "signals" of the U.S. market has affected two main
consumer lines: that of fresh fruits and vegetables

during the winter and early spring, when there is a decrease in the production of certain items in the United States; and that of widely consumed frozen and processed products.

This is the result of certain comparative advantages of Mexican horticultural and fruit production. Since harvest times were different, Mexico was able to supply the U.S. market in times of relative scarcity. There were also substantial differences in labor costs and in the general context of production, given the overall protection that the Mexican government gave to its producers. These advantages, however, have not resulted in better conditions of accumulation for direct producers, because of the intervention of U.S. distributors and brokerage agents in Mexican production.

To ensure control of the productive process, agribusiness intermediaries have used financial, commercial and technical assistance mechanisms in two main ways: agricultural contracts, and the leasing of land. This has enabled agribusiness to incorporate direct producers into its system of crop cultivation, thereby absorbing *campesino* labor deprived of direct control over its own production.

Under the agricultural contract scheme, the commitment between agribusiness and producers is not simply a contract of sale, that is, it is not restricted merely to the delivery of a predetermined quantity of production, but implies the adoption of a complex set of productive practices: type of plants used, machinery, fertilizers, insecticides, irrigation systems, etc. Such "commited" inputs have to be acquired by credit from the State, a private bank or the agribusiness. The productive processes themselves are controlled through "technical assistance services" that agribusiness makes available. This means that direct producers are reduced to fulfilling merely operative functions, as if they were overseers, yet at the same time, they must assume the risks and uncertainties involved in a basically unfamiliar productive process.

In the latter case, when agribusiness leases plots of land, it assumes an owner-function directly contracting workers and fixing wage levels. This model is only used when the other cannot be applied,

because of the inherent risks involved in this kind
of illegal exploitation and because it does not allow
the direct producers to maximize the resources
yield   through an increase in the rate of exploitation.

International agribusiness usually finds it can
best operate in association with large national capitalist producers and local or regional *caciques* who
are able to use direct coercion or monopolistic, commercial mechanisms to establish local or subregional
collection systems linked to packaging and export
loading centers. The direct application of agricultural contract or land leasing schemes, frees agribusiness of risks, inefficiencies and a variety of
limitations; and makes the need for profit sharing
an acceptable cost.

Obviously, the expansion of this system generates a permanent pressure on the land which is
controlled by *campesinos*, both small land holders
and *ejidatarios*, as well as on their cultivation
habits. This pressure is an indication of the contradiction existing between the social protagonists in their far-reaching struggle for control of
productive resources and over the use and final destination of production. It also reflects the dispute
on a national level over how to define the role of
production organizers, and the mechanisms with which
to regulate the relations between them.

The fact that national intermediary agents are
found in the production and marketing processes,
means that a local circuit for appropriating surplus can be established. This accumulation increases
and reproduces itself through investment in complementary areas of agricultural trade (agencies for
the sale of machinery, industrial inputs, etc.) and
in the field of financial capital. All of this links
the interests of these sectors to those of agribusiness.

b) The "Industrial Agriculture" Model

For the last ten years in rural Mexico there
has been a tendency in the productive forms of
capital controlled by multinational agroindustrial
corporations, to dominate over other agribusiness
forms.

Since it appeared in this country, this sector
has regulated its activities in terms of the internal market, while at the same time reshaping the
dynamics of this market, diversifying it by promoting
new eating habits, defined by producer convenience and
not by consumer necessity. Although this constitutes
the principal aim of its operations, it also performs
according to U.S. demands, especially in the line of
frozen and canned fruits, and textiles.

Even though agroindustry adopts different attitudes towards internal and external demands, it always tends to impose norms with the following characteristics: change in cultivation patterns, where
traditional grains are replaced by industrial crops;
specialization of processable products at local and
regional levels; change in cultivation habits, related not only to an increase in profit, but also
to product adaptability in industrial processing
requirements; change in technological patterns,
leading towards an intensive use of capital through
imported agricultural inputs that replace labor.

Agroindustry usually operates, as does agribusiness, through intermediaries, whose direct or
indirect character depends on whether control is
exercised at the level of the productive process or in
the area of commercialization. When it uses technological and financial, as well as marketing mechanisms,
as is generally the case, it manages to capture a
growing volume of the surplus generated by direct
producers. Both agribusiness and agroindustry have
in this way widened the process of rural differentiation and of total or partial conversion of
campesinos to a wage system. It has also tended
to encourage the reclassification of the agricultural
protagonists through systems of land leasing, thus
accentuating and consolidating the subordination of
labor to capital and its inclusion in the logic of
the latter.

c)   The "Public Capitalist Agriculture" Model

The Mexican government, consistent with the
State's overall project, has directly intervened
in the propagation of rural capitalist relations in
the three main ways: by creating and administrating

irrigated areas and by regulating agrarian redistribution; by introducing State commercialization
and processing of production; and by the drawing up
of "integral plans" for agrarian reform, in many
cases following the guidelines of international
financing agencies.

Irrigated areas had, originally, been created
for obvious agrarian reasons, as a way of overcoming the limitations of *campesino* economy within the
framework of promoting collective organization of
production within the *ejidos*. Since 1940, however,
a variety of new conditions has redirected this
process. Those producers in irrigated areas capable
of accumulating, began to put pressure on the then
current land tenure system. They thus identified
themselves with those who wanted to bring an end to
Cardenist ways, in order to initiate "productive
modernization" in conventional capitalist terms.
Old revolutionaries and new civil servants, specu-
lators and former Porfirian *latifundistas*, some of
them U.S. citizens (4) strengthened mutual bonds,
and renewed efforts to pressure the government,
using their new identity: they were spokesmen of the
regime, the unheard voice of Mexico's rural *empresarios*, the incarnation of modern ideas needed in
rural areas to counteract the newly implemented industrial urban development project. The beneficiaries of technological innovations, of credit, of
technical assistance and of guaranteed prices joined
forces with them, thereby closely linking them to
the commercial agricultural plan directed by multinational agribusiness. This kind of support ensured
the intensive and short-term accumulation prospects
for these "modernized *empresarios*." The changes in
production which had come about encompassed all commercial agricultural operations, making its functions more complex and facilitating an increased
participation of these "farmers" in the widened
sphere of commercial and financial capital, towards
which they were directing their investments.

Another line of government intervention involved regulating the basic grain market. This has encompassed strictly commercial activities as well as

(4) See Cynthia H. de Alcántara, LA MODERNIZACION
DE LA AGRICULTURA MEXICANA, Siglo XXI Editores, México, 1978.

those related to the partial processing of products.
On the one hand, many public enterprises have operated monopolies that control the commercialization of
certain products or have marginally intervened in
the markets of others. The objective in both in-
stances, has been to subject the commercialization
of agricultural and cattle-raising products to overall fixed conditions, intended to stabilize prices
for the consumer (within the protective policies of
industrial development) and to channel resources towards producers. The logic of these activities has
tended to encourage producers to adopt capitalistic
ways rather than maximize entrepreneur profits or
subject production to social necessities, although
efforts have also been made along these lines. On
the other hand, these same public enterprises, along
with others, have been directly concerned with the
industrial processing of production. When this processing is not completed, which often is the case,
such enterprises serve as intermediaries for national or international agribusiness, which final-
izes the productive process and initiates marketing.
Throughout all these commercial or industrial operations, public enterprises have managed to integrate
many producers into their sphere of influence, under
similar and parallel terms to those of agribusiness.

Finally, the government has also organized "integrated agrarian reform" programs, adjusting them,
in many cases, to the specific requirements of international financial organizations. The difficulties inherent in trying to integrate the collective
organizations of producers subject (because of Constitutional limitations) to the *ejidal* system into
the orbit of capital, has provided a permanent obstacle to direct intervention of national and multinational agribusiness in these enterprises. To overcome this obstacle, the Government has acted, on a
number of occasions, as intermediary or substitute
for agribusiness, by promoting and controlling the
collective organization of production. Through
these mechanisms, the collectively organized producers retain the formal ownership of their land
and their capacity for deciding on its use, although in reality this is transferred to public
enterprises or institutions. In this way, technical
organizations assume power without responsibility
and the producers, responsibilities without

power (5). The use of the land, cultivation habits, conditions under which production is organized and carried out, and all the other aspects of the productive and commercial process, in one way or another, become matters depending on the decisions of public agencies which thus reproduce and extend agribusiness patterns and serve as their intermediaries.

d) The "Extensive Cattle-Raising" Model

Capitalist development of cattle raising has imposed its peculiarities on the agricultural and cattle raising sector in different ways. In the first place, it puts great pressure on the system of land use (through extensive exploitation, and as a "legal" mechanism for property expansion), affecting the very pattern of land control. Secondly, such pressure modifies the use of agricultural land by introducing cultivation patterns directly related to animal feeding. Thirdly, this new order integrates and subordinates forms of production and social organization which were previously outside it.

The basic feature of this kind of exploitation comes from the association of northern calf breeders with the important beef farmers in the United States, and their intensive feeding units. The demand for export livestock of maximum weight, to be produced in as short a time as possible, created a demand by cattle producers for the production of fodder, balanced foods, etc. This in turn, affected crop structure and the organization of production.

Attention given to the export market altered productive patterns for the domestic supply of meat, as traditional areas began to devote more effort to the foreign market. This in turn gave rise to pressure, extending cattle raising to agricultural land, much of it *ejidal* and communal, and furthering subordinated *campesino* cattle raising to the logic of capitalist enterprises.

---

(5) See, among others, David Barkin, DESARROLLO REGIONAL Y REORGANIZACION CAMPESINA, Editorial Nueva Imagen, México, 1978.

THE OVERALL DYNAMICS

The tendency towards the transnationalization of
the Mexican agricultural sector, encouraged by the
agroindustrial system, is based on two movements.
On one hand, from a productive point of view, the
dynamics of intermediate demand directs agricultural production and imposes crop patterns which displace direct food production. This movement is
complemented by the tendency to expand extensive
cattle raising activities, thus putting pressure
on land use and restricting subsistence agricultural production areas, forcing them to move to
eroded or forested areas, with the resulting deterioration of the ecosystem. On the other hand,
the trend towards transnationalization is based on
the integration of direct producers into the sphere
of the market economy and into the productive logic
and accumulation of agribusiness. This subordination
of labor to capital will not disappear with the dis-
solution of pre-existing social relations, nor with
the destruction of previous productive logic. It
seeks to adapt forms of land tenure and legally recognized labor organization to its own mechanisms
for the extraction of surplus, which it introduces
in the spheres of production, circulation and
finance.

The basis for an overall strategy to spread the
agribusiness market economy in this country, is
concretely in a tendency to intervene in productive
processes through an intermediary system. This system is made up of capitalist entrepreneurs, the
main agents of agroindustrial effort in rural areas,
and of *campesino* labor subordinated to capital. In
this way, agribusiness manages to transfer the bulk
of exploitation risks to the direct producers (who
in fact they no longer are), and permits them to
take care of the "organization" of their own production. Thus, in the case of *campesino* labor, a
type of fiction of a class which possesses its own
productive factors, and exploits (under the form of
wage labor) members of its own collective organizations is created. Some careless authors,
unaware of this fiction, that is, the vicarious
function of the "direct producer," place these "direct producers" amongst the land owners, although
they are distinguished by size and other aspects.

Finally the coexistence of *campesino* productive forms with market relations, means that within the overall strategy, a labor force is available at a lower cost than the average wage, a fact that contributes to the strengthening of *campesino* reproduction as a productive agent.

2

FARMERS, CATTLE RAISERS AND AGRIBUSINESS

"The town is full of echoes. They seem to be locked up in hollow walls or under stones. When you walk, you feel someone Treading on your shadow. You hear creaks. Laughter. Old, weary laughter. And worn-out voices. You can hear all of this. I'm sure the day will come when these sounds will be no more."

Juan Rulfo, PEDRO PARAMO.

The protagonists of rural Mexico described in this chapter live in a very special way: they are never what they seem to be. The distance produced between the tangible manifestations of their being and their intimate reality determine this. They are very rarely what they think they are. Those who act as if they were the protagonists, the authentic stars of the show wearing known disguises, turn out only to be emanations or some other representation of the real ones. But these very same people, who lead the movement and capture all the dynamism, tend to disappear into thin air. It is difficult to find their concrete personifications in daily life. To tear apart this world of shadows, to trap them in their ghost-like dance, is a task long since fulfilled by artistic imagination. The first to do so was Juan Rulfo in his Pedro Páramo, but science is still struggling with this hope, trapped in its own inertia and clumsiness. For the moment all attempts have to admit their experimental nature.

PHANTOMS

> Phantom - an illusion or fabrication of the
> mind, like those produced by a dream or by
> heated discussion // The image of an object
> as imprinted in fantasy // A proud, grave
> and presumptuous individual // A fright to
> scare simple people.

Farmers (small private landholders)

Deeply individualistic, clinging to their land
(as if it were an eggshell they dare not peck at except
that it is an opportunity of life) often innovative as
to technique but rather conservative or reactionary
as to politics, farmers are a dying species in rural
Mexico. Those who still are believers, due to their
age or naïveté, are fierce, proud, serious and
haughty. Those who are already coming out of this
long-held illusion, cannot hide their unbearable
sadness. All of them are experts in agriculture and
have explored their land inch by inch. But that,
maybe, is all they know.

They are the product of two main trends towards
land tenure: the colonial and the liberal.

As children of the colony, they were born and
grew up on the outskirts of the large *haciendas*,
with which they maintained a contradictory relationship of tension-necessity, characteristic of the bas-
tard status they had. Sometimes they supplied the
food requirements of the *haciendas*, which were mainly interested in monocultivation for exportation.
Sometimes they were granted a piece of land as a re-
ward for their support of domination campaigns promoted by their bosses, the *hacendados* and other
agents. Some obtained land with a lifetime's savings,
or as a consolation prize for an adventure that
never achieved its ultimate goal. Attacked by both
communities and *haciendas*, they installed themselves
with difficulty, in the empty leftover crevices without ever achieving great splendour.

Later, in the *República Restaurada* in 1867, they
were a promised paradise: they swore this to themselves as well as the destiny they so desired; they

also promised it to the liberals who had great
hopes for them: they were the foundations on which
to build an equal and modern country, the anarchist
republic of small producers, the ever present element of the liberal dream. But it was all a dream.
They could not do anything against the power of the
compañías deslindadoras and the unlimited expansion
of the *haciendas*. It is clear that "the boss was
boss."

Another movement of illusion, in the third decade of this century, gave them perhaps their most
active period in rural Mexico. The 1917 Constitution had already foreseen their situation. The Constitution gave the nation ownership of land, but
also entrusted to it the "establishment of private
property." On September 1, 1925, President Calles
presented a bill on the division of plots of land
and the granting of *ejidal* lands as personal property. He claimed that the introduction of the individual property principle would increase agricultural production and would involve the *campesino*
more closely in the improvement of cultivation methods. Luis I. León, Calles' *Secretario de Agricultura*, argued in defense of the project that people
should not be afraid of *campesino* impoverishment,
because the *ejidal* plot was not the classical bourgeois model of smallholdings: "We are sure," he
said "that there are *campesinos* who, thanks to
their energy, intelligence and character, are above
the rest of the *campesinos* and consequently have
far-reaching tasks ahead of them." These tasks were
very concrete: to acquire land from their neighbors
to become modern farmers who might eventually penetrate the sectors of commerce and industry as well.
As will be remembered, in the 1920s, improvement
plans for this type of producer were drawn up, the
rhetorical arguments against the *hacienda* were forgotten, and land redistribution was kept at as low
an ebb as the *campesinos* would allow. The agrarian
winds, which blew again in the Cárdenas government,
opened the way for all these small producers, whose
numbers increased at the same rate as the *ejidos*,
and although they had less land, it was of better
quality.

This is the state in which the model, later to
be associated with the Green Revolution, found them.
They became social protagonists hiding the real

process of land concentration. In some villages there are still old posters from President Miguel Alemán's period (1946-52), which show a fat, dark skinned <u>farmer</u>* smiling optimistically towards the future, on his well-cultivated farm, with his trac- tor, cows, poultry and everything else desirable. Opposed to Cárdenas' dream of a Mexico made up of *ejidos* and small industrial communities, was the vigorous dream of great urban industry and of pros- perous individual rural producers, full of entre- prenurial spirit and innovative capacity. Scientific research, technology and improvement plans were and have always been directed towards them, although only in rhetoric appearance.

This was really only fiction: some assumed it was a true project and suffered the consequences of their naïveté; others consciously used it in order to give "social protection" to the concentration process they were promoting. After a few years, a new term began to appear distinguishing this group from that which was forming alongside of it. People began to talk about <u>authentic</u> smallholders. The implication was that some owners were not in fact authentic, i.e. *latifundistas* and agricultural and cattle raising enterprises which adopted the legal appearance of the constitutionally permitted small- holdings. These were thus able to hide their true intentions and activities, which will be described later. The <u>authentic</u> smallholders were, thus, those who existed within the legal limits of smallholdings, as independent producers who really tried to be such. They were really not far from Zapata's prin- ciple "The land for those who work it." But they adopted this particular tenure system, and not that of the *ejidos* and communities, probably because they did not have any other practical opinion. They preferred the promise of autonomy apparently offered by this modality or had other reasons. Many had work- ed for the Porfirian *haciendas* and had never had access to the *ejidos* and communities, nor had they taken part in their struggle. They did not have land to recover. In order to become landowners for the first time, they opted for this modality or adopted it for this purpose.

---

*In English in the original.

Little by little, this group began to disintegrate. A good many became *minifundistas* who found
themselves in worse conditions than the *ejidatarios*
and *comuneros*, both with regard to the size of their
plots of land and their socio-economic situation.
Evidently, they were the favorites of those who were
guiding the process since the *ejidos* and communities
offered greater resistance. Eventually, most of
these <u>authentic smallholders</u> became workers subordinated to capital under different modalities and
conditions. We will deal with their situation in the
following chapter. This much diminished group has
only a few survivors throughout the country. In fact,
they only become relevant when rural Mexico's dominant protagonists use them as an effective shield
to resist pressure for land redistribution. Their
authenticity, the individualism which keeps them
irrationally tied to living conditions over which
they no longer have control, makes them inflammable
material of great usefulness for those who cannot
show their real face.

The fact that they are producers who combine personal and family work with temporary or permanent
employment as wage-earners, is one of the crucial
points for their survival. As transitory protagonists, they have not been able to differentiate
between the personal function of their job and the
organization of salaried work. This means there is
permanent debate over their own salaries and attainment of an average profit rate. Year after year they
begin their task with an ever present dream: they
remember the time when "they had a good stroke of
luck," without knowing either how or why, when they
suddenly accumulated an amazing profit and this they
try to repeat with the utmost diligence and inge-
nuity. Nevertheless year after year, they are limited
to carrying out their own work or fearfully watching
debts accumulate.

The fate of this protagonist, almost completely
subordinated to agribusiness, is objectively similar
to that of the *campesinos* and other agricultural
workers. Yet it is difficult for them to perceive
this as such, for that would mean giving up a life-
long dream, backed by generations of people fighting for the impossible, constantly encouraged by
rhetoric used to glorify and stimulate them. It
also means accepting themselves as proletarians.

This not only bothers them deeply, leading to rejection, but also awakens a very real concern about the lack of prospects for this group to date.

Independent of the functions they still perform in the overall logic, it is possible that their persistence is due to their historical substance. It is true that they do not come from the Mesoamerican past associated with a community-minded impulse, but they did emerge from profound forces developed under a variety of circumstances. It can be argued that Villa's forces represented those protagonists. Let us go into this in more detail.

General Francisco Villa's Northern Division has a mottled history, compared with that of Zapata's forces. The southern leader probably never had the number of men Villa had ready for fighting and whom he managed to turn into a real army. Zapata's men concentrated on different types of guerrilla fighting, while Villa fought on the open field against professional armies and succeeded in defeating them for several years. But Villa never had Zapata's strength which was based on village autonomy: he did not promote community development. Zapata did, and his people laid down their ploughs for rifles to return to their lands later. Armies were formed by aggregation, that is, men from every social condition willingly joined; they came along in small groups or even, at times, whole villages. Integrated social groups were not common in Villa's forces. The Northern Division was an army of masses, based on the homogeneous integration of more or less individualized fighters. It was not the organized combination of a living social corpus.

Some authors have seen only outcasts of the Mexican society in Villa's armies. For many, Villa's men were simply bandits, cattle-rustlers, vagabonds, men without a past or future, unknown adventurers ready for violence and robbery. Doubtlessly there were some of these men in the Northern Division, but they were not the only ones. Their behavior was different because they came from the North; they lacked the Mesoamerican social background and the community integration found in the central or southeastern areas; they had been more exposed to the individualizing process of the northern system of exploitation and its context. Thus, hunger for land was as

strong as among Zapata's people, but they tended to
express it through other productive options. Even
their anarchism was not that of the villages dealing with internal problems that revolved around
their own life, trapped by localism. It was the
vague anarchism of a people lacking experience and
notions of organic integration as the origin of
social existence, who join others from personal de-
fenselessness, linked to them for little more than
sheer exploitation. This last point was not the
foundation for solidarity through which the proletariat can turn into an organic force, that is,
it tended to propitiate reinforcing individual and
family development, cells which are interrelated
but constantly claim their fierce independence.

Villa often said that he dreamt of spending his
last days on a small *rancho*. He was killed on one.
He hoped for small plots of land for his men,
complete with cows and chickens, but like Zapata,
he was not a government man. The stubborness of his
agrarian claims, the profound and popular response
to his commitment, and maybe the uncontrollable
nature of a force which was incapable of recognizing its true nature, made his acceptance impossible
by those who were trying to constitute a government
along constitutionalist lines. Villa's agrarian law,
published on June 7, 1915, only six months after
Carranza published his, in order to reduce Zapata's
strength, had very little ideological influence on
the revolutionary process. It was promulgated after
the Northern Division had been completely defeated,
and before Villa could express his ideas on what he
would do if he won. All that remains of these ideas
is what he agreed upon with Zapata.

Villa's movement has provided material for intense discussion which continues even today. Whatever his role might have been during the Revolution,
it is still possible to trace his influence in
those smallholders who cling to their plots of land.

Their number, however, is not precise. It is
difficult to separate them from other natural protagonists and agents who have already taken over.
Empirical research has proven that there are, in
fact, very few of them and that their number is
decreasing.

Cooperatives

Some of these smallholders have grouped themselves into cooperatives in order to survive, and
express themselves through, what in the long run,
has proved to be an extension of their agony.

This is not the most appropriate place for a
description of Mexican history of cooperativism
(which has a special place in this country). Cooperatives, necessarily included here, originated
with the grouping together of smallholdings sharing some common elements in the productive process
or performing similar commercial or other types of
activities. Division of labor and its uses are
individual decisions made as a result of complex
interaction. This interaction divides collective
commitments from autonomous decisions of individual
cooperative members.

The fundamental framework within which these
institutions develop includes the relationship between technological and input needs so as to confront the market or financing sources collectively.
The different ways of combining resources as well
as the different ways of facing the contradictions
between individual-family accumulation and that of
collective commitments, give rise to emergency
processes of internal differentiation, which place
cooperative operations under tension which in turn
leads to their disintegration. While some seem to,
or really do, advance towards the characteristic
behavior of a capitalist entrepreneur, others tend
to be assimilated into the wage-earner context.

Theoretically, the cooperative outlook could be
the basis for collective organization, which would
place small landholders in a different historical
and social perspective, and, this in fact has
happened in some cases. But, in general, external
pressures of disintegration are added to yet another
basic limitation blocking their development,
which is, the initial drive coming from smallholders who see the cooperative system as a way of
extending rather than denying themselves. Each of
the cooperative members tries to "utilize" the
system for personal and direct benefit. Because of
this, success is always circumstantial and transitory:

it carries the seeds of its own destruction.

Some cooperatives have emerged from strictly capitalist forms, that is, they dispense with co-operative and self-management mechanisms which strictly speaking could help to define them, and instead use mechanisms of discipline, hierarchy and profit sharing based on economic participation. Their success or failure has been related to their size and dynamics: some of them have been evolved toward higher forms of mercantile societies, which in turn become any one of the protagonists later described; others have retreated to their original position, re-establishing the smallholdings where the attempt began.

In spite of the periodic support cooperatives have received from the government or other social forces, they have not been able to come up with one important specific productive form for rural Mexico. Rather they tend to join forces with other prota-gonists, sharing with them their determinations and behavior.

Rentistas

Undeniably a left-over from previous structures or a marginal product of new processes, the *rentis-ta* leads a polyfacetic existence, characteristic of rural Mexico. Sometimes, he represents the impov-erished existence of Porfirian *latifundistas*, at other times the absent expression of the smallhold-ers or even *ejidatarios*, who have tried other oc-cupations or activities, outside the rural context.

To keep this particular case in perspective, he must be distinguished from the others, who are in fact linked to the general practice of illegal leasing of plots of land, as a mechanism of capitalist expansion in the Mexican context. In the latter case, the owner of the rented plot of land is consistent with the logic of the capitalistic system, in different ways i.e. hiring himself as a *jornalero* on his own land, carrying out the pro-ductive process on behalf of others, under pre-established commercial conditions, etc. Therefore he will be described in the following chapter, since, strictly speaking, he is a rural worker, that is, a protagonist who depends on his own labor

for survival, even though the "right" to do this
-the employment guarantee- is based on the usufruct
of the plot of land. In contrast, the *rentista* is
an agent who uses his title deeds as a specific
source of income.

Some members of this group find themselves in
a peculiar situation which practically excludes them
from this category. For example, certain *ejidatarios*
or private *minifundistas* who depend on other activities for their labor-income, i.e. trade, handicrafts,
etc., retain their plot of land not as a source of
income, but as "something to come back to" if their
efforts in other fields fail. In fact, the lease
is often merely symbolic. At times the owner of the
plot of land leases it in order to increase his
income from other sources and accumulate capital
which will allow him to cultivate the land again
himself eventually, with better chances of success
or development, backed by the investment of the
capital accumulated.

Since the *rentistas* are removed from the overall logic of the evolution of the Mexican agricultural sector, they are leading towards extinction.
Legal proceedings are taken against those who do not
work their plots of land, regardless of size. Law
enforcement is far more rigorous in these cases
than against those who lease land as a way of placing themselves within the general operation of the
system.

ECTOPLASMS

Ectoplasm.- Material emanation that some
mediums claim to produce // Outer layer
of the cell.

Caciques

"See this fine gentle humid land... It's good
land, I swear it is!... But next year things will be
just as bad, 'cause we're in the hands of *coyotes,*
middlemen, *agiotistas,* and *tiendas de raya* owners,
who sell sacks of ammonium sulphate at 75 pesos
when we know it only costs 37 pesos. And the same
goes for insecticides and pesticides. It just ain't

fair. And then they try and convince us what wonder-
ful people they are, 'cause they lend us all the
money we need at 8 or 9% monthly interest rates,
taking the crop in payment. So the crop already belongs to them, long before it's even harvested."
(Agustín Torres, 39 years old, *ejidatario* from San
José de Chuen, 12 kilometers from Ario de Rosales,
Michoacán, January 30, 1975).

"In spite of everything, the *caciques* in Hidalgo continue to maintain gangs of riflemen and
invading *ejidal* lands in 28 communities in the District of Tepehuacán, Hidalgo, where terror and
violence are everyday events. This complaint was
filed by members of the Cuatolol *ejido* before the
provisional governor of the State. They accused
both Francisco Austria Cabrera (colonel and lawyer)
who comes from a family with one of the longest
traditions as *caciques* in the region, but which
supposedly had been wiped out long ago, and also Is-
mael Martínez Angeles, who is the deputy of *cacique*
Austria Cabrera. Some years ago, they said, Austria
Cabrera gave control of the *ejido* to members of his
gang, as well as to some *terratenientes*. These
people have threatened us, ambushed us, persecuted
us, imprisoned us, robbed us, perjured us, and
even killed some of our group. Nothing of course
has been done to them." (Ultimas Noticias May 15,
1975).

"Merchants, influential people, bankers, industrialists, and even a former President of the Republic have taken illegal possession of more than
half of the 160,000 hectares of the Cabo Corrientes
Ejidos, a district in one of Jalisco's richest sea-
shore strips. One of the *caciques*, Alfonso García
Castillón, knew that sooner or later his lands
would be affected, so he decided to give them away
to those in powerful positions in order to protect
himself. Antonio Zepeda Pacheco, mayor and *comisa-
rio* of the *Ejidos* Union 'Alfredo V. Bonfil', inform-
ed this newspaper that García had given almost half
of his 42,000 hectares to 120 name-lenders. 'El Tui-
to' is the name of this dusty town, located at the
foot of the Sierra, 43 kilometers from Puerto
Vallarta. "Before, nobody was interested in these
places, they said, but now that the road between
Puerto Vallarta and Barra de Navidad has been
opened, everybody wants the land." He then added

"García Castillón illegally took over 42,000 hectares when Nabor Estrada died, and he was the most
important *latifundista* in Cabo Corrientes. Now we
have applied for land for the Las Juntas de los Ve-
ranos *Ejido,* and this affected El Carrizal, which
belongs to García Castillón, so he immediately tried
to find a way of protecting himself. For the time
being at least, he has managed to prevent this
endowment from taking place. Some time later he
took over 20,000 hectares more; this means he now
has a total of 62,000 hectares which belong to the
Indian communities and *ejidos* of the district.
Later, García Castillón simulated a land-division
project and divided the land up into 21 parts. He's
distributed these among his own *mozos* -who never
had access to the usufruct of the land- as well as
to rich merchants, bankers and industrialists from
Guadalajara, so that they will defend it for him.
He gave half of his *latifundios* to a lawyer called
Urzua, who has since distributed it among others.
But I'd rather not give their names because I know
they'd do something to me." (Excélsior, March 28,
1975).

One can bet with absolute certainty that
daily there will be news items in the Mexican press
on similar accusations about *caciques*. No sociological study on rural Mexico can afford to omit such
character.

Who are these protagonists so important in
agrarian affairs? It is possible to go way back in
history and find, for example, the *Cacique Gordo* of
Tlaxcala who helped Hernán Cortés, the Spanish con-
queror in his campaigns against the primitive Mexicans. It is also possible to keep track of these
caciques throughout the most varied periods and
circumstances.

Today's *cacique,* however, has very concrete
origins. Because of all the given legal restrictions
and the socio-political context within which rural
capitalist expansion took place, a significant portion of the participants in this process used
corruption as the necessary mortar with which to
build the modern economic apparatus. And the agent
used to produce and handle this mortar was a protagonist whose obviously villainous profile had
very little to do with his capacity as the star of

the show, i.e. the *cacique*. Doubtless, he is the
world's worst "agricultural manager": he neither
organizes nor participates in production. As part of
the intermediary economic structure, between the
rural community and the "rest of the society" his
role is one of extracting resources from agriculture
But just as he is incapable of stimulating rural
productive forces, he is also the worst urban manager. His urban "investments" merely serve to reproduce the predatory scheme which initially gave
him power.

In spite of this, or probably because of it,
the *cacique* is a key agent in the economic operation of the Mexican agricultural sector. The *hacienda* had been destroyed as a productive unit
and the *ejido* had been incapable of taking over at
the appropriate time its collective exploitation,
so the *campesinos* had no other choice than to
develop the individual or family-mode of exploiting
their plots of land. The *cacique*, who originally had
often been an authentic agrarian leader at the forefront of the struggle for land, thus became a cohesive element in the productive effort, able to control it but not to organize it.

The initial states of exploitation took on
several characteristics: the successful use of his
own land, the operation of trade centers, availability of ready cash, his relationship with the outside world as well as many other facets. Eventually
his activities spread like cancer throughout all
areas of community life. He was equally capable of
obtaining for the community either state funds or
police repression. In the same way, he either financed crops or bought them, he would sell consumer goods
and would pay wedding or funeral expenses and organize religious festivities. He was incapable of revo-
lutionizing productive forces because, among other
reasons, he operated from an illegal, violent basis
with doubtful political representation. Any permanent investment in the land carries with it unacceptable risks. His "investments", even in agriculture,
had to be on a short-term basis, extremely short
term, sometimes hardly even that of an agricultural
cycle. He prevented the *campesinos'* accumulated
economic surplus from being invested in productive
improvements, by taking it from them or diverting it
towards consumption. Even when it was actually in his

hands, he did not use it to any productive purpose
but instead to extend his own activities in order to
consolidate his economic and political power, or
make conservative investments in urban centers.

As a structural agent in the functioning of rural communities, the *cacique* was also a liason with
other social groups which determined "from the outside" what happened on the rural scene. This is
where both his strength and his weakness can be
found. He is effectively an articulating agent,
subordinating producers to the sphere of capital,
but without any genuine life of his own, and with no
economic force to ensure expansion. Although he is
a vital link in the chain of relations between the
true protagonists of the productive process, he does
not really take part in this process, but depends
increasingly on the managerial structure which employs him as an intermediary.

A very important factor in the rise and persistence of *caciques* is the lack of real integration
throughout the country. To the ethnic and cultural
plurality which divides Mexicans, even as far as
language is concerned, one also has to add the total
isolation in which large sectors of the rural population have lived until very recently, and in which
some sectors still do. The *cacique* was the liason who
fulfilled the ambivalent function of integration-
disintegration.

Caciques persist because of a very specific re-
generative process: the old revolutionary politics
which allowed them to develop the material basis of
their economic power is used to increase their political position and this, in turn, allows them to
extend their material basis of operation. Some of
their functions are related to the manipulation and
control of *campesino* communities in order to guide
them along the political lines laid down by the
government. At the same time, together with direct
coercive mechanisms, the *cacique* also becomes a
quasi-political representative of the *campesino*
group, in order to solve specific problems and obtain, among other things, state funds.

The speculative nature of management prevails
in their economic activities. Their actions do not
permit true integration into a productive structure

which of itself, ensures the accumulation of capital in the strict sense of the term: they buy and
sell land, rent plots of land, cultivate from time
to time land obtained as credit guarantee, use
"private armies", and even the police to invade or
control land, etc. By using both, their own resources and those obtained from official credit institutions, they are able to impose their own
usurious credit practices, thus bringing to heel the
bulk of the *campesino* population, most of which
(75% in 1970), has no direct access to the state or
private institutional credit.

Nevertheless, the *cacique* no longer fulfills
these objectives. He arose from the heart of the
rural world, but has been left in a gap in the
functioning of the global system of production. Unless he is able genuinely to change his character
and become an authentic rural or urban entrepreneur,
he will remain little more than a physical representation of the true forces which move the system. He
has been a useful and sometimes necessary tool but
increasingly less and less vital to the dominating
structures. He has carried out the "dirty work" of
others, as well as the paternalistic tasks of those
economic agents who guide the process needed to
correct the existing contradiction between legal
standards (and their socio-political context), and
economic reality.

Under the critical conditions of recent years,
their role seems to have increased, as it has been
necessary to use direct domination, when political
formulae for negotiation, manipulation and control
have been exhausted. But even this is only the result of appearances. Once the real forces involved
in the crisis have to come face to face, the shadow-
y fiction, which tends to cover up the real economic
and social relationships in rural Mexico, ceases to
be of significance. The intermediaries thus lose
importance, and their ambivalence becomes meaningless.

Rancheros

They are found in the most unlikely situations.
They might be equally found trying to break the bank in
Las Vegas as enjoying life to the full on their
land, or helping their favorite mare give birth, or

acting as a doctor to the cowhands, or with tie and
everything, sitting behind an impressive ministerial
desk worrying about a speech to be delivered before
an international audience.

Obviously they prefer cattle raising, but can
just as well produce fruit, vegetables, grains or
anything else. As cattle raisers, their general
behavior is very similar to that of the *neolatifundistas* (who will be described later); as farmers
they follow the lines of agribusiness, agroindustry,
rural enterprise or agrocommerce, according to the
agent with whom they are directly associated.

Their origin varies. Some arose from the dreams
of expansion of smallholdings which, thanks to
strong capitalization, became profitable, without
surpassing the legal limits of their property.
Others had urban origins, i.e. banking, government
officials, politicians, businessmen and even em-
ployees and workers. All of them had some sort of
mental fixation about having a *rancho*, as a status
symbol and a way of getting into regional or national elites. In those cases, it is no rarity to find
that the *rancho* is a non-profitmaking concern, and
represents a permanent expense of its owner, or
rather its profitability stems from the use of staff
and resources of state institutions, where the *ranchero* appears to work or to which he has access. But
even here, the *rancho* is not, strictly speaking, a
source of income or power, but an expression of the
political or economic power he already holds.

In general, the *ranchos* can be described as
medium capitalist investment according to their
size, the capital with which they operate, the degree of wage earners employed, and the volume of
production. When they operate under this logic in
the area of cattle raising, their activities are
closely tied to the extensive practice of breeding
calves for export. Thus, they have been largely
responsible for the links between the cattle fattening business in the states which border the U.S.,
where most of their production goes. In these cases,
their main economic activity has kept them closely
linked to the commercial capital which controls exports. This relationship has also given rise to
different ideological and cultural ways of thinking,
especially with regard to consumer habits and atti-

tudes towards life which have been assimilated
through this kind of contact. Recently their extensive cattle raising activities have been modified
through the adoption of semi-intensive patterns,
by fodder cultivation aimed at obtaining fatter
animals in less time. In certain regions they have
combined raising bovine with other species such as,
for example, porcines. In tropical areas, they have
dedicated their efforts to grazing calves (raised on
ejidos and communities), fattening them in natural
or artificial meadows. Their main link with the
domestic commercial system (which has recently been
opening up to foreign markets), allows them to add
to their already existing productive activities,
those of intermediary between *campesino* producers
and commercial or industrial meat chains.

Certain *rancheros* behave in their "own" way,
i.e. they represent a stage between the "independent" smallholder, and the large capitalist enterprise. In this way they exaggerate even more the
pioneer image, that of the "self-made man". In
general, however, the *rancheros* are ectoplasmatic
characters, simple emanations of the urban world,
expressing their political or economic power through
the rural world without actually having stemmed from
there. They are the physical representation of the
economic dynamics of those productive agents which
control the global logic of productive processes in
the Mexican agricultural sector.

Neolatifundistas

Originating during the period of Porfirio Díaz,
temporarily blocked by the Revolution, and then
expanded during the modernization process which has
developed since 1940, the *neolatifundistas* is a
symbol of the continuity of an economic and political
process which resisted attack from the *agraristas*
and found fertile channels through which to develop
a project of capitalist expansion within the Mexican
agricultural sector. The creation of large irrigation
systems opened up the possibility of speculation with
rural land for former Porfirian agents who had been
hidden in a thousand different ways within the revolutionary regime, and who were now mingling with the
newly powerful families and urban dealers.

Once they came in contact with land which had increased its productive potential (because of the new irrigation systems) without yet needing immediate large capital investment, their vast hunger for land control was awakened. The initial process was anything but innovative with regard to technology, i.e. the rapid process of accumulation basically depended on the amount of land they were able to occupy or control. This they did in many ways: they registered several "fractions" of land under the name of different members of their families; they used *presta-nombres* (name lenders) from the people within their sphere of influence; they leased directly or indirectly, private or *ejidal* plots of land. Their access to credit and their ability to obtain state investment funds, gave them a privileged position compared to that of the *campesino* producer, who lacked resources and support.

The accumulation of the initial years resulted from the above mentioned improvement mechanisms. In the 1970s, they began to react to the stimulus of fixed high prices for their crops, and they made investments which opened the way for technological innovations. These developments however, corresponded more to pressure from the organization in charge of promoting development than to a genuine "innovative mentality": in reality, many years of frustrated efforts by technological and assistance agencies were needed for the objectives of those efforts to be effectively assimilated by these agents.

These facts accentuated even more their hunger for land. While they tried to intensify the handling of their plots, they also tried to widen the productive scale of their operations, with the argument that technological resources should not be restricted to the "limited" field of their plots. In this way, they projected throughout the country an image of keeping up with the times, as well as the idea that they formed the only group capable of ensuring food supplies for the population.

The *neolatifundista* benefited most from the Green Revolution. His accelerated process of accumulation was based on extensive land control. Recently a variety of factors have led him to undertake mechanization (sometimes excessively) and this is causing

changes in crop cultivation patterns. Although he
originally grew fruit, vegetables and cotton, he
now turned to wheat and other products, during the
biggest expansion period, in order to take advantage of official guaranteed prices and other state
incentives. He still, although without having yet
left these lines of production, increasingly adapts
to market needs within the established overall
norms of agribusiness. In the long run he has become
increasingly dependent on this for survival and
concrete behavior. His highly irrational consumption (which has been given as an example of his
wastefulness) has engendered a close relationship
with national and multinational financing and
commercial systems which in turn, progressively
impose their productive guidelines on him.

Rural entrepreneurs

Although they often emerge from the *neolatifundista* group, rural entrepreneurs differ from the
former in the diversification of their commercial
and financial activities, and even in their initial
processing of agricultural production. Thus their
own pace of accumulation takes on quite different
characteristics, i.e., as a *latifundista* he is
helped by resources obtained from financing and
commercial systems.

The rural entrepreneur soon became linked to
the marketing aspect of industrial inputs needed in
agriculture, thus opening up new prospects. His
access to official credit, as an agricultural producer, provided him with the possibility of having
a cash-flow which facilitated his commercial tran-
sactions. Eventually he used these accumulated resources to ensure his regional function as a grain
stockpiler through financial means. He took the
classical route of commercial capital and began to
intervene in the productive process itself, by
imposing on the producers under his control the
conditions under which the production should be
carried out. In this way he was able to subordinate
the totality of activities related to his own
accumulation model.

This same process led him towards a closer
relationship with existing U.S. interests linked to

agribusiness throughout the country. His personal
field of reference can be found in western North
America. From Houston to Las Vegas, the indelible
footsteps of his depredatory consumerism can be
followed. And it was for this very reason that the
real control of his operations was taken from his
hands. Although some still believe or seem to believe that they have real power of decision, the
fact is that they have been loosing this in the face
of the constant advance of those who really direct
this process.

PLASMA

> Plasma. Liquid constituent of blood //
> *Plasmar*. To give shape. Used especially
> regarding clay handcrafts.

> *"The winds continued blowing. The very same
> winds which had brought the rains. The rains
> had left but the winds remained. The corn
> patch spread out its leaves to dry and then
> lay down in the furrows to hide from the
> wind. By day it was bearable, it twisted
> the vines and made the tiles on the roofs
> creak; but at night it howled, long-drawn-
> out howls. Canopies of clouds passed silent-
> ly through the sky just skimming the earth."*

> Juan Rulfo, PEDRO PARAMO

And here, at the end of the description of the protagonists in rural Mexico, the result is, that on
the side of capital, there is nothing to describe.
Apparent reality vanishes into thin air. Only
shadows remain.

It is, of course, possible to make conventional
approaches. The well-known list of enterprises and
managers of agribusiness, whether national or multinational, which appear as the incarnation of capital
could be included. Their complete names, as well as
how many there are and their characteristics, could
be given. All this information is being collected by
prominent researchers who are exploring this phenom-

enon. The mechanisms for land concentration could
be identified along with the purchase or merging
of capital; administrative council links, as well
as data from the stock market. We could easily
give the usual descriptions of high company execu-
tives, of the already familiar decadent capitalists,
of the many notorious members of the revolutionary
family and of the efficient representatives of bran-
ches and subsidiaries. It would be almost impossible
to resist the temptation to denounce the large octo-
pus, together with its accomplices, obscure transac-
tions, international pressure...

But it would be to no avail. When one tries to
get at the true picture, the existence of strong,
impressive and ever present forces mean that concrete
phenomena slip through the fingers. Once the puppets
had been seen and identified, and their subordination
proved, it became necessary to follow the strings
which moved them, and reach the stirring hands. And
here nothing is clear. We have to return to the
previous chapter: logical functioning can be seen
through effects, manifestations and consequences, at
an abstract level which allows profiles to be drawn
and speculation on its character in order to form a
hypothesis. The actions of agribusiness cannot be
"proved" through a final description merely by adding
new figures or intuitions. The "proof of the pudding
is in the eating."* The proof of the hypothesis is
in change, and this cannot find a concrete field of
expression here.

---

*In English in the original.

3

CAMPESINOS, **AGRICULTURAL AND OTHER RURAL WORKERS**

On December 5, 1810 the priest Miguel Hidalgo
declared that land should be returned to those to
whom it rightfully belonged (the natives). Hidalgo's
statements therefore, were to constitute, according
to Jesús Silva Herzog, the first agrarian document
of independent Mexico. Hardly three months earlier,
the popular movement which would lead to the independence from Spain, had exploded.

The *campesinos* are the natives of this country.
They have always provided the basis for its development and have always been a keystone in any changes
which have taken place. Even today, numerically they
are the largest group in Mexican society. At the
beginning of this century they represented 80% or
90% of the population. And today the ever-increasing
urban population is made up of children and grandchildren of *campesinos*.

These facts gave rise to the historically
false picture of bucolic agrarianism within which
an ever-constant *campesino* played one and the same
role throughout history. He has thus come to be seen
as some kind of formal entity walking on and off
different stage sets, endlessly playing the same
monotonous role for different audiences. This fairy
tale view was the one which gave the world the
picture of the Mexican as an Indian sitting crouched
under his hat. It was also responsible, paradoxically, for the *campesino* being denied any historical
roots, and for his being seen merely as a puppet of
the dominant structures.

In the XVI century, Father Bartolomé de las
Casas, the Great defender of the Indians felt oblig-

ed to paint a true picture of the Indian. He did
this in his famous "Apologética," refuting the
idea that the Indian lacked the rational capacity
for self-government in a civil manner and within a
system of public order. After the publication of
the book, and because of it, "the American Indian
was integrated conceptually as an equal among all
social levels within the universal vision of the
Christian community." However, because of the
Aristotelian maxim which states that whatever is
superior and better must dominate whatever is inferior and imperfect, the following aphorism was
propagated: "civilized nations do not only have the
right but also the supreme moral obligation to intervene in the life of barbarian nations. They
should use their sovereignty to guide and help these
nations only with spiritual advice, but by imposing
upon them, through force if necessary, benevolent
and paternal institutions to lead them to the path-
ways of true religion and civilized traditions."
This meant that, although Fr. Bartolomé's work
placed the Indian in the social environment of the
historical vision of the time, this integration was
not seen "as fraternal communion between all men
and peoples but as communion taking place under
paternalistic Spanish banners." (1)

Varying trends of thinking prevailed at different times during the four centuries of colonial
rule; trends such as medieval imperialism -like that
of the historian Oviedo- or modern nationalism, but
whatever the trend, the Indians were always an
oppressed, colonized people living under the strict-
est domination. Even though they fought for their
communities' autonomy, their condition always oscil-
lated between that of "slave" and servant.

In 1841, two decades after Independence had
been established, a distinguished traveler described the situation of the Indians in the following
terms: "There are two classes of Indians: cowhands,
who receive 12 pesos a year and 5 sacks of corn a
week; and ploughmen known as luneros (Monday men)
because they have to work on Mondays. When they

(1) Edmundo O'Gorman, CUATRO HISTORIADORES DE
INDIAS, Sepsetentas, México, 1972, pp. 101, 107 and
110.

marry and have a family and consequently need more
water, they are obliged to till, sow and harvest
twenty *mecates* of corn for their masters (each *mecate* has 24 square *varas*). When the chapel bell
rings, all the Indians have to go immediately to
the *hacienda* and do whatever work is assigned to
them by their master or his substitute. For this
they receive one *real* and three *centavos* worth of
corn. The authority of the master or his substitute
is absolute. They settle disputes between the Indians, punish any wrongdoing... the Indians only
have to stay on the *hacienda* if they are in debt and
being in debt ties them hand and foot. A malicious
master can make sure they are always in debt." (2)

Around the same time, a distinguished Mexican,
Melchor Ocampo, described the position of the *peones*
as follows: "Working six days a week, *peones*
receive 9 *reales*: they spend three on corn, half a
real on chili, half a *real* on salt, all these being
necessities. Four of the remaining *reales* are
used to pay a debt; then they would only have
half a *real* left to buy meat, thread, ciga-
rettes, fruit, medicine. In order to pay off a debt
of ten pesos, giving four *reales* each week, they
need five months..." (3)

On December 3, 1912, while Emiliano Zapata was
fighting for the land in Morelos, Luis Cabrera,
together with 62 other Federal representatives,
presented the draft of a law. The first article declared "the reconstitution and endowment of *ejidos*
to villages" to be of public interest. The speech
he made defending the project immediately became
famous and remains so today. It contains a passion-
ate picture of the situation of the *campesinos*,
valuable in spite of the penetrating ideology of
the speaker. To quote from it at length will save
us many pages of free description. Here then, are
some excerpts:

---

(2) I.L. Stephen, "Incidents of Travel in Central
America, Chiapas and Yucatán," quoted by José Mancisidor in SINTESIS DEL MOVIMIENTO SOCIAL EN MEXICO,
Centro de Estudios Históricos del Movimiento Obrero
Mexicano, México, 1976, pp. 13-14.
(3) Melchor Ocampo, "Polémicas Religiosas," quoted
by José Mancisidor, OP. CIT.

"Whether conditions found by the Spaniards at
the time of the conquest, were to be respected -as
wisely advised by Phillip II- and consequently the
Indians were to be left untouched, whether towns
were to be founded by means of *reducciones* or
through settlements, the population could not survive
according to the Spanish or the colonial criteria unless it had the *casco* of the *ejido* and the *propio*.
The *casco* circumscribed the limits of what really
constituted urban life; the *ejidos* that related to
the communal life of the inhabitants, and the *propios*
have been the source of many important economic phenomena in our country. Anyone who has read any title
deeds of the Colonial period, must have felt how the
struggle between the *hacienda* and the village stands
out on every page. In the rural economic battle that
took place during the Colonial period between villages and *haciendas*, victory was gradually gained by
the villages as a result of their privileges, their
organizational ability, the effective cooperation
learnt over the centuries and above all, because of
the vast power obtained through the control of *propios*, as elements of conservation. The *ejidos* se-
cured subsistence for the villages, the *propios*
guaranteed the power of district governments. The
ejidos provided peace for neighboring families
nestled round a church, the *propios* represented the
economic power of municipal authority for villages,
which were nothing less than huge landholdings in
relation to the *latifundio* known as *hacienda*. This
was the secret of how villages were able to survive
vis a vis the *hacienda*, in spite of the enormously
advantageous privileges of the Spanish landowners
during the Colonial period. The *propios* were misused,
when it was seen just how far they could be used for
entailment purposes. But when later laws required
the disentailment of unused land, almost immediately
the *propios* were considered a very risky form of
mortgaging which had to be destroyed, together with
amortizations of religious orders and lay corporations. The situation of the villages compared with
that of the *haciendas* was notoriously privileged in the
eyes of the 1856 disentailment law. These laws,
which were applied to the *ejidos* resolved that
instead of the *ejidatarios* appropriating the land,
it should be distributed among the members of the
village. This was the beginning of the end of the
ejidos, and the origin of the absolute impoverish-

ment of the villages. At the present time, I won't
say because of usurpation, although there has been;
I won't say because of theft or complicity of the
authorities, although there have been thousands of
cases, but because of the way in which the *ejidos*
were disentailed, it was obvious that for economic
reasons they fell into hands which were able to
profit from them. Sooner or later, this distribution
was going to lead to the formation of a new *latifundio* with the characteristics of the *hacienda*, or
it would become part of neighboring *haciendas*(...)
There were some voices heard against the disintegration of the *ejidos*(...) There were not just one or
a few villages, there were many which, at the right
moment, managed to resist the disintegration of the
ejidos. After the redistribution of the land, many
of the people began to give their title deeds to
the most trusted person in the village. Let's call
him the *cacique* in the good sense of the word. This
meant that he came to have in his hands all the
title deeds, in order to keep and defend village
lands, through communal administration, which in
fact still continued.

In the State of Mexico, this system was very
common and had reached such a level of perfection
that cooperative or public limited companies were
formed by all the villagers, in an attempt to return to the communal situation. It was this situation which the law had tried to change through procedures more in keeping with modern tendencies of
social organization. This was the only way they
found to defend themselves against the extinction
of communal property. But obviously it was insufficient, in view of the great attraction of the
neighboring *latifundios* for small landowners. Whatever the reason, either negligence of small landowners or abuse by the authorities, the fact is
that the *ejidos* passed almost entirely from the hand
of the villages to those of the *hacendados*. Consequently, a great number of villages, at present,
have no way of satisfying their most basic needs (...)
The disentailment laws of 1856, which did away with
the *ejidos*, left no alternative means of subsistence
for the villagers. Even though previously they had
been able to make their living throughout the year
from the cultivation of the *ejidos*, now they became
'de facto' slaves or servants in the *haciendas*.

Slavery in the *haciendas* was inversely related to
the existence of *ejidos* around villages. Industrialization began to develop after 1884, and changed the
condition of the rural classes somewhat, especially
in places where there was industrial activity or
where they were close to mining centers (...) But
where these conditions do not exist, *ejidos* are
vital for small villages, and where there are no
villages, only vast tracts of land with entire areas
occupied by *haciendas*, there undoubtedly slavery
exists (...) Over the last fifteen years the *hacienda,* in this part of the central plateau, has
used two types of servants or *jornaleros*: the yearly
contracted *peón*, and the specific task *peón*. The
yearly contracted *peón*, the so-called *acasillado,*
is given special privileges over other *peones*, under
the condition that he brings his family and lives in
the *casco* of the *hacienda* and remains in service
there for a year. The specific task *peón* (*peón de
tarea*), on the other hand, is someone who comes from
time to time to sow or harvest. The yearly *peón* has
an insignificant salary, one on which he cannot possibly live, one which would not suffice to feed a
mule. How is it possible for such salary levels to
exist? Is it possible, theoretically speaking, that
a man can live on it? No, it is not possible, but
this happens for the following reasons: the *hacienda* can pay or calculate for instance, an average of
120 pesos, for the four months it needs the *peón's*
labor; this would mean that the *haciendas* should pay
$30.00 monthly or $1.00 daily for a good *peón* capable
of doing all the yearly tasks. But if the *hacienda*
contracts a *peón* and then allows him to leave, it
would have difficulties in hiring a new one. It has
somehow, therefore, to ensure that the *peón* stays on
the *hacienda*. This it does by dividing four months'
salary throughout the whole year, by paying a day's
work at $0.31, that is, the same $120.00 yearly salary. Seen in this light, the daily wage of $0.31 is
an excellent salary that the *peón* cannot find any-
where. Generally speaking, the yearly *peón* gets
$0.25 daily wage. The yearly *peón* has a minimal sal-
ary but on the condition that he and his family remain at the *hacienda*. He has a secure job for a
year, even though it is at the expense of his freedom and at a daily wage which is insufficient to
cover his needs. A salary, in fact, less than the
cost of hiring out some poor nag. The owner of the

hacienda, therefore, pays a salary of around $0.25 daily, that is not enough to fulfill the *peón's* needs; the *hacendado*, therefore, has to find a way of keeping this *peón acasillado*. If he gets along with the local political administrator, who is usually no more than a servant of the *hacendado*; and if he has access to the army, that tremendous, ever-present threat hanging over our rural classes; and if he has a *tlapixquera* to throw the *peón* in when he tries to run away -in fact if he has the power and means- he can have as many *peones* as he wishes and can be sure they will remain there. But when an *hacendado* does not have all the repressive means at hand, then he has to find other ways. He becomes a little more flexible and uses other means for his purposes. For instance: the price of corn, to which the yearly *peones* have a right, constitutes the first complement to his salary. If the price of corn on the market is usually $8.00 or $10.00 this is of little importance, because part of the *hacienda* harvest has been put aside in order to be able to sell corn to the yearly *peón* at $6.00 per *cuartilla*. Half a *cuartilla* is the weekly allowance for his family; this, in itself, is an economic incentive and, in fact, constitutes a small increase in salary, since the *campesino* buys the corn at a lower price and gets it as a complement to his salary; not a very large one, but just enough to ensure that he does not die of hunger. And this is looked upon as a favor on the part of the master towards his yearly *peones*. In areas where *pulque* (fermented juice of the agave) is extracted, another salary complement is given to the *tlaquichero peón*: it is called the *tlaxilole*. This is the portion of *pulque* that at sunset and after singing praises to the Lord, the *tlaquichero* gets to cover his family's needs. He can do whatever he wants with it: sell it, drink it, or put it in what is known as a *panal*, which is the hollowed out stem of the maguey cactus where it is secretly fermented. He generally drinks it or sells it, but, in any case, the *tlaxilole* is a small extra salary for the *tlaquichero*. Something I should have mentioned earlier, which is also a complement to his salary, is the *casilla*. This is the half, third, or eighth portion of a *casilla*, which one of these poor souls gets as living quarters; it is true that the "*acasillado*" *peón* has to share the hard floor he sleeps on with other *peones* or servants of the *ha-*

cienda, in very unchristian promiscuity; but he does
have a small section to call home and this is also
considered as a complement to his salary. While he
is a yearly *peón*, he also has the right to school,
on rare occasions, but under what conditions? In
1895, when I was a teacher in a *hacienda pulquera*,
I was instructed by the administrator -who was not
the person who paid my salary because I was an
official employee- that I was to teach only how to
read and write and the Catechism of the Roman Catholic Church. I was absolutely forbidden to teach
arithmetic and especially "things to do with Civic
instruction that you people bring with you and are
of no use! (...)" Anyway, school is a small increase
in salary, but it is not always provided by the *hacienda*. Next on the list are the <u>credits</u> given in
the *tienda de raya*. The *tienda de raya* is not a
simple imposition of the *hacendados*, it is an essential part of the economic system of *hacienda*
management. It is impossible to think of an *hacienda* without one (...) The *tienda de raya* is a place
where the *hacendado* gives credit to the *peón* and
this is considered as a benefit for the *peón*, but,
at the same time it becomes the *hacendado*'s bank.
The salary complements talked about before, constitute the *hacendado*'s generosity given to the *campesinos* by his right hand. However, the left hand
through the *tienda de raya*, then, takes back any
excess salary that the *peón* might have been paid
through his corn allowance, *casilla*, and the *tlaxilole*; everything is returned to the *hacendado*
through the *tienda de raya*. And the *peón* unfailingly
returns it because the system of perpetual credit,
an incurable evil among our social classes, and even
ourselves is the economic death of our poorer
classes. The most characteristic application in the
credit system is the *tienda de raya* , where every
day the *peón* obtains what he needs to eat on credit.
All the discounts mean that his weekly salary will
only amount to a few cents; all the rest is merely a
question of accounts. When Holy Week comes, the wife
needs special petticoats, the children new sandals,
and he, a belt or a shirt. Since the *peón* has absolutely no chance of any source of income apart from
his daily salary, his only resource is to ask his
master for a Holy Week loan (...) The *hacendado*
takes it all in his stride as yet another of his
expenses. Even though he does not expect to get paid

back, the amount is dutifully written down in the
hacienda account books under "indebted *peones*." Why,
if the *peón* is unable to pay it back and the *hacendado* will not charge him? Its importance does not
lie in the present, but in the future, for it is
the *peón*'s children and grandchildren and their
children's grandchildren who will be required to
pay (...) The three yearly loans would not appear to
be salary increases, but they are, in effect, the
most insidious of the increases, for they constitute
the true chain of slavery (...) The indebted *peón*
remains on the *hacienda* not through fear or even
force but through a kind of fascination brought
about by his own debt. He sees this debt, written
irrevocably in the *hacienda* account books as his
chains, a mark of slavery, his fetters. He rarely
knows the exact amount of his debt; it might even
reach the tremendous sum of $400.00 or $500.00. An
apparently humane, interest-free debt, which remains
unchanged on the books until the *peón* dies. Then,
the total amount is divided between three or four of
his young descendents, who are already working on the
hacienda. There is one last salary increase which
only very special *peones* are allowed, that is the
so-called *piojal* or *pegujal*. The *pegujal* is a small
piece of land, which hardly consists of more than a
quarter of hectare. But the *peón* who has proved himself worthy has the right to sow it. In this way,
he can supplement his salary with the corn harvested
from it. However, he does not reap the corn himself
but sells it, often even before harvesting, to his
master. He can thus pay off some of his debt or use
it for his family needs. The *pegujal* is not granted
to just any *peón*, only to those who have risen to
the status of captain or have become servants, such
as houseboys or grooms. The *pegujal*, therefore, can
represent the beginning of independence for those
peones who have become *medieros* or tenants. Consequently, it is the most important and interesting
kind of salary complement. With the exception of this
complement, all the others are links in a chain,
which only serve to further enslave the *peón* to the
hacienda."

Much of the strength and vigour of this excellent description is due to the fact that it was
delivered as a spontaneous speech. But it also
gives the image and idea of an immutable, unchanging
campesino, by alluding to other than colonial times.

Father Bartolomé de las Casas' work did not have to deal with the "slander" that the Indians were neither human, nor rational beings, but with that which stated that they were not capable of governing themselves "in a civil manner and within a system of public order." Nevertheless, even Bartolomé de las Casas himself, along with the entire colonial population, acted according to this assumption. Even today in Mexico, in daily life, in academic circles or in politics, many think that *campesinos* are incapable of governing themselves.

"A scheming master can always keep (the Indians) in debt," remarked the same famous traveller from last century, and the same thing happens today through the *Banco de Crédito Rural*, which is not without its own rogues; or through the *caciques* established in each *campesino* village.

Phrases could be added to Luis Cabrera's description to replace those referring to institutions and situations, which in "the light of our time" seem to be things of the past. But the occasional observer would not find many differences between today's *campesino* and the ones described by Luis Cabrera. The *campesinos* would thus be mere shadows from history, a left-over from the past, which must be "done away with" as quickly as possible. This image easily slots into common prejudice. It is relatively easy to admit that *campesinos* have made history. It can even be accepted, without too much resistance, that the structuring of modern societies has resulted, to a large extent, from their participation. It may even be thought that dictatorships and democracies have been founded on their attitudes and reactions (Barrington Moore). But they have been, and they still are, the damned of the earth (Fanon, Dumont); they are the pariahs of all cultures; they are putty, demolition material, mere rubble. Sometimes they are the amorphous mass to be shaped by other social forces, those forces which are apparently the carriers of social life, as well as the builders and changers of its course. Compared with pharaohs and emperors, mandarins and kings, feudal overlords and landlords, *encomenderos* and *hacendados*, *latifundistas* and farmers, agribusinessmen and modern agricultural entrepreneurs, all people who viewed themselves as pioneers of history, decisive

elements in the rise, splendor and fall of empires,
the *campesinos* are -so it is said- a pale, immutable
shadow drifting through history from one century to
another, from one continent to another, whose fate
is to adapt themselves, as best as they can, to their
current master: giving in to him, accepting his laws,
or becoming masters themselves, as some have tried
to do successfully. Their resistance, passive or
violent, illusory or otherwise, intermittent or persistent has hardly any other option -that is, if it
is noticed at all- than that of adapting or dying.
Even today, as many projects are drawn up to bring
about their "liberation" (according to various
approaches) the underlying idea is that they cannot
free themselves: either they will be "liberated" by
the forces of capitalism that will turn them into
workers or by the forces of the latter, who will
make the revolution for all. In the first case they
will have to accept the notion of agriculture without people: stop being what they are -*campesinos*-
and trust that society will offer them another role
(today, for the great majority, that of marginal
population). In the latter case, it seems they will
have to accept the role of "mass of militancy"
based on an alliance with those claiming to be both
their peers and their leaders at the same time.

In Luis Cabrera's brilliant speech, he pointed
out that he would not have recourse to "the background of the history of Rome, nor the English Revolution, nor the French Revolution, nor Austra-
lia's, New Zealand's, or Argentina's, but to that
of the only country that can show us how to solve
our problems, the only country we can imitate: New
Spain." And he emphasized: "New Spain is the only
country Mexico can imitate." And possibly he repeated it so much that notice was taken of him.
Some would say that, besides copying New Spain,
Mexico has been imitating the Porfirian structure,
thus imposing its past on its future, and with this
produce figures or data, images or gestures, situations or policies, to confirm such statements.
They would even quote those in power who have supported this idea.

But it is important to look beyond appearances.
However painfully similar the conditions under
which today's *campesinos* live are to those of their

counterparts from the past, they are nevertheless
different people. We have to take into account the
deep, substantial changes, which have taken place,
changes which cannot always be perceived seeing or speaking to them, changes which have, for
the better or the worse, caused transformations in
their social structure and which have even affected
those forces oppressing them. But above all, we
must take into account how much they themselves
have changed through the dynamics of their contradictions, through the difficult task of interaction
with others, through the accumulated experience of
the long history of their struggle. It would finally
seem that all the "false routes" have been exhausted, those routes which led them time and again to
waste their energy and resources on solutions which
took them nowhere, or on slogans for freedom which
were eventually used against them.

Who, today, are the Mexican *campesinos*?

Rodolfo Stavenhagen has summarized some elements which create an overall picture:

- If the *campesino* is a tenant, then he has to
  pay rent in money or in kind; if he is an
  owner, then he has heavy overhead due to interest, premium, and other payments.

- The poorest *campesinos*, who work the poorest quality land, pay a differential rent
  compared with the rest of the agricultural
  sector.

- The price of land (or its rent) is higher
  for the *campesino*, given the monopoly and
  oligopoly over it.

- Credit is both generally and frequently
  given at usurious rates, thus leading the
  campesino into a systematic process of
  permanent debt.

- Modern physical inputs can only be acquired
  on a small scale at higher prices than for
  large producers, because of the structure
  of trade and the existence of intermediaries.

- Output is low and production, in general,
  is of low quality, and sold at low prices.

- Work productivity is, consequently, very low.

- Crops are sold immediately, independent of
  market conditions (i.e. they sell, even if
  the prices are not advantageous), to satisfy
  immediate cash needs or because of inadequate storage facilities. They often sell
  what they have produced to cover their own
  needs and then have to buy again at higher
  prices. Intermediaries, as well as existing
  monopolies compel them to sell below market
  prices.

- Transportation difficulties increase the
  cost of their products even more.

- The family labor force is not assured
  steady work throughout the year and the
  level of payment for their work is lower
  than that of the rest of society.

- The *campesino* and his family offer their
  services outside their own holdings,
  accepting salary conditions below the legal
  minimum wage, which do not cover their cost
  of living. (4)

Another study points out that 78% of agricultural land does not produce sufficient for the *campesinos'* own consumption contributing only 15% of
production value. On the other hand, 13% of agricultural land provides three quarters of the total production, but employs only 20% of the *campesino* population with half of this percentage working regularly.

Campesino units of production are found all over
the country, but are concentrated mainly in the states of Durango, Zacatecas, San Luis Potosí, Jalisco,

---

(4) Rodolfo Stavenhagen et al, CAPITALISMO Y EL
CAMPESINO EN MEXICO, INAH, 1976, pp. 20-21.

Michoacán, Morelos, Puebla, Oaxaca and Yucatán. (5)

In areas where other forms of organized production exist (Chihuahua, Sonora, etc.), most of the
campesino lands are located in arid or mountainous
regions, i.e. in the most inhospitable areas,
usually with poor quality agricultural land.

Specific characteristics of some key agrarian
protagonists, can be distinguished from this overall description.

Managers and employees: the Master's Voice

These characters do not fit exactly into this
chapter, but must be included here because they receive a salary. However, their objectives, interests
and idelogoy would better place them in the previous
chapter.

They are the "staff personnel" of *rancheros*,
cattle raisers, farmers and agribusinessmen, who
hold managment, administrative, or service positions. They receive a salary throughout the year,
as well as different kinds of compensation, varying
from profit-sharing when they have powerful administrative positions, to room and board if they are
peones, cowhands, or domestic servants. Some also
have the equivalent of the *pegujal* and work available pieces of land, either directly or through
tenants or salaried workers. Occasionally, they are
able to become "independent" and are integrated
into different rural or urban social groups.

Those who make up this reduced segment of the
rural population, almost always act in their master's name and interests. Since they identify with
controlling capital, they usually have difficulty
in identifying themselves with other workers and
their relationship with them is often antagonistic.
In many cases, it is tenser and more aggressive than
that between the master and the other workers. Their

(5) Kirsten A. Appendini, and Vania A. Salles, "Agricultura capitalista y agricultura campesina en México (diferencias regionales con base en el análisis
de datos censales)", in CUADERNOS DEL CES, No. 10,
El Colegio de México, México, 1977, p. 22.

work occasionally consists of finding and directing
"rural guards," those who take care of the dirty
work of repression in certain regions.

"Golondrinas" (or wandering souls)

These destitute people wander from place to
place, either inside the country or abroad. It is
impossible to calculate their numbers correctly,
because of their wandering rootless life. From time
to time, some empirical research touches on them,
but they soon slip through the researcher's fingers.
They are the dramatic clochards of rural Mexico,
prisoners of their own miserable freedom, dragging
their way through a meaningless and usually short
life, except in the case where fortune smiles upon
them and keeps them in one place. One of them, a
prisoner on the Islas Marías, was able to cultivate
a piece of land and, walking through the streets,
while serving a long murder sentence said with no
regrets, "Here I feel freer than on the mainland.
There I do not even have a village to go to."

The "golondrinas" seem to be people expelled
from their own community because of some social or
family crisis which led them to break all ties. They
offer their services as day workers in the fields
according to harvest needs, or go to towns where
they are prepared to work doing anything. Their lack
of initiative or spirit of adventure, results from
a melancholic or aggressive resignation which led
them to cut all ties with the past and the future.
They carry their home on their backs. They live for
their own resources, hiring themselves out as laborers or resorting to crime. If no unexpected "re-
demption" arises, the chance of a stable job, a
girlfriend who will tie them to one place, or access
to an established group, they will vegetate and die
as imperceptibly as they appeared.

Our estimate has put this group at 1,200,000, (6)
but this is obviously the result of confusion with
a group we will talk about later: that of _jornaleros_,
who roam from one farm to another, often taking their
families with them but never losing contact with

(6) Francisco Schnabel, "Vivienda transitoria para
trabajadores migratorios", in VIVIENDA, INFONAVIT,
México, 1978.

their home towns. The true *"golondrinas,"* who have broken these links, appear occasionally in the census in the slots and regions where they happen to be at the time, but statistics are unable to give precise details as to their numbers. Some data, however, indicate that they have increased: data such as the cruel disappearance of many rural communities, which have literally been wiped off the map, or the proliferation in villages and towns of those the authorities consider to be "vagabonds." They form the dregs of Mexican society, politically neglected and a constant reminder of its evolutionary pattern. Thus described and in contrast with "swallows" that appear in literature, perhaps they should be rather called albatrosses that nest temporarily on passing boats. Or, maybe they should be considered wandering souls in search of a body in which to materialize.

Farm workers

There is another small group which must be mentioned. This is made up of permanent, salaried farm workers, with formal work relations in specific places. Their numbers are small because the demand for them is limited to relatively few units of production: generally in highly capitalized areas with specific crops, or paradoxically in areas where traditional economy prevails. Although many operations need workers, they tend to contract them to perform specific tasks for limited periods of time. In this way, they avoid serious labor obligations and hire only the required numbers.

These farm workers are similar to industrial workers in terms of their objective class condition and some of their attitudes. However, they seldom share similar working conditions. They rarely receive individual contracts or minimum wage. This results from their lack of negotiating power and the fact that they are so disperse, that they are unable to organize themselves. Their numbers, however, do not have very much bearing on the total.

A recent survey stated that 12% of the employed rural population was made up of permanent salaried workers: roughly 800,000. Officially this group corresponds to farm workers. However, certain empirical research projects have questioned this estimate.

They ascertain that in many *campesino* operations, the salary received is an important element for its functioning. This obviously implies deep and integral interactions between salaried and non-salaried workers, which sometimes presuppose a transfer of value from the boss to his employee and not vice versa. (7)

In the analytical context of this book, farm workers are defined as those who are completely disconnected from *campesino* agricultural operations and whose earning capacity, as well as that of their families, comes exclusively from selling their labor. Many of them, similar to industrial workers, take upon themselves a large part of their costs of living (they build their own homes, make their own clothes and household utensils, etc.), or receive them through public services. In spite of this, they have lost their authentic productive capacity, for their activity itself does not generate either profit or consumer goods for others; it merely produces enough to cover their own needs. In this sense, even though they possess tools, they lack a means of production. Consequently, it could be thought that the actual number of farm workers is less than calculated, and that they are scattered, given the non-existence of large concentrated capitalistic units of production because of constitutional stipulations. A large number of these workers are found in operations where no more than five permanent salaried workers are employed.

Campesinos

Most of the rural population of Mexico can be classified under this heading. Their common characteristics are few, although enough to distinguish them from other social groups: they basically depend on their work for subsistence and reproduction; they maintain a special relationship with the land, either directly or indirectly, and they are integrated -albeit weakly it would seem- into a community structure, the outer signs of which are social or

(7) Marielle P. L. Martínez and Teresa Rendón, "Fuerza de trabajo y producción campesina," in COMERCIO EXTERIOR, Vol. 28, No. 6, June, 1978, p. 663.

superstructural, although these indicate an economic basis of organizational functioning. Any attempt at generalization beyond these characteristics, only further emphasizes their heterogeneity. However, within the methodological framework of this book, it is possible to present some subgroups under this heading, without losing sight of the fact that the members of each subgroup share the same general characteristics presented above. Before describing these groups, perhaps some of their common characteristics should be studied in more detail.

First of all, the dialectics of the contradictions characterizing present day Mexican *campesinos* must be explained: on the one hand, they depend upon their own work to produce and to survive, and, on the other, they maintain a special relationship with the land. This contradiction, seen in a strict sense is what separates Mexican *campesinos* from their own and other pasts, while at the same time defining them as a class and their differences with other groups within the same class: they are proletarian but are distinguished from others (such as the workers) because they are subject to different mechanisms of exploitation.

Work, in this sense, is not equivalent to effort. Throughout history *campesinos* have survived by relying on their own efforts and on creative energy capable of transforming nature and of producing objects to satisfy their own needs and those of their oppressors. Work in this case is productive work, which in a capitalist context, means the capacity to generate profit for capital. *Campesinos*, as well as industrial or service workers, are subordinated to capital along the lines of the logic described in the previous chapter. This subordination does not always mean, however, being tied to capital in concrete productive activities. Neither does it necessarily imply being tied to it in terms of a worker-capitalist relationship, materialized on the one hand by salary and in the other by a series of duties subject to discipline and hierarchy. *Campesino* subordination to capital is, in fact, part of its logic, that is, functioning in such a way that the results of their productive process become their own reproduction process as well as a profit for capital.

The other side of the condition of the *campesinos'* existence -the dialectic one- is that of the ties they have with the land, which are a substantive part of their relation to capital, or rather, of the specific relation of capital to them. Capital cannot (and very specifically does not want to) concern itself with *campesino* reproduction. And it must not, as is the case of the industrial and service workers, for the *campesinos* take on this responsibility with their own means. This has nothing to do with the problem of unemployment, a "natural" condition in modern capitalist societies, of the so-called industrial reserve army of the unemployed or "marginalization." What it deals with is the specific form this relationship takes on.

First, capitalist production in agriculture should not and cannot, in the terms of its own logic, cover the annual salary of the worker since it only needs him part of the year (Luis Cabrera already foresaw this). Second, capitalist operations are centered on activities other than cultivation itself, either because of preference (due to profitability), or because it is obliged to (due to the socio-economic context). Agribusiness, as we have already seen, is centered on control of the productive process to ensure it over industrial, agricultural and cattle raising inputs. The risks of crop production must be undertaken by the direct producer. Capital merely guides the productive process, leaving the technological patterns untouched, in the initial stages of intervention. In this case, it works from the "outside" as a conditioning and determining factor, and can therefore intensify the productive activity, although it is not concerned with transforming it. However, agribusiness tends to transform the productive process itself radically in order to subject it to its own patterns both to create the need for its own inputs, and to adapt the product to the form and needs of its own requirements, while remaining "outside" direct production.

The relationship between agribusiness and the *campesinos* frequently follows tortuous paths through an increasing number of middlemen and other people between them. This does not deviate greatly from basic capitalist logic, the main tendency of which is to disassociate workers from their means of production. The *campesinos'* situation, on the contrary, confirms this tendency since this disassociation has generally already taken place. What happens is that land and work instruments are not means of production, proper for the *campesino*: rather they are the space and the condition for their productive activity to materialize. In fact, the strength of this link with land generally means that his usufruct guarantees the materialization of his productive activity, a guarantee he would not otherwise have.

This phenomenon results of course from the fact that according to the Constitution of the Republic, the ownership of all land corresponds to the Nation. But it also results, above all, from the fact that usufruct of the land, which gave rise to the different forms of land tenure, has been encroached upon by capitalist evolution. In Mexico, capital has a <u>legal</u> limit for its direct access to agriculture, since law prohibits commercial capital participating in land exploitation. There is also a <u>political</u> limit, indicated by the presence of the *campesinos* and their struggle to be heard. Consequently, agricultural capitalists only become what they are, through the illegality of open or simulated *latifundios*. Since the judicial system of the country rejects the entrepreneur structure of exploitation and restricts the hiring of permanent salaried workers, capital is obliged -and in this way adjusts to world norms- to operate from "outside" the productive process. This is generally done through openly illegal mechanisms which allow it to direct and subordinate this activity, according to its own logic. "The form of land tenure -Rodolfo Stavenhagen has said- has not yet been an obstacle for the development of capitalism. Capitalism has, in one way or another, total control over production." (8) Gradually, land tenure (or usufruct) has become simply a form no longer associated with specific types of social relations. *Campesinos* appear to be direct producers, "dressed" according to the tenure structure: they can be *comuneros, ejidatarios*, small landholders, small *minifundio* owners... Their relationship with

(8) Rodolfo Stavenhagen, an interview in PROCESO, No. 81, June 19, 1978, p. 9.

capital -understanding capital as a relationship-
does not necessarily take the form of salary, even
though they are workers at the service of capital.
The relationship with land produces yet another dialectics. On one hand, the *campesino* is guaranteed to
be able to channel his productive activity. Since
this is subordinated to capital and acts within the
framework of its logic, this means that the guarantee
for subsistence is related to the capacity of acting
within this framework. To lack this capacity means
risking, in real concrete terms, subsistence on daily
terms. On the other hand, however, the ties with land
provide a way of belonging to a socio-economic structure which guarantees a stable condition for subsistence: the rural community. While it is true that
being able to fit into the framework of capital logic
is the conditioning and determining factor of *campesino* life, it is also true that this is a fleeting,
volatile pre-requisite for survival. It can be destroyed at any moment and only offers insecure, reversible guarantees because of the demands made by this
very logic. The other guarantee is lasting and stable; it has resisted the passage of time and the
worst of natural and socio-economic hazards. The
community appears as an indestructible force of
resistance, even when it serves as the "besieged
fortress" in the words of Arturo Warman. It is true
that every day some villages come in to being, while
others die; and that the organization process continues its unchecked march forward. But the fact is
that those rural communities with under 2,500 inhabitants, have remained surprisingly stable over recent decades.

A slight digression is necessary here if rural
Mexico is to be fully understood. Like *campesinos*,
the rural community represents a "way of life" which
appears to have been the first kind of human settlements and perhaps the least studied. Its origin and
personality have aroused both interest and mistaken
opinions. One mistake, for instance, has been that
of trying to trace the likely antiquity and strength
of present communities in history. This again has
resulted in the myth of "primitivism" being put forth,
which confuses instead of clarifying present reality.
In the name of history, real history is denied. "The
past is frequently lost for those who do not analyze
it carefully, establishing it in the seemingly imme-

diate present on an anachronic, disused block of
time." The "urban eye" with its ethnocentric shrouds,
approaches a qualitatively different reality and cannot see it. Those who live within cannot talk about
it either, because its very organization and consciousness "are hidden in the individual lives of
those who dwell in it: sensitive reality is as secret as it is immediate." (9) City dwellers are
prone to consider people from rural areas as gossips.
But we are the gossips. For them, talking about somebody else means talking about themselves; in their
shared reality, no one is foreign to anyone; a comment on a neighbor is an act of introspection.

The rural community is a form, but it is not
merely a façade: if we do not search in history for
its various contents -in its static and changing
dynamics- we will never discover them. The fact that
it persists, in the same way the family does, -under
the most heterogeneous conditions, in totally different periods of time, separated by history or geo-
graphy- and the fact that it remains, disappears,
reappears under different production systems, mean
that it is an organic entity with strength and dynamics, rooted in history, and in legend, in constant reproduction and transformation. It has a past
from which nothing remains yet everything is felt.
We cannot take it as it was. We cannot see its present reality as a residual product or a strange left-
over from the past. We cannot cling to the rigid
frame of prejudice that tends to characterize our
analyses of rural reality. Just as U.S. rural communities were an urban product -because fugitives of
the cities were the ones who built towns on a social
vaccum-U.S. sociology, that of a country lacking
historical breadth, has given shape to a cosmopolitan
image of a rural community that has little to do with
it. And this image seems to have permeated virtually
any analysis we make of the subject.

---

(9) Henry Lefevre, "Problemas de sociología rural:
la comunidad rural y sus problemas histórico-socio-
lógicos", in DE LO RURAL A LO URBANO, Lotus Mare,
Buenos Aires, 1976, pp. 19-20

The rural community "is not a productive force nor is it a mode of production (...) It is a kind of organic community which cannot be reduced to the total sum of its individual elements (...) its relation cannot be exhausted through land tenure relationships since it is also made up of collective rulings which are extremely flexible according to their circumstances and strength (...) This gives us the elements for a definition of a rural community (a *campesino* one): it is a form of social group, organizing, according to historically determined characteristics, a set of families tied to the land. These primary groupings have on the one hand, collective or individual wealth, and on the other, "private" wealth from varying relationship, but these are always historically determined. They are ruled by collective forms of power and assign -even when the community keeps to itself- responsible leaders to direct the implementation of these tasks of general interest. (10) It is certainly true that "nowadays *campesino* life lacks autonomy. It cannot develop according to its own laws, in many ways it is related to general economy, national life, and modern technology." But if it also is true, as Lefevre pointed out thirty years ago, that the *campesino* community can spring up again in modern times, according to modern needs and on a modern basis, it would be a fascinating rebirth perhaps from which a new sense of earth would be born." (11)

The rural community as such is not a productive force nor a mode of production but it is inextricably related to the forms of organized labor. When conflicts arise from the development of productive forces, specifically during capitalist expansion, its disintegration is planned in the classic way. The advance of capitalism in agriculture, apart from appropriating productive and natural resources, has also demanded the "individualization" of the rural workers, their radical separation from the means of production and from the social relations tying up their lives. The organic nature of the community means that individuals exist within it in as much as they are differentiated from it. It is precisely

(10) Lefevre, OP. CIT., pp. 26-31.
(11) Lefevre, OP. CIT., pp. 37-38.

these differences that form the group and through
which its cohesion is developed. Capitalist development needs to eradicate this social form of existence,
because in order to function it requires the homogenization of individuals. It needs to produce
human atoms immersed in the mass, with each of them,
establishing new forms of social relationships with
the economic agent which allows the process: the
capitalist. Some of the "individualized" *campesinos*
are absorbed by industrial work as a part of this
sequence which increases social entropy, opening up
thus, the possibility of chaos. The organic relationship among themselves is limited and disrupted, it is
transformed into mechanical solidarity within the
productive unit and can only be reconstructed in the
long process of integrating the new group. It starts
in the way dictated by labor unions, until the new
group emerges through organic solidarity, in a class
organization. The rest of the *campesinos*, those who
remain in the rural areas without "proletarianization" in terms of the classic sequence, constitute
the rural communities. But they generally remain under conditions that do not respond to their historical characteristics. Mechanical solidarity often
prevails over organic solidarity which has been
broken down by social and productive transformation.
In this way the definition of rural community given
by Kolb and Brunner can be understood as an example
which clearly contrasts with the one presented above.
They define it as "the interaction of people and
their institutions on a local level." This interaction results from a kind of individualism which is
continually exacerbated -keeping pace with the substantive homogenization of individuals and the growing disintegration of links with their community.
The individual has been alienated from his community
and clings to what he has, while at the same time
changing his traditional values for those given to
him by the impersonal forces of the market through
the mass media. It is this social context that gives
origin to the traditional conservatism of the *campesino*, but simultaneously it also is the background
against which all the prejudices towards the *campesino* flourish. (12)

---

(12) It is not only a case of prejudice. The modern
catonism to which Barrington Moore refers is populist
rhetoric, which alludes to real content. This proc-

This classic sequence of events, however, has
not generally occured in Mexico or in many other
countries. The social forces that initiated the disintegration of rural communities did not see this
disintegration through to its end. As soon as the
campesinos realized that they were not being offered
a new framework of social relations within which
they could subsist and develop, their reaction was
one of survival and of resistance to the change
which only seemed to be leading them to their own
extinction. The organic strength of their communities provided them with a concrete option, that is
it gave them a guarantee for survival that they
could no longer obtain in any other way. However,
this strength was seldom enough to encourage development because external pressures remained blocking
the possibilities of accumulation. The existence of
this kind of solidarity at the heart of many rural
communities may give way to new options for rural
development at this moment in history. It means that
the conventional "proletarianization process" (the
transformation of the direct producer into a salaried or unemployed worker) is not a fatal or inevitable event: neither, of course, is it the only option for capital or for workers. It also means that
the inherent irrationality of a process, such as the
capitalist process, which needs to break down society into individual elements in order to reintegrate
them is not an inescapable process. It means that
reality can be transformed through a drive towards
development which can be found in this organic
strength instead of going against it, trying to dis-
solve it and inciting fruitless social conflict.
When the salaried worker notices that his contradictory situation with capital cannot be overcome by
his status of a "free" worker, his only alternative
is to integrate himself into a long process promoting
organic solidarity, first within his own productive
unit, and then within his own social class.

---

ess of individualization is an irreversible and universal fact, although levels and goals vary according to context. The appearance of "lonely crowds"
(in the sense used by Riesman) is a fact which has
to be taken into account. Gustavo Esteva, "Movimien-
tos Campesinos y Política Nacional", in CUADERNOS DE
DISCUSION, CENAPRO, No. 2, 1978.

The *campesino*, however, from the start already has a social organization from which the
capitalist system has not as yet been able to dis-
connect him. This organization can be used once he
becomes aware of the economic contradictions that
result directly and immediately from the political
climate of the real conditions under which Mexico
is developing.

Community organizations

The degree and type of solidarity found in
Mexican rural communities show, in fact, great
heterogeneity. It is important to distinguish between the community structure which developed on
the basis of Indian tradition, and that which
resulted from later colonization processes. The
Mesoamerican residuum in the central and southern
regions of the country gives rise to communities
that constitute literally, forms of social organization, living and organic bodies, from which
"individuals" progressively break away -although
never completely- to appear as emanations of an
active social substance. In the northern part of
the country, however, patterns similar to those from
North America were adopted, that is, "individuals"
or families who were already constituted as such,
coming from different places with varying characteristics, gathered together in a common, relatively
open space. Unification results -as in other com-
munities- from mutual help against both a hostile
environment and common enemies. But the lack of
pressure for land tenure, characteristic of long
periods of colonization, encourages the formation
and strengthening of socio-economic differences between the members of the community who for some time
merely share the physical space of the community.
(An obvious exception, of course, is the Indian
"enclave" of the Yaqui, Maya, Tarahumara and other
tribes, although even here one can see differences
compared with the ethnic groups in the central and
southern states.)

Another perceivable difference is found in the
legal form of land tenure, which in some cases
offers modern legal systems whithin a clearly
defined historical reality, and in others it offers

new ways of social existence arising from a variety
of experiences. Within this diversity, *ejidos* and
Indian communities, agricultural and cattle raising
groups and villages have to be distinguished.

Ejidos and Indian Communities. The term *ejido*
was first used in Mexico as an extrapolation from an
old Spanish institution. It was the term the conquerors were most familiar with, when they tried to
adapt Indian organizational traditions to their own
requirements. The original structuring of the *ejidos*
in Mexico is, therefore, a *mestizo* achievement whose
long Indian history has been transformed by Spanish
domination. It represents a triumph for the Indians,
since it meant their recognition by the Spanish
Crown and the obtaining of their title deeds. But it
was also used as an instrument of domination over
them, since the *ejidos* were incorporated into institutions of colonization.

During the Colonial period and the first years
after Independence, the *ejido* was the key in the
constant struggle between communities and *haciendas*. The liberal laws of the *República Restaurada*,
which affected the confiscated church lands also
affected the communities. In answer to these abrupt
losses, the communities tried throughout the Porfirian dictatorship to reconquer their communal properties. This led them at the turn of this century
to the situation described by Luis Cabrera at the
beginning of this chapter.

The first years of the Revolution are characterized by a process of reconstitution of the *ejidos*.
For Luis Cabrera and others who shared his line of
thought, this was all there was to matter. The *ejido*
would be a parallel and complementary institution to
the *hacienda* and to the smallholdings. Here the *campesinos* would be able· to work by themselves during
their periods of unemployment on *haciendas*
or smallholdings. It was to be, therefore, a transitory institution which would gradually disappear in
the face of economic expansion. The 1917 Constitution,
which gave the nation ownership of the land also
entrusted it with the obligation of endowing land to
campesinos. It thus paved the way for *ejidos* to become a permanent institution of great historical
density. Even though many years were to go by before

this endowment come into effect, according to which new centers of population would be created (already in existence in the case of reconstituted *ejidos*), such an action has a clear legal and constitutional inception and deep socio-political roots. In Lázaro Cárdenas' time, the *ejidos* occupied as much as half the land under cultivation. In a now famous dispute, Cárdenas defended his agrarian policy as a direct consequence of the Mexican Revolution that would bring about the autonomous existence of the *ejidos* as a form of production. Luis Cabrera, on the other hand, maintains that this is a novelty: an invention of "today's" revolutionaries because "yesterday's", those who actually carried out the Revolution, thought that the *ejido* would merely be a mechanism for complementing the *campesinos'* means of subsistence. (13)

The present day *ejido*, therefore, stems from the constitutional provision which establishes that "the centers of population which lack or do not have sufficient land or water... have the right to be given these from neighboring properties, provided smallholdings under cultivation are respected." The reconstitution of *ejidos* follows the lines of communal legal deeds although they are no longer known as such. The *ejido* thus becomes a product of an agrarian policy of endowment or enlargement.

Strictly speaking, just like communities, *ejidos* have a legal character and internal mechanisms of decision. These are the General Assembly made up of all *ejidatarios* and *comuneros* with full power of decision and the *Comisariados Ejidales*, the *Comisariados de Bienes Comunales*, and the *Consejos de Vigilancia*, all elected by the Assembly. The provisional or definitive endowment of land to *ejidos*, or the enlargement of these, can only have legal validity, however, if a representative of the *Comisión Agraria Mixta* or the *Delegación Agraria* is present. This permits direct government intervention in internal *ejido* matters.

---

(13) Blas Urrea (Luis Cabrera), "La Revolución de entonces (y la de ahora)", in VEINTE AÑOS DESPUES, Ediciones Botas, México, 1938, pp. 240 and following.

Ejidal endowment grants social rights of usufruct over the land, and is always the result of community struggle. The *ejidal* configuration, however,
is based on "units of *ejidal* endowment" which are
individually distributed. This fact gives rise to
permanent friction between the two trends in *ejido*
organization; one fueled by the necessity for dividing the *ejido* into small plots, similar to those of
small private property and the other by the need for
collective organization for land development. The
latter respects the title deeds which grant the
right to the usufruct of the plot of land, but
changes them into guarantees of participation in the
productive process and in the distribution of profits according to decisions made by the *ejidatarios*.
In fact, the degree of integration of *ejido* functioning varies greatly: from total division into individual disarticulated plots to total collectivization (that sometimes even reach the level of *Ejidal*
Unions). A whole range of variations can be found
between these two extremes, from compact groups of
differing sizes and characteristics, to total or
partial collective organizations which undertake
specific tasks within the productive and commercial
processes.

Indian communities have a legal character similar to that of the *ejidos*, but their historical
basis gives them legal and explicit preference in
the agrarian policy of endowment of land they have
owned (Article 199 of the *Ley de la Reforma Agraria*).
The restitution of lands expressly respects "the
title deeds of land and water redistributed according to the law of June 25th, 1856" (the only section
of communal land property still valid according to
Law).

In Indian communities, formal legal structure
often runs parallel to actual organization, according to ethnic norms. Once a community exercises
autonomy from the political and economic authorities on both national and local levels, formal official duties tend to coincide with the community
responsibilities of those involved in the internal
social life of the communities.

At present, there are some 25,000 *ejidos* and
communities, occupying approximately 95 million

hectares (more than 15 of which are in the hands of
Indians). The *ejido* and Indian community population
(including families) is made up of approximately 18
million. This figure represents three quarters of
the total rural population and one quarter of national population.

   Agricultural and cattle raising colonias. These
are hybrid institutions, created in the 1940s as an
alternative to the *ejidal* and communal structure.
The *colonia* grants private usufruct over federal property to those who promise to fulfill the *Reglamento
de la Colonia* once they have plots of land for agriculture or cattle raising. The *colonia* expressly
stipulates that "no *colono* has the right to prevent
any other *colono* from peacefully enjoying his ground,
plot for cultivation, or any other rented or titled
land. Consequently the size of these cannot be changed and any trespass will warrant sanctions" (Article
XII of the *Reglamento General de Colonias Agrícolas
y Ganaderas*). It also stipulates that "the *colono*
must support government efforts to increase agricultural and cattle raising production while at the
same time promoting harmony both within the *Colonia*
and among the *campesinos* of the area" (Article XIII).

   After a good start in the 1940s, the agricultural and cattle raising *colonias* have not progres-
sed because of a basic inherent contradiction. Those
who form part of an organic structure which give a
social content to their struggle for the land, usually opt for *ejidal* or communal agrarian endowments.
Those who possess means for acquiring land, with
individual title deeds, opt for smallholdings. In
this latter case they are not restricted by the *Reglamento General de las Colonias* which imposes limits,
although it does also give some guarantee of immunity
to land expropriation. It is still interesting to
note, however, that this *Reglamento* establishes that
the *colonos* can either cultivate their plot or "direct its cultivation" (even though they do not intervene directly). This is substantially different from
Zapata's principle which states that the land belongs
to those who work it. Here, what is being openly
recognized is that "owner" can be an entrepreneur
rather than a worker. Even though this principle is
frequently violated on smallholdings and even on *ejidos* and communities, it is only in the *colonia* structure that it is explicitly permitted.

At the present time there are 784 agricultural *colonias*, occupying 7.5 million hectares. Together with these, and also on federal land, there are about 300 thousand *nacionaleros* whose situation has still to be legalized. Arguments and political conflicts arise from time to time to the best way to resolve this legalization, whether as small private holdings, *colonias* or *ejidos*.

Over the years, and in a few cases since their foundation, some of these *colonias* have acquired a certain organic solidarity with the *ejido* or communitary structure. Others have remained at the level of a kind of mechanical solidarity similar to that of private and disarticulated *minifundios*. Yet others have been integrated into the organic solidarity of the villages where they are located.

Villages. These are defined as circumscribed territory with its own legal character, whose destiny and fate is linked to the heterogeneous and changing situation of the *municipio libre*, a basic institution in the country's republican way of life. The *municipio libre* reflects the constant latent contradictions between the forces of federal centralized power, and those that intend to use the *municipios libres* as a pivot or focal point for the redistribution of economic and political power through a process of descentralization.

Many villages came into being as part of the *ejido* and community reconstitution process, and the creation of new population centers resulting from agrarian policies of endowment and expansion. In many of them, one or more *ejidos* or communities still make up the central nucleus of their organic structures around which the rest of the village gathers. In other cases, however, such as those where villages came into being through the processes of colonization, or merely through occurring together in the same physical space, the *ejido* has lost that agglutinative capacity.

Besides the *ejidatarios* and *comuneros*, private *minifundistas* also live in the villages: one million heads of family have received about 83 million hectares (almost as many as the *ejidatarios*) for their own private usufruct. Some of them use legal tenure

to become one of the agrarian protagonists described
in the previous chapter. The rest operate under conditions similar to those of the *ejidatarios*, sometimes
with smaller and inadequate plots of land, which they
cultivate individually or in cooperatives which manifest the same variety of levels of integration as the
ejidos.

A group which is tied to the land but which has
not yet been mentioned is that of the *avecindados*.
These cultivate the land under many different systems
of land tenure, as a result of individual or collective arrangements which the communities accept, even
though these are not covered by any legal definition.
Also, there are those, such as merchants, craftsmen,
domestic servants, etc., who do not work directly in
agricultural or cattle raising activities.

The villages operate within the limits of their
legally established power. In some areas such as
Oaxaca, these directly coincide with those in the
municipalities. The *caciques* are decisive cohesive
elements, even if, as previously mentioned, they do
not actually participate in the organization of production. Civil servants developed capitalist operations -in their myriad forms-, school teachers,
priests and others, all have similar roles in the social structure.

At first sight the villages appear as class
structures, authentic small-scale societies with
corporate traditions and tendencies, especially
accentuated in areas of Indian concentrations. However, recent *campesino* behavior, especially as the
agricultural crisis intensified, has given rise to
the hypothesis that the community itself becomes a
specific organization, within a class in each of the
villages.

Many Indian traditions entail social procedures
that prevent individual accumulation. The *sistema de
cargos*, for instance, deprived them of their "savings"
and even leases those have managed to obtain them in
debt. The weakening of these traditions or the
strength of capitalist expansion, however, has created
class differences within rural communities: their own
authorities, leaders or others become *caciques* or
acquire economic power over the rest. In such cases,

even when these people maintain their positions within the community, as well as their formal links to
it, there is a process of community reconstitution
that takes place apart from them, usually behind
their backs and even against them. The strength of
class definitions determines organized behaviors
that are related to class interests, with which the
rural communities only retain some of their characteristics within the limits of class and established
differences between this kind of organization and
that which is formally or apparently devised by the
people.

Forms of insertion into the logic of capital

These community structures, dependent on their
own labor for production and reproduction of life-
style, and with strong bonds to the land, manifest
generalized, consistent *campesino* characteristics.
The way they fit into the logic of capitalist accumulation, which defines forms of exploitation, allows
for further typological comments.

Agricultural jornaleros. A substantial number
of *campesinos* (perhaps more than half of the economically active agricultural population) hires itself out regularly for temporary work on other farms
or in a variety of urban or rural activities. This
is done for periods which range from one day to six
or eight months and, in some cases, perhaps for
several years.

Some authors consider that the *jornaleros*
should be treated as wage-earning workers whose situation, in this sense, is the same as that of agricultural or industrial workers. In this way they
would fit into the classic process of "proletarianization." To support this argument, some estimates
have been made of the quantitative importance of
wages for the total income of the *campesinos*. These
calculations have been made by giving monetary value
to their non-wage income. It has also been pointed
out that many *jornaleros* travel for long periods
throughout the year with their families, looking
for those areas which need to hire labor to harvest
crops. (These workers, as previously mentioned, are
thus included among the *golondrinas*.)

Other studies, however, have shown that wage income makes up a substantial part of the logic of the
campesino economy and this, in turn, part of the wage
system. It is important to differentiate between these
workers and truly salaried ones for several reasons.
As previously mentioned, capitalist operations are
neither able nor wish to absorb the total reproduction
costs of these workers, who are only hired as long as
they cover part of these costs themselves. Secondly,
income obtained through the hiring of the labor force
is part of the context of belonging to a community
group. This income becomes part of the logic of its
functioning, thus, contributing to the reproduction of
operating conditions at the service of capital. Moreover, wages sometimes constitute a peculiar procedure
of accumulation which in some cases gives them a transitory nature, especially when they are obtained over
a long period or when they are relatively high.
Through this mechanism, on an individual, family or
community level, conditions are created for a process
of development which for a time at least, gives the
producer a certain autonomy. The labor force, then, is
just another commodity -not the only one, nor the most
important- which the *campesinos* use to safeguard their
production and reproduction. Their integral insertion
into the logic of capital through many different mechanisms, determines that their relation to capital be
manifest in the context of the circulation process,
thus, they appear to be of a mercantile nature (producers concurring freely to the market). In reality, however, they are relations of production which identify
them as workers at the service of capital, disguised as
direct producers. If this means that the exploitation
to which they are subjected is worse, it also means
that because of the relative control of resources
which characterizes it, possibilities are open for
negotiating as well as for fighting and expanding, as
the last few years have begun to make evident.

The landless *jornaleros* ("*campesinos* with safeguarded rights" according to the *Ley de la Reforma
Agraria*) would seem to fit better into the category of
salaried workers rather than that of *campesinos*. However, unless they are *golondrinas* who have broken all
ties with their communities, the *jornaleros* remain
linked to them through diverse economic and social
mechanisms. For some of them, a wage is a way of

getting land; survival is generally attained through
genuinely belonging to a group which assimilates them
into its patterns of economic functioning and "takes
care" of them when they are unemployed, helping them
to stretch out their meager income through internal
distribution mechanisms.

For these reasons, *jornaleros* should be seen
within a temporary dimension of *campesino* life and
not as a characteristic that differentiates two social groups. It should also be recognized that this
phenomenon creates constant tension with wide ranging consequences, within daily life of the *campesino*.
It is a fact that the *jornaleros* make up a large part
of the rural migrants settling in the cities. For
them, at least, obtaining a wage was no encouragement to stay in rural areas and improve their operations. Quite the contrary in fact. It led them to
abandon their fields and look for new horizons in
cities. (However, growing difficulties in the cities
have opened the door to a process of "*recampesinización*", through which the migrant returns to his rural roots, after a long period of time in the city.)

Gil Victoria, a *campesino* from Atlapulco, in the
State of Mexico, illustrates an extreme case of today's prevalent situation. "He was born a *campesino*
and has no desire to cease being one. But twice a
week he walks a few kilometers to the highway where
he takes a bus which in two hours takes him into a
contaminated industrial zone of Mexico City. There he
works a 24 hour shift in a piston factory, after
which he returns to the mountains to work for a couple of days on his plot before going back to work
another shift at the factory. This job as a salaried
worker does not earn him more than a thousand pesos
a week, but this bridges a vital gap for his family's
well being. It means the difference between an annual
income of less than five thousand pesos and one of
more than 50 thousand; between rags and clothes; between a diet of corn *tortillas* and one which includes
meat two or three times a week." Gil Victoria feels
satisfied with his situation in comparison with that
of other *campesinos* who never leave their land. "It's
not that I feel so tied to the land" he explained,
"but the closer I am to the city, the harder it becomes for me to feed my family." Gil Victoria is
planning to enlarge his operation with the savings he

has obtained as a salaried worker. He has already asked the community to allow him to work a piece of uncultivated land. Gil's older brother, Angel, has settled in a depressing *barrio* of Mexico City, where he leads a wretched life. For him, however, *campesinos* are dormant beings in a hopeless situation: "they don't really want to change and never will." But for Gil Victoria, being a *campesino* means having a real future: "I want to stay here on the land and I want my children to live here. I don't want them to go to Mexico City where there are already too many people. Someday they'll all have to return to the land or they'll suffocate." (14)

In many *campesino* families, craft or commercial activities function similarly to that of a wage-earning position. In some extreme cases, when the market situation is favorable or craft skills open up new perspectives for development, the *campesino* may even abandon his plot of land or rent it until he officially or really loses it. But generally, craftwork is a way of complementing *campesino* subsistence -either at a family or community level. The same thing happens with forest exploitation, mining, cattle raising or other activities.

Special attention should be paid to the *braceros*. As many as a million *campesinos* year after year go up to the south of the United States (and sometimes to the north and even as far as Canada) to hire themselves out temporarily as *jornaleros*. This phenomenon has a long tradition and is a permanent thorn in the relations between the two countries. The "illegal" situation of these migrant workers lends itself to tremendous exploitation. Studies have shown that a large proportion of these *jornaleros* are the most capable *campesinos* and those with most initiative in their communities. They have found this to be a way of improving their living and production conditions but at the high cost of frequent maltreatment, danger and humiliation. Although *braceros* come from all over the country, they are mainly from medium-level development operations from the central and northern states.

---

(14) An interview with John Huey, in THE WALL STREET JOURNAL, November 22nd, 1979, p. 1.

"Independent" producers. Many _ejidatarios_, _comuneros_, _colonos_, _nacionaleros_, private _minifundistas_, tenants or _aparceros_ clearly appear to be direct producers because of the individual or "independent" exploitation of their plots of land. At first sight, it seems that as well as the usufruct, they also have the capacity for decision over their land, their traditional technology and pure commercial relation with other economic agents. Whether they work as temporal _jornaleros_ or not, they seem to maintain a certain relative autonomy in their agricultural activity. For some authors, these operations correspond to the simple mercantile mode of production which they purport are linked to capitalist production and subordinated to it. Others see in them similarities to the French paysan or the German bauer, if not with the American farmer, and they imagine that because of the restrictions on the free transfer of land ownership as well as on its concentration, these factors, which otherwise would, cannot give rise to the agglutinating process characteristic of the agricultural development which has taken place in more advanced nations. For many others, these producers have been left so far behind simply because of the lack of one or several of the conventional factors for development: capital, education, technology, organization, etc.

Empirical studies, however, have proven that the so-called "free" access of these producers to the market falls within an interplay of social relations which has placed them deep in the logic of the capitalist system, in accordance with the dynamics described in the previous chapter. Their cumulative economic surplus is systematically transferred -through different mechanisms- to other agents who, in turn, determine their productive decisions as well as the conditions under which they perform their activities through multiple mechanisms.

Colectivados. The tendency to insert labor fully into the logic of capital is already present in the "independent producers", but it finds its most obvious expression in those who are collectively organized. In some cases, collective organization of production has been the product of _campesino_ initiative or the product of the efforts made in Cárdenas' time. In other cases, it is the result of actions

taken, especially in the 1970s, through which both
government and private companies promoted collectivization of the *ejidos* as well as the cooperative organizations of private *minifundios*.

In certain cases, the collective organization of
production and commercialization has undoubtedly
opened the way for autonomous *campesino* development.
It has enabled them to strengthen their capacity for
retaining their cumulative economic surplus, as well
as increasing possibilities for negotiation with
other economic agents. In general, however, collective
organization has tended to function as a mechanism
for subordinating labor to capital, adapted to the
specific condition of the socio-political context.
Here in effect, *campesinos* retain their title deeds
over the land as well as official autonomy for deci-
sion-making in the productive process and in labor
organization. Decisions are made in assemblies and
requirements of self-administration are fulfilled.
In practice, however, these are mere token actions.

Decisions are often made externally by State
enterprises or private agribusiness (the former tend-
ing always to function as intermediary of the latter).
These normally make decisions on production and
define in "commercial" terms the producer's income,
which has to function as the equivalent of a wage.
What and how to produce; how the land is to be used;
what inputs are to be used and when; how to overcome
plagues, pests, and diseases, and how to harvest;
when and to whom it is to be sold; etc. All these are
decisions made outside the collective organization,
and are merely ratified through assemblies.

Reality, and above all, the prospects of Mexican
campesinos are areas which are still open to research
and historical exercises. We now know that they are
not left-overs from the remote past, and that there
is no way they can fall into the classic pattern of
capitalist agricultural development. The trends established by modern multinational agribusiness on a
world scale have had repercussions on a highly dynamic reality which has continually shown its creative
and innovative capacity.

A recent empirical study on the *Unión de Ejidos
Emiliano Zapata*, in the eastern portion of the State

of Morelos came to this conclusion: "The analysis of
ejidal organization challenges the structure characterized by the existence of relations between independent owners who clash with one another as producers: the relation between those who occupy land and
make up the labor force with those who only control
the labor force; between seasonal *jornaleros* who own
land and *jornaleros* without land; between the process of labor generated by family division of labor
and the social division of labor; between wage-earning and non-wage earning labor. An analysis of these
relations and a classification of their impact on
ejidos is beyond the scope of this study but it is a
study which has to be made." (15) This kind of study
can only be made if the global impact of multinational
agribusiness is taken explicitly into account.

To sum up, the Mexican *campesinos*' possibilities
are obviously linked to their capacity for making
their common objectives heard through a consciously
organized body, capable of expressing itself politically. Their economic, social and political organizations have generally arisen from heterogeneous forms
of social existence. This makes their organic global
articulation very difficult, especially when it has
to face obstacles and opposition at both the structural and superstructural levels. This means that,
as well as a clearly defined political program to
help overcome the traditional prejudices *campesinos*
have had to face, there has to be a sharply defined
interplay of alliances. It seems that in these terms
a ray of hope is beginning to appear. As the President of the *Unión de Ejidos Emiliano Zapata* in the
eastern portion of the State of Morelos has said:
"What it boils down to is that those who are worse
off are those who have joined forces with us. The
others are only taking advantage of us. But the time
will come when things will have to change." (16)

(15) Clarisa Hardy Raskovan,, "La Unión de Ejidos Emiliano Zapata en el oriente de Morelos (perspectivas de
una organización económica independiente)", in ORGANI-
ZACION, LUCHA y DEPENDENCIA ECONOMICA, Editorial Nueva
Imagen, México, 1978, p. 191.
(16) Quoted by Clarisa Hardy Raskovan, OP. CIT., p.
12.

4

CROPS AND REGIONS

CORN

Little remains to be said about corn in Mexico
which has not already been said, for the history
of corn is, to a large extent, the history of Mexico. Corn is related to religion, money, and culture,
besides being a staple of the Mexican diet.

Corn has been cultivated on this continent for
more than 5,000 years. Its first name, Teocintli,
underlines its divine origin (Teotl - god and
cintli - corn), and from this comes the name of Teocinta, the forerunner of today's corn. Teocinta is
a perennial plant whose recent localization in the
north of the state of Jalisco, Mexico, has led to
heated argument, as well as research projects,
which may radically modify future agricultural practices.

Nowadays, more than 10 million people are involved, in one way or another, with the cultivation
of corn in Mexico. Almost half the land under cultivation is used for corn, which represents almost
a quarter of the total value of agricultural production. Over the last 15 years, production has
fluctuated at around nine million tons per year,
while consumption has tended to rise, mainly due to
population increases. This meant that whilst from
1965 to 1975, almost five million tons were ex-
ported, from 1972 to 1977, 7.4 million tons were imported; some three million tons had to be imported
to satisfy demand in 1980.

Over the last decades, corn growing has come
under heavy discussion, both as it relates to the

nature and the development conditions in the agricultural and cattle raising sector and as to the
role *campesinos* play in the overall model. Periodically important campaigns have been made to promote cultivation, only to be followed by objective
tendencies and concrete efforts to encourage the
abandoning of it.

Unlike other corn-producing countries, Mexico
basically produces this crop for human consumption:
three-fifths of the total. 35% never reaches the
market, 20% is directly consumed by producers and
15% is alloted to animal consumption or planting.
More than 40% of the total demand (domestic production as well as imports) is used for *tortillas*, and
the rest is converted into other foodstuffs or used
as raw material for other products. Internal production difficulties, along with other factors,
have meant that consumption per capita has decreased
from 200 kilograms to 156 kilograms over the past
15 years. Predictions for the 1980s suggest that
demand will rise with demographic growth, but that
consumption per capita will remain at about 150
kilograms per annum.

Only 10% of corn-producing areas use improved
seeds. Almost 80% of the producers still use primitive agricultural implements. Four-fifths of the
land used for corn cultivation by *ejidatarios* or
private *minifundistas* consist of less than 10
hectares, and 90% of the surface area destined to
corn cultivation is under seasonal use; that is,
more than seven million hectares. Only half the
irrigated corn fields are fertilized, and only one
fifth of lands under seasonal use. The spring-sum-
mer harvest, which is sown between March and August
and harvested between September and January, accounts for 90% of the total production. Five states
(Guanajuato, Jalisco, México, Michoacán, and Puebla)
produce 50% of the total and another four (Veracruz,
Chiapas, Tamaulipas and Oaxaca) produce 20%, in
spite of the fact that corn is cultivated in every
state of the Republic. Even though high yields have
been achieved by using improved varieties on irrigated land or on good seasonal land, the national
average is still relatively low: just over 1,200
kilograms per hectare.

Apart from *tortilla* production (using *nixtamal*
dough or corn flour), the industrialization of corn
is restricted to only a few products. While in
other countries corn is used as raw material for
more than 800 articles, the "damp milling" process
found in Mexico is used only to produce caramel-
colored liquid and solid glucose, starch, dextrine,
fecula, syrup, oil and a few other products. Only
5% of the total available grain is used for these
products.

One-fifth of the two million corn producers do
not produce enough grain even for their own consumption, which means they also buy corn. This is the
poorest sector and is predominantly Indian. Another
40% produces only enough for its own consumption.
The role this group plays in the market is marginal;
that is, when occasionally a modest surplus is produced, or when urgent needs require selling reserves,
even though they may have to be later repurchased
at much higher prices than the original reserves
were sold for.

Official policies supporting corn producers
have been directed mainly towards commercial aspects:
guaranteed prices, storage facilities and auxiliary
services. According to the expansive model set for
commercial agriculture in the 1950s, guaranteed
prices, which were higher than international prices,
encouraged production and even resulted in export
surplus in the 1970s. In 1963, when a new guaranteed
price for corn was fixed, it was stipulated that
this should be considered as the *campesino*'s wage.
But this price was frozen for the next ten years,
while prices of other crops increased, in accordance
with the requirements of the global model, which
demanded that profitability conditions for commercial farmers and stability for urban wages be maintained. To encourage corn cultivation this policy
was reconsidered in the 1970s, but an increase in
guaranteed prices would have come up against a series of contradictions. Any feasible increase in
guaranteed prices could not be too high, since due
to inflationary pressures prices had to be controlled for the final consumer; but if increases were
not sufficient, then commercial farmers would have
no reason for reverting to corn production, in
lieu of more profitable crops. The fact is that the

logic of subsidies, which had been given in increasing quantities in an effort to overcome this limitation, cannot displace implicit economic rationale. Besides, when the guaranteed price increases, and with it all other articles consumed by the corn producers, many of them are then forced to reduce the cultivated areas and, sometimes, give them up. This means that if they are net buyers, then the price increase also increases their financial deficit and forces them to look for other sources of income as *jornaleros*. If they are self-sufficient, since their highest production cost is their own maintenance, then this measure represents an increase in the cost of production, with the result that their physical possibilities of continuing to cultivate corn become more and more limited, promoting them to look for other options.

This situation led to other measures after 1973. Once it was realized that guaranteed prices, as a regular commercial device, implied uniform treatment to non-uniform groups, then systems of direct aid for *campesino* producers were applied. To avoid guaranteed prices reaching only large farmers, or the intermediaries who control *campesinos*, storage centers were set up with *campesino* participation, as were collective systems of commercialization entailing bonuses which ensured the correct allotment of subsidies. Based on these premises, auxiliary services of commercialization were also provided: sacks, grain threshing, transport, input supply, etc. Of particular interest was a consumer credit system established in the hope that it would help liberate the *campesino* from his traditional bottlenecks, and encourage his commitment to production.

This approach was not only in contradiction to other more conventional government measures, but it also reflected existing tensions within the very institution responsible for operating the system, CONASUPO, and between this institution and the *campesinos*. On one hand, there was a constant tendency to use government agencies as a way to intervene and control producers in order to subordinate them to the overall logic of capitalist development.

On the other hand, it seemed that an attempt
was being made to remodel official institutions so
that these would, in fact, back the *campesino* movement towards autonomy which would tend to affect
the terms of their relationship with other agents.
Progress made in this aspect may help explain, along
with other factors, the widespread crisis towards
the end of 1976, which coincided with the change of
government. It may also help explain the decision
made at the beginning of 1977 to cancel policies
being followed by CONASUPO, by reducing many of the
auxiliary services for the *campesinos*, thus returning to more conventional policies.

Problems arising over corn production are
generally related to the overall direction taken by
Mexican agricultural expansion, which after the
1940s tended to concentrate more on commercial
agriculture, while "giving up" the *campesino* economy, which was left in the hands of agents who
merely tried to exploit it in a predatory fashion.
This phenomenon is clearly illustrated by the research and technical assistance policies adopted
throughout the period. As previously mentioned,
corn was segregated to a certain extent from the
endeavors of the Green Revolution. Although important research did result in highly productive hy-
brids, seeds and complementary resources -credits,
technical assistance, etc.- these were channelled
into the most developed areas, where corn is cultivated only in a marginal way. Paradoxically, these
endeavors have even led to a decrease in corn cultivation, since the technical assistance given has
encouraged producers to reconsider profitability
and relative costs carefully, which, in turn, has
led them to examine other possibilities and eventually adopt them.

Another contradictory aspect of official policy
lies in the increasing use of corn as fodder. The
need to maintain low selling prices in order to
protect consumers by stabilizing urban wages, has
led to an increase in the use of corn for the
manufacture of balanced diets for cattle.

An overall view makes it clear that a model
which concentrates on commercial agriculture while
marginalizing *campesinos* (mainly corn producers),
together with the low profitability of corn (due to

controlled price policies), are decisive factors in the crisis of domestic corn production. Nevertheless, the implications of an increasing participation by multinational agribusiness in Mexican agriculture must also be taken into account.

Agribusiness is excluded from corn production for a variety of reasons. The producers' real life situation makes them unattractive prospects as buyers, and the few needs they have are catered for by State enterprises. As far as their production goes, it is unappealing to multinational agribusiness. 60% of the total consumption, as previously indicated, is used for *tortilla* production. Most of this comes from *nixtamal* dough prepared either directly by the producers, or in many small mills which supply tens of thousands of *tortillerías*. The very nature of the dough makes its processing on an industrial scale impossible. A monopolistic distribution would be unprofitable because of the regulations imposed by the *Comisión Nacional de la Industria del Maíz para Consumo Humano*, an inter-ministerial agency which very efficiently controls distribution. One obvious way in which agribusiness could encourage modernization and control would be through corn flour production, but this process is under a Mexican Government patent, which has been granted to multinational corporations on the condition that it whould not be used in Mexico. Corn flour is produced in Mexico by a State-controlled company that belongs to CONASUPO and by a private company which belongs to an economically and politically powerful group. All this means that only a few corn by-products are left for multinational agribusiness, and these, for a variety of reasons, cannot absorb any significant proportion of the corn produced.

On the other hand, cattle raising, fruit and vegetable production offer ample and real possibilities for exploitation by agribusiness. This means a tendency to displace both commercial and *campesino* corn cultivation on available land. Another factor in this sense is the increased interest of multinational agribusiness in compensating for increasing corn deficits, since they completely control corn cultivation in many countries, especially the United States. In the face of this double "disincentive" a crisis in corn production was an

almost inevitable result of this ongoing process,
and it also illustrates the role of State mechanisms in the overall operation, especially when
apparently unrelated government measures reinforce
the process, only to contradict it from time to
time when effective aid is given to the *campesinos*.

WHEAT AND OTHER GRAINS

As already pointed out, the endeavors of the Green
Revolution were basically directed toward wheat.
Mexico thus became the cradle of improved grains,
which have spread all over the world.

Since the Colonial period, wheat has been cultivated throughout the central areas of the country
because of the excellent ecological conditions. The
post-1940 modernization trends led to wheat cultivation in the northwestern irrigated areas where
commercial farmers made progress using the improvement devices already described. However, this
process embraced some inherent contradictions. The
vast profits obtained from this crop, thanks to
State aid, began to diminish as a result of the
price-control policy aimed at keeping consumer
prices at a certain level. Although spectacular
yield increases meant continued expansion for some
time, producers were beginning to familiarize themselves with other profitable crops which gradually
began to drive wheat out. Wheat, which needs a great
deal of water, was being affected by increasingly
saline irrigation systems in the north-western region. If the water resources of these areas are to
be regenerated, less wheat and more crops which require less water, must be grown there in the 1980s.

National wheat production constitutes a good
example of how farmers are inserted into the logic
of capital, through modern development conditions.
In spite of strong State intervention, particularly
related to price regulations of certain kinds of
bread for the consumer, there is ample room for
agribusiness to operate, and agribusiness has been
intervening on an increasing scale in agricultural
production itself, controlling all aspects of the
productive processes and imposing different agricultural modalities through contracts, while at the
same time playing a more important role in indus-

trial processing without participating in the gov-
ernment-controlled production of white bread, it
has concentrated on the production of wheat-derived
foodstuffs, which have less nutritional value. To
achieve this it has had to adjust consumer patterns
to the industrial producers' needs and conveniences.

Rice, barley and sorghum are also important in
Mexican grain production although they do not account for a significant part of all cultivated land.

National self-sufficiency in rice production
has been achieved through the participation of commercial farmers and *campesinos*. A large part of production is controlled by a small group of industrialists who are involved in rice processing and
who increasingly intervene in the financing and control of productive processes.

Barley is basically in the hands of the *campesinos*, but is strongly subjected to control by the
brewing industry. Even great efforts by this heav-
ily concentrated industry to increase yields and
extend the surface area under exploitation have
failed to cover the deficit in production, which is
mainly located in the central plateau areas.

Sorghum has undergone spectacular increases
over the last 20 years, displacing corn from large
areas. But, in spite of this, the deficit has also
increased. This is related, on one hand, to a noticeable increase in fodder consumption, and on the
other, to the production and marketing advantages
this cereal has over corn.

Oats are of minimal importance in the national
crop structure, but they are of great regional importance in Chihuahua, where they are cultivated by
the Menhonites, who have created a peculiar productive enclave in the area. Less than a quarter of
the production is used for human consumption and
the rest is mostly used to feed the Mennonites'
cattle. The crop has spread to other areas in the
State, and a subsidiary of Quaker Oats is trying to
encourage more production in the central areas of
the country, in order to satisfy the demands of the
domestic market.

OILSEED CROPS

The cultivation of these crops has been concentrated both regionally and socially. Cultivation takes place mainly in the North of the country, using modern techniques, improved seeds, and fertilizers. The main sources of oil are sesame, cotton, safflower and soybean.

Sesame and in particular copra production, have a long *campesino* tradition. Cotton, from which oil can be extracted as a by-product, has long been cultivated in the North of the country and has had important boom periods both for *campesino* producers and commercial farmers, who channelled their efforts toward the export markets. Two large companies, one Mexican and the other multinational, played a fundamental role in the expansion of cotton production. The evolution of safflower and soybean production has shown exceptional progress from insignificant levels in 1965 to a quarter of a million hectares in the first half of the 1970s. More than half of the total oilseed production is located on *ejidal* lands.

In spite of this increase in oilseed production, large imports have been required of grains, pasta and oil -particularly soybean- to be used in the manufacture of balanced cattle feed. This industry, as well as the oil industry, are closely linked to multinational agribusiness.

FRUITS AND VEGETABLES

An increase in opportunities offered by foreign markets -the U.S. in particular- has fostered an important increase in fruit and vegetable production. The areas of cultivation increased from two million hectares in 1960, to 2.7 million today; their value has also increased during the same period from 20% to 30% of the total. There has been a significant increase in yields as a result of private participation in the supply of seeds and other inputs required.

A recent study pointed out that "the increase in fruit and vegetable production implies the redirecting of land, technology and capital resources from production of food requirements for the majority of the population, towards agricultural produce aimed at the medium and higher income brackets. There are also differences within this type of agriculture. Popular crop consumption does not align itself with the dynamics emanating from the core, induced by the strategies of the multinational companies." These companies have encouraged high value products which are more labor-intensive, both for the export market and for domestic luxury consumption. Outstanding examples of this are strawberry harvests in the Bajío and tomatoes in the Northwest, both obviously to serve the U.S. market. In both cases the producer faces great risks: price fluctuations and U.S. policy regarding these imports. Buyers do in fact finance a good part of the production of the *ejidatarios* in the Bajío and private commercial farmers in the Northeast mainly through intermediaries, processing and packing companies. The high costs of tomato crops reduce the participation of *ejidatarios*, and as far as strawberry production is concerned, the *ejidatarios* are unable to participate in the substantial profits associated with it.

Vegetables represent a small but important part of this productive complex. A significant proportion is alloted to the processing industries, the majority of which are multinational. Much of the production is carried out under contract.

Most of the fruit and fresh vegetable production is absorbed by the domestic market. A fairly strict monopolistic control of the main marketing channels exists. In spite of high and irregular prices paid by consumers, the profit received by producers has not allowed appropriate technification of the crops.

COFFEE, TOBACCO, SUGAR, AND *HENEQUEN*

These heterogeneous products are included under the same heading because of the similarities in their productive conditions. In each case, a government agency has virtually total control over the market. Producers have little land and most of them belong to the poorest sector of the population. In spite

of official intervention, international price fluctuations for these products have greatly affected
producers.

   A large part of the <u>coffee</u> is grown in Indian-
dominated areas. Many people there do not speak
Spanish and the majority are women. The *Instituto
Mexicano del Café* (*INMECAFE*), a State agency, has
increasingly intervened to oppose middlemen who
have traditionally controlled the market. A small
group of large landowners and coffee exporters, as
well as a large multinational instant coffee company used to control marketing channels and much of
the first hand processing; through financial mechanisms as well as commercial and technical control
they were responsible for keeping the producers in
subsistence conditions. At the end of the 1970s
when frosts in Brazil caused tremendous increases
in international prices, coffee was the second most
important Mexican export, after oil. The same period saw the parallel expansion of INMECAFE, which
in turn eliminated a number of important intermediaries, thereby offering better prices to producers and encouraging production. However, it has
not, on the whole, been able to modify the local
production structure, where poverty and exploitation still prevail.

   The majority of <u>tobacco</u> producers are *ejidatarios* concentrated in two states of the Republic.
Traditionally, they have had to deal with a strongly monopolized market, biased towards exports and
catering mainly to the multinational cigarette industry. Partly as a result of pressure from *campesinos* working in this area, the tobacco processing
industry was nationalized in the 1970s, and *Tabacos Mexicanos* (*TABAMEX*) a State enterprise was
formed. Recently several studies have tried to show
that it is an intermediary for large cigarette companies which operate both in Mexico and abroad. The
Mexican enterprise strictly controls all aspects
of production, from the production and marketing
of seeds to the distribution of tobacco to industrial consumers. Many attempts have been made at
organizing producers, including thorough collectivization of *ejidos* to no avail, in terms of improving the *ejidatario*'s economic situation. Internal
contradictions have also arisen among the *ejidal*
producers and those who cut the tobacco. The former have taken it upon themselves to impose strict

harvest conditions on those who cut tobacco, for the benefit of the final consumers.

The <u>sugar</u> industry presents a somewhat different picture because of changes which have occurred over the last decades. Since colonial times it has played an important role and was responsible, during the Porfirio Díaz period, for highlighting some of the main contradictions that arose during the Revolution and subsequent years. Zapatismo had its initial roots in land belonging to a large sugar mill, and it was here that Zapata had one of his greatest triumphs, confirmed a quarter of a century later, during Cárdenas' government. Since 1940, however, increasing inefficiency and sharp social disputes have marked its development. While a powerful trade union of industrial workers was being formed, the *ejidatarios* responsible for planting sugar cane found themselves under strict control. Confined by the conditions laid down by the sugar mills, they in turn imposed virtually unbearable conditions on sugar cane cutters, who were one of the most severely exploited groups in the country. Government subsidies were provided in the hope of appeasing these political and social disputes as well as keeping prices at a low level for domestic consumption. The subsidies, however, only resulted in further corruption and inefficiency at an industrial level, as well as in the progressive disarticulation of agroproduction, which was characterized by proliferation of land leasing among *ejidatarios*, together with a decrease in production. In the 1970s, State intervention reached as far as direct operation of the sugar mills and virtually took over control. The Government now has a financing company for this industry, a monopolistic commercial enterprise, an agency which deals with most of the industrial production and a National Commission controlling the industry. This sector also enjoys a subsidy of several billion pesos per annum. In spite of all these measures, the country no longer exports sugar and in 1980 became a net importer. Sugar mills have begun, very inefficiently, to administer the agricultural process. This has produced a kind of *ejidal* rent for sugar cane *ejidatarios*, who work as paid laborers on their own lands or devote themselves to other activities.

Henequén has evolved along similar lines to
sugar. As a result of intense social disputes,
which caused the well known "*Guerra de Castas*" in
Yucatán during the last century, production of henequen has come under State regulation since the
1940s. The producers have to deliver henequen over
to government processing plants, not because of
legal provisions, but because of the lack of any
profitable alternatives for land or labor use. An
official bank takes care of financing production,
and CORDEMEX, another State enterprise, deals with
its marketing and industrialization. Large State
subsidies have done little to improve the condition
of *henequén campesinos*. Their situation is an excellent example of how producers are inserted into
the overall logic, as well as the subsequent kinds
of consciousness raised by this process. *Henequén
campesinos* are oficially considered direct producers who receive bank credits and maintain commercial relations with CORDEMEX. However, a few years
ago, a group of them demanded a yearly bonus from
the bank -which gives them weekly payments- similar
to that which wage-earning industrial and service
workers normally receive. The bank refused on the
grounds of the merely financial nature of its presence in the industry; the *campesinos* were able to
show that they did not actually have any decision-
making power over their operations or working conditions, and that the bank inspectors were those
who defined the terms in which the harvest had to
take place and CORDEMEX was responsible for regulating sales. Moreover, among the producers there
is a very common practice, known as *henequen de
luna* (moonlight *henequén*), which consists of
"stealing" the *henequén* from their own plots at
night and delivering it to intermediaries who sell
it to CORDEMEX, in an attempt to overcome bank
control and increase their income.

CATTLE RAISING

As shown throughout this book, cattle-raising constitutes a characteristic example of concentration
of economic and political power. Cattle raising activities integrated during the Colonial period and
strengthened by the great cattle *haciendas* of the
Porfirian period, lasted until after the Revolution

since there was no legal limitation on the size of
cattle raising areas which were judged not in terms
of hectares but on the basis of heads of cattle.
This fact, together with the vagueness of grazing
field coefficients -which supposedly related the
number of hectares according to a Constitutional
decree- encouraged cattle raising interests among
those in favor of concentrating land in private
hands. It should also be remembered that the vast
operations which still existed in 1940 were concentrated in the northern states of the Republic, where
natural conditions limited agricultural expansion
without irrigation systems.

Over the past decades, a combined system of
cattle raising has developed which assigns to Mexican producers the task of breeding and fattening
cattle for southern U.S. producers. Within this
framework the Mexican meat packing industry, was
developed, characterized by its use of lean meat,
which was not in high demand on the domestic market but destined for U.S. consumption combined with
other types of meat, used for products typical of
the U.S. diet. The sausage and other meat by-products industry was developed along parallel lines.
In all these activities -the production of balanced
cattle food, veterinary medicines, etc.- multinational companies played an important role and also
participated significantly in industrial milk production.

All this favored continuous cattle raising
activities, and expansion of these activities resulted in an ever-increasing takeover and control
of *ejidal* and communal agricultural lands. Within
the global model, meat production in the north of
the Republic was aimed at the U.S. market, and
that of the Southern and central areas at the domestic market. However, when international prices are
high, production from the southern and central
areas has often gone to the U.S., creating scarcity
and speculation on the domestic market.

An example may help illustrate what is happening. The State of Chiapas is an important corn producer and, in some areas, it is even possible to
obtain up to three harvests per annum, without
using fertilizers. However, over a period of 12
years, corn production stagnated, while the number

of heads of cattle and the area used to raise them
on has doubled. An analysis of 115 serious agrarian
disputes revealed that 86 of them had been caused
by cattle raisers' invasion of *ejidal* and communal
lands. Their activities have also been decisive
factors in the destruction of the Lacandon jungle,
and the ensuing ecological damage to one of the
country's most important strategic natural resources.
(Cattle raising expansion has had the same effect in
the neighboring state of Tabasco, where forest reserves have been reduced by a fifth in only a few
years for the same reason.)

Cattle raisers' activities throughout the country have been a decisive factor in local and regional power structures and *cacique* domination. Their
activities also help explain the lawlessness in
rural areas and the prevailing climate of violence.
Tensions and contradictions between *campesinos* and
cattle raisers are caused by the irrational and
coercive use of the political and economic power,
wielded by the ranchers. It is probably the most
important single factor in the exceptionally violent conditions of rural Mexico.

FORESTRY

Mexico is one of the richest countries in the world
in forest resources. Nevertheless the fact that she
has to import large quantities of forestry products, is proof of the great obstacles faced by this
sector.

The existing difficulties are related, to some
extent, to prevailing legal provisions and to the
absence or inefficiency of the systems controlling
the present irrational exploitation. A large proportion of forested lands is in the hands of *ejidos*
and communities which can only exploit them under
government-issued licenses. The *ejidatarios* and
comuneros lack of resources on the one hand, and
the conditions under which the licenses are granted,
on the other, have meant that both the impoverished
campesinos as well as numerous commercial agents
have inefficiently over-exploited forest resources.
Campesino income is barely increased by their weak
but constant forestry activities. Commercial ex-

ploitation is usually carried out under more or less
illegal conditions, which result in the instability
of this kind of operation and in little benefit for
the forest owners, since it is based on quick profits with little regard for conservation.

This, combined with the above mentioned cattle
raising activities, is causing accelerated destruction of forest resources in the south of the country,
in the States of Chiapas, Tabasco and Campeche,
while at the same time displacing thousands of *campesino* producers.

REGIONS

Mexican commercial agriculture is concentrated in
the Northwest and in some Gulf states, extensive
cattle raising in the North, the *campesino* economy
in the South and Southeast, while in the central
areas farmers, cattle raisers and *campesinos* coexist.

Three States of the Republic (Mexico, Oaxaca,
and Michoacán) absorb a quarter of the economically
active population in agricultural and cattle raising
activities; and these states, together with another
five (Puebla, Veracruz, Chiapas, Jalisco and Chihuahua) absorb more than 50%. In six states (Tlaxcala, Oaxaca, Durango, Michoacán, Chiapas and Hidalgo) more than three quarters of the total population is dedicated to agriculture and cattle raising, with the *campesino* economy clearly predominant
in the productive structure. At the other extreme,
in three states (Baja California Norte, Baja California Sur and Nuevo León) less than one-fifth of
the population works in agriculture or cattle raising; in the two former states because of the scarcity of agricultural resources, and in the latter
because of the preponderance of industrial activity.

Unemployment in the rural sector also tends to
be geographically concentrated. In three States
(México, Michoacán, and Hidalgo) more than 50% of
the rural population is unemployed. In another seven
(Chiapas, Chihuahua, Guanajuato, Sinaloa, Tlaxcala,
Jalisco and Oaxaca), the proportion reaches four-
fifths of the total.

It is worth noticing that permanently salaried workers are concentrated in states where the *campesino* economy predominates (Yucatán, Campeche, Tabasco).

In the South and Southeast, labor mobility tends to be scarce, although not in the central states (particularly Jalisco, Michoacán, Guanajuato and México). The State of Sonora absorbs an important amount of labor from other states. The States which provide most migrant labor are Oaxaca and Michoacán, as well as Guanajuato, Durango, Veracruz, Jalisco and Zacatecas. The migrating labor force which goes abroad (*braceros*) comes mainly from the States of Jalisco, México, Oaxaca, Veracruz and Nayarit, i.e., the central and Northern states.

This regional count does not throw much light on the way in which the country is integrated. A final account relating regions and crops will take us out of the dangerous world of figures. In the northwestern regions of the country, in the States of Coahuila, Chihuahua, Baja California Norte, Sinaloa and Sonora, commercial crops of wheat, oilseeds, vegetables, etc., thrive side by side with intensive and extensive cattle raising. In these regions there are virtually no plots of land of less than a hectare. In the South-central region, the States of Hidalgo, Oaxaca, Puebla, Querétaro, San Luis Potosí, and Tlaxcala, corn is the predominant crop. Half of the private *minifundios* or *ejidal* lands of less than one hectare were found in this region in 1950. Twenty years later this proportion had increased to 60%. The former region encompasses half of the irrigated land in the country; the latter only 10%. The first region absorbs one third of the fertilizers used in the country and 40% of agricultural machinery, while the second uses less than 10% of the fertilizers and machinery.

It is worth trying to make some general remarks at the end of this chapter. The North of the country, along the U.S. border, is a colonized underpopulated land with little Mesoamerican background. This region is where modern commercial agriculture and extensive cattle raising activities developed, always concentrated in few hands and

aimed at export. The central and southern regions of
the country are Indian *campesino* lands, with some
densely populated zones. These developed within a
campesino economy which returned the land to its
original owners, and concentrated production of foodstuffs for domestic consumption. The central and
southern areas showed the way for the nation's historical project, pointing towards national independence and social justice, that were being negated in
the North. But it was Northerners who imposed the
overall orientation. Paradoxically, Francisco Villa
and his Northern Division suffered defeat after defeat until they were wiped out; Emiliano Zapata and
his Southern Liberating Army were never militarily
defeated. Yet the North prevailed over the South.
When the Revolution used the Nation's resources to
build a modern society and committed itself to planning and improving agriculture, these efforts were
concentrated in the North. In 1970, the Northern
Pacific region possessed 53% of the cultivated and
irrigated areas of the country, while the South had
only 1.7%. These facts do not relate in any way to
nature's gifts. In the state of Chiapas alone, (the
South) a quarter of the country's hydraulic resources are to be found. In spite of this, it hardly
has any irrigated land, but it does have the highest
concentration of Indian groups and is considered by
some to be the poorest part of the country. Socio-
economically, Chiapas is the most backward of the
States, a situation which has worsened over the last
25 years. The differences, therefore, are not the
result of geographical fate and this fact should be
taken into account when attempts at change are made.
The differences have been brought about by men, by
power.

"The Constitutional agrarian concept (drawn up
by northerners) shaped by political and tactical
necessities, visualized the return of lands to the
communities, but its well-known dream was always
that of the old Mexican liberals, i.e. a system of
modern, capable, self-sufficient, smallholdings.
This was precisely what inspired the governments of
Sonora from 1916 to 1920." (1) While Zapata went on

---

(1) Héctor Aguilar Camín, LA FRONTERA NOMADA: SONORA
Y LA REVOLUCION MEXICANA, Siglo XXI Editores, México, 1977, p. 434.

fighting, Calles enacted laws protecting private property and stimulating "autonomous farmers," as De la
Huerta called them. In 1918, while attempts to "incorporate" Zapata into constitutionalism had been
exhausted, and his murder was being planned, in Sonora, programs were being devised "to create and
protect smallholdings." Through agreements with
"known farmers," i.e. efficient ones, good lands
would be given to those who would act as managers of
"cooperatives" from which the old *peones* would receive a salary. These associations would be assisted
by the Government with seeds, funds and legal aid,
as well as investments and auxiliary services. De la
Huerta said, "The application of this kind of system to agriculture will make it an inexhaustible
source of national wealth, as well as the best way
of giving social and political freedom to those
poor farmers who have long been nothing but *peones*."
As Aguilar Camín stressed: "In an agricultural tradition such as that of Sonora, irrigation, export
and machinery are not isolated elements but vital
ones because of the scarcity of labor and water
supplies, where the modern *hacendado* was an obvious
example to be followed, a regional paradigm more
than a focal point of hatred. In this situation,
nothing could crystallize more easily or naturally
than an agrarian policy which encouraged profitable
and technified agricultural enterprises." And the
"ideal manager" dreamt of by De la Huerta for this
type of operation was Alvaro Obregón, the personi-
fication of the virtues of productive management,
the representative of modern agriculture, the ne-
gotiator for federal funds and local facilities,
the executive manager, the true molding element of
colonization and of the post-revolutionary boom* of
the Mayo and Yaqui Valleys." (2)   And it was precisely these men, Obregón, de la Huerta and Calles,
who occupied the Presidency of the Republic during
the 1920s from where they tried to project Sonora's
influence over the entire country. Calles' decision
in 1930 to declare agrarianism concluded was somewhat hasty; Mexico is not Sonora. The vigorous
campesino answer to agrarian trends gave rise instead to agrarian actions, which aimed at creating

*In English in the original.
(2) Aguilar Camín, IBIDEM.

a different national plan, that is, of *ejidos* and
small industrial communities where modern techniques
would be at the service of the people and not vice-
versa. Paradoxically, Cárdenas' achievement of
redistributing 20 million hectares of land and its
consequent social peace, favored the aggressive return of the dominating restless factions. What Calles could not do in 1930 was again attempted in
1940, and it was nothing but the Sonora plan.

    In order to explain this, it may help to take
into account the brutal violence which gave origin
to the Sonora dynasty. This violence provided the
foundations for her present economic, political and
productive victory. "If we live, as Elias Canetti
maintains, on a mound of dead men and animals, and
our identity feeds on all those we have outlived,
then it could well be said that Sonora's power is
based on graves -hence its strength. Moreover,
this firm identity actually thrives on having outlived one of the most extensive lists of enemies
which anyone has ever overcome in the whole history
of Mexico. It could not have been made up of any
harder or older clay, than what came from the power
obtained from the domination and killing of the
Yaquis, those people from Sonora who were deprived
of their vital space, their vital lands. They per-
sonified "the enemy" for Sonora, both before and
after the Civil War. The new inhabitants forced the
Yaquis to succumb to the "civilization" which Sonora wanted to build and discovered instinctively
and essentially,what they were not,what they did
not want to be, as well as what they needed to
exterminate in order to give themselves the type of
life they wanted." (3)

    In November 1979, the *Coalición de Ejidos del
Yaqui y Mayo* were celebrating the third anniversary
of the recuperation of their lands. The expropriation had taken place ten days before the change of
government and gave rise to one of Mexico's most
serious crises of modern times, and to the most
hard felt pressures ever exerted on Government by
a single powerful group. Before the assembled gathering of guests -Union members, independent *campe-*

---

(3) Aguilar Camín, OP. CIT., p. 446.

sino organizations, Indians and intellectuals-, the *Coalición* related its brilliant achievements. Despite all predictions of failure on these lands, which up to then had been worked efficiently by regional agricultural entrepreneurs, the *campesinos* had managed to increase, year after year, the already high yields of the lands recovered. When financial sources and auxiliary services were canceled, the *campesinos* opened their own "*Caja*" (savings bank) -based on an age-old tradition- and successfully overcame the enormous difficulties opposing them, and they remembered the names of all those who had died on the way. Among others they mentioned those who had died a short time before in San Ignacio Río Muerto, when an attempt was made to stop *campesino* progress at the heart of the monster. They also mentioned the bloody deeds of 1975 which originated in the expropriation of the *latifundio* of former President Calles' daughter, Alicia Calles de Almada. History always seems to find a way of expressing its deepest roots through anecdotes.

PART THREE

PROSPECTS

This part of the book will try to summarize the terms which are being used in present-day Mexico to discuss, either explicitly or implicitly, current problems, proposed solutions, prospects for rural development and the possible outcome of the violent history of the struggle for rural Mexico.

1

THE ACADEMIC AND
POLITICAL DEBATE

Since 1965 the growing rural crisis has been the
subject of ever more heated debate within Mexican
society. All sectors have taken part, from the most
varied of ideological positions, and similar inten-
sity has been shown in academic institutions and
political gatherings. The interests involved seem to
make it natural for this debate to take place in a
highly ideological context. The terms of the discussion tend to lead to dogmatic definitions which
reflect, through a hundred distortions, the interests at stake. This is partly due to a lack of information on the present situation, as well as to a
biased intellectual tradition, which has been incapable of getting at the heart of the more recent
aspects of the present situation. In spite of this,
however, over the last decade, various attempts have
been made to carry out empirical as well as theoretical research projects, which have been placing the
current debate in a new light.

In this kind of debate, which has led to thousands of printed pages in academic texts and mil-
lions of lines in newspapers, there is always the
risk of oversimplification: omissions and prejudices
are inevitable — a risk taken in this book.
However, it is better to take the risk than to keep
silent over a central issue of concern at present.

It is no exaggeration to say that Mexico is at
a turning point in its history: the problem is that
this now sounds like a cliché and merely brings
tired smiles from those who hear it, for it represents yet another example of the empty rhetoric
which has characterized discussions up to now. At
this turning point only utopia -which has not yet
found a place in this world- seems possible. What

cannot be done is to maintain the conventional course
whose trends have been accentuated over the last few
years: the Apocalypse is just around the corner. Perhaps no one doubts the need for change. The seventies gave Mexican society the opportunity to know itself: it saw its evils, it faced the truth, it denounced its weaknesses and limitations, it showed
the frustration of long-held expectations, it declared the failure of its development model -even if
there are still discussions on the criterion that
led to its adoption and of the extent of other alternatives. But now a choice has to be made. While the
possibilities for change are analyzed or the opposing
forces clash over how this should be done, the need
 to formulate a   national program becomes increasingly evident. Obviously, the program could become
trapped in the very inertia of the process from
which it evolved, in which case the same old story
will be repeated, but it also could turn away from
this trend and open up the way to new prospects,
becoming a guiding light in this transforming action.
This is really what the national debate is all about.

THE NATURE OF THE STATE

The nature of the Mexican State is at the heart of
this discussion. Although time has passed, the debate continues -perhaps more vigorously than ever-
on the nature of the Revolution from which it e-
volved. Some happily accept the old definition: a
democratic-bourgeois revolution which enabled the
dominant class of modern capitalist society, the
bourgeoisie, to take control. Others point out that
the Mexican Revolution was the first social revolution of the century, and not the last bourgeois
one. Even though this does not tell us very much, it
opens the door to a wide interplay of positions: the
revolution can be considered a failure, or merely
interrupted or unfinished; it can be seen as tired,
destroyed, exhausted, renewed, predictive or promising... all of which can be synthesized in one
alternative: in order to bring about any kind of
change, a new revolution with different characteristics must be initiated; while others want to
reactivate the past one, either taking it to its
final conclusion or gaining strength from it to give
form and meaning to unfulfilled hopes. Or perhaps,
as others claim, the most important thing is to

"sweep" the country clean of all popular rhetorical
trends and enter the scene of modern politics, understood as liberal democracy.

In Mexico, the liberal ideal of "government for
all" has not earned much credibility. On the one
hand, there is the question of its legitimacy: for
some, effective suffrage is not sufficient (even its
effectiveness is questionable) for it results in
formal, not real, representation of the dominated
classes. On the other hand, there is the theoretical
and political question of the very nature of government. Even diverse points of view agree that it
should be put <u>above</u> all the social protagonists, as
the coercive power of society: as the legal-politi-
cal instance, which can impose its authority on
individuals and classes, as a kind of reference.
Others however, are more concerned with the nature
and affiliation of effective government power. Most
people reject the idea of government being a simple
combination of juxtaposed individual opinions, or
that of a "loyal interpreter" -and no more than an
interpreter- of "popular will." Some see it simply
as an instrument of the dominant classes: "the
specialized apparatus of "repression" or "domination" used by them to enforce their power. They
suspect that the "populist" nuances or even authentically popular trends, are nothing more than mani-
pulative devices for maintaining necessary control
over the masses. Others claim that these "mass
politics" are not confined to the Mexican Government, but a very coherent action on the part of
the authorities, who are perfectly aware that any
modern capitalist society has to develop social consensus in order to govern. Since the Constitution
of the Republic answers to a specific productive
regime, that is, the capitalist system, and sets
political guidelines for the solution of its contradictions, the main task of government would then
be to maintain and reproduce the power necessary to
enforce these political guidelines. In order to do
this, <u>partial</u> violence would be acceptable as a
means of avoiding <u>generalized</u> violence, which would
only reveal society's inability to channel its
inherent contradictions politically. Mass politics
would be a fundamental instrument for this purpose,
but its inadequacy occasionally opens the door to
violence against the masses in situations where
emotions become heated and the global stability of

the system finds itself threatened. Finally, there
are others who claim that the Nation is the ring or
arena where society's class conflicts are played out
or processed, and that Government is the <u>expression</u>
(something more than a mere reflection or representation) of the political correlation of social
forces. Its levels of autonomy would be related to
its expressive capacity. Its role as a referee
(Caesarism, Bonapartism, etc.) would merely be for
the sake of appearance: when welding power, government does not express itself but the historical,
social and political forces from which it evolved.
Since these are always highly dynamic forces, acted
out against a background of constantly changing
alliances and correlations within the Constitutional
limits of Mexican society as such, and its inter-
relation with the new strategic areas of world power,
government itself undergoes constant change (although it never goes beyond these limits). The real
contradictions of society would thus be reflected
internally, when reproducing this interplay of alliances and correlations through which "internal
forces" express preferences and options.

     All these factors are explicitly present in the
debate on rural Mexico, since the *campesino* situation within the Mexican State and its relationship
with Government are determining elements in the conceptions of the State which in turn affect the *campesino* and his perspective. Mexican society was,
and still is, mainly *campesino*. Social consensus is
inconceivable if it excludes or subordinates a group
which makes up more than half the total population,
and which at the beginning of the century embraced
all areas of society. Both the *campesinos'* admission
to, or exclusion from the Mexican State and its Government, necessarily imply some kind of rupture. To
include them explicitly with full rights, means
giving them strength and mobility to oppose the
interests of other social classes radically -be these
permanent or not, tactical or strategic. This would
obviously make impossible the social consensus necessary for government. A direct decision to exclude
them explicitly would mean the State and Government's
loss of the numerically most important social
group, which would also make the Government's task
impossible; and violence would be the only way to
enforce this kind of exclusion. This situation

may help to explain the little success achieved by
explicit positions which go beyond mere rhetoric.
The reactions they evoke -both at verbal and real
levels- mean they are soon blocked. Hence an implicit definition on the issue tends to be maintained,
while a deep, quiet struggle evolves round the dialectics of admission- exclusion, which varies according to the continuously changing circumstances.

THE ORIGINS OF THE RURAL CRISIS

These problems are highlighted by the interpreta-
tions made of the origins and development of the
rural crisis and the efforts being made to resolve
it.

    The conventional version of "structural dual-
ism" obviously exists. Because of original sin or
the "polarizing dynamics" of society, the existence
of two sectors in the agrarian structure is taken
for granted: one modern and dynamic, the other backward and stagnant. Even though some say the crisis
is a result of the loss of dynamism of the former
sector, analytical studies tend to concentrate on
the cause of the latter's backwardness as a way of
also explaining the loss of dynamism of the former.

    This line of thought leads some to look for the
problem in the backward sector by using static comparisons: they detect the "missing elements" which
hinder development. Obviously, it is impossible to
see a missing element; however, since this is a
comparative exercise, the idea is to observe what
is missing in the backward sector, by comparing it
to the advanced sector: capital, education, technology, business-mindedness, etc. Then, according
to this kind of reasoning, the solution would
merely be to inject the missing elements in order
to stimulate development. Another point of view,
along these same lines, simply describes it within
the framework of a linear process of development,
where the backward sector is merely at an earlier
stage and its "natural" -or artificially acceler-
ated- evolution will lead it to the developed
stages of the modern sector.

    Other approaches tautologically suggest that
the crisis is related to the rupture of the postwar

expansion model which had led to a boom, especially
in the 1950s and the first half of the 1960s. The
real problem lies in looking for the cause of this
rupture. Theories about the exhaustion of the model,
exhaust themselves. What was feasible at a given
moment, is no longer so, an alternative has to be
found. Others, who still believe in the validity of
the model, look for its limiting factors. Thus, some
claim that there are no more "progressive farmers"
able to take advantage of the technology of the
Green Revolution or that it is impossible to take
the Revolution any further along the same lines
(irrigation, etc.) for a variety of reasons; they
propose, therefore, to create adequate conditions
for its continuation, by modifying its limiting
factors. They propose, for example, new technological packages to be used under seasonal conditions,
so that new "progressive farmers" may undertake the
task. Others think that the cause of the problem is
to be found in extra-economic conditions, particularly in political action which they consider
demagogic. They suggest that legal insecurity and
the problems of tenure, for example, prevent private investment in agricultural land, thus blocking
the progress of the model.

And finally there are those who reject both the
dualist hypothesis and the expansive model. They
consider that the dynamism of one sector can only
be attained at the expense of the other, and see
the cause of the crisis in this interaction; a
model biased towards the developed sector necessarily led to deterioration of the *campesino* economy,
to the point that it was impossible for it to
accommodate the vigor of commercial agriculture
which it had never achieved in the first place. Although it would be possible to reinstate this by
directing public resources towards creating and
strengthening it, it would be useless and insufficient to do so, due to the level of deterioration which already characterizes the *campesino*
economy. Hence, it was suggested that these funds
be directly channelled to the *campesinos*: for some
this simply means increasing the net amount of the
budget for agriculture and cattle raising; other
suspect that funds used in this way would eventually reach the same people as before, having
passed ineffectively through *campesino* hands. They
suggest the need for a change in policy, that would

remove those resources which continue strengthening
commercial agriculture (and which enable it, in effect, to support itself at *campesino* development's
expense, in order to seriously cater to the needs of
the *campesino* economy.

The attempts made in the 1970s to face the crisis, reflect the fluctuation and confluence of these
positions. What has happened in practice is that an
attempt has been made to follow the guidelines implicit in all these positions, all at the same time,
which obviously nullified any effort and clouded any
panoramic view of the situation.

THE NATURE OF THE CAMPESINO ECONOMY

Against this background, it was inevitable that attention be focused on *campesino* economy. For the
most varied reasons and purposes the so-called "traditional or subsistence agriculture" -evidently
biased in its outlook- or the *campesino* economy
-again biased- became the focal point of interest.
In order to explain what had happened and bring
about some kind of change, it was of primary importance to ascertain the characteristics of the reality to be transformed.

When those involved in the debate decided to
look at the experience and knowledge of other nations, they were disappointed. As far as theory
goes, *campesino* history is still remarkably obscure.
Economics deals with this area in a very haphazard
way: from its very inception *campesinos* were given
and deprived of the main role. Since land was -for
the physiocrats- the key element in economic life,
today it seems possible that countrymen, the *campesinos* should have had such a predominant place in
this theoretical context. But those considered to
have been the first "real" economists, hardly took
them into account. They were practically looked upon
as part of the natural resources, little more than
an extra element in the landscape.

It has been said that classical theorists have
been tested, that they really become what they are
when they apply their theory to land rent. Only
those who develop their own interpretation of the
problem transcend, but here the *campesinos* are again

mere shadows flitting around the agents of change:
the capitalist entrepreneurs locked in battle a-
gainst landlords. They emerge only to disappear;
they only begin to exist in theory when they cease
to be what they are and become part of the rural or
urban proletariat. The subjects in this process are
tenants, gentry, junkers, farmers, or *hacendados*,
never *campesinos*.

As the crowning glory to these classical theories, Marx barely mentions them in his basic writ-
ings. For him they seem to represent little more
than a "sack of potatoes", a class which could never
function as such on its own, and that was destined
to disappear, torn apart by the contradictions between two living classes -the bourgeoisie and the
proletariat. However, towards the end of his life,
Marx turned his attention to the peasant issue and
became "peasantized." When the subject of his studies was the Russian peasant (not the European peasant to whom he applied the previous expression),
he comes to very different conclusions. He even
claims, that the mir, the Russian rural community,
has a different historical option from that of the
primitive community. Instead of entering a dis-
integrating phase, it could become a "regenerating
factor" in Russian society, as well as the "point
of departure" for the building of a new society. (1)
However, for over a century the orthodox line of
Marxist theorists disregarded these final conclusions, so critical for the Marxist debate over the
campesino economy. This debate seemed to have been
reduced theoretically and historically to the
'sack of potatoes' image.

---

(1) See, Karl Marx and Frederic Engels, "The class
struggles in Russia", in THE RUSSIAN MENACE TO
EUROPE (Collection of articles and speeches, letters
and other documents, compiled by Paul W. Bladstock
and Bert F. Hoselitz), The Free Press, Glencoe,
Illinois, 1952, pp. 203 and ff., and Michael Dugget,
"Marx on Peasants", in THE JOURNAL OF PEASANT
STUDIES, Vol. 2, No. 2, London, January, 1975.

Since Marx closed the classical position -which
had become politically dangerous in academic cir-
cles- it became vital to search for new horizons.
The propositions, turned out by the Austrian school,
totally ignored the *campesino* position. The rare
times they referred to it was as some anomalous
left-over not worth their while. It did not even
arouse any theoretical uneasiness.

The *campesino* was no better off in the hands of
the neoclassicals, the Keynesians nor the marginal-
ists. From Marshall to Mills, they only appear as
a theoretical concept once they have lost their
specific characteristics. Thus, once they no longer
fit into their own intimate reality, they can be
classified into one of the preconceived (urbanly
conceived) pigeonholes: those corresponding to
optimizing, market oriented homo economicus. The
ultramodern attitude of the monetarist school is
even narrower. What is the use of worrying over
social agents who operate on the fringe of monetary
circulation?

Anthropology comes on the social science scene
as a direct link with certain agrarian societies,
but it takes a long time for this discipline to
redirect its primary interest to the past. It only
deals with the *campesino* issue when it appears as
part of primitive exotic societies, and these societies, themselves surviving entities from the
past, are only of interest as far as they relate
to the urban present, inasmuch as they can offer
clues for interpreting or understanding overall
present societies or their history. Thus *campesinos*
once again fall into obscurity: as left-overs from
economic processes, shadowy hangers-on of history,
the ignored and ignorant anonymous masses.

Finally, sociology for its part, when it is not
trying to squeeze *campesinos* into some kind of
taxonomy without which it cannot seem to function,
tries -as does economics- to exterminate them. They
are only of interest in their resistance to be what
they are not. Variation, modernization, mobility,
are all concepts which have been defined in terms
alien to *campesino* reality. What is interesting
about *campesinos*, if there is anything interesting,
is how they internalize outside reality which

shapes their destiny. Even if the sociological analysis of the *campesino* issue is turned into a
specialized area of study -rural sociology- it is
still unable -as is agricultural economics- to
venture authentically into a particular and novel
reality. It is merely an extrapolation.

This state of affairs in the social sciences
-which fortunately has begun to show signs of change
in recent years- strongly influenced debate on the
matter in Mexico. For some time, there was a con-
formist attitude towards formal generalizations,
such as that of Redfield: *campesinos* are "a species
of human organization with certain universal
traits." (2) However, the inadequacy of this notion
soon became evident. This was mainly due to the
fact that the *campesino* life-style did not easily
fit into the theoretical framework of those disci-
plines, which might have been able to deal with it.
These theories have to be distorted to a greater or
lesser extent, if they are to shed some light on
that evanescent and multi-faceted reality.

Present *campesino* reality cannot be understood
if we assume it merely to be the extension of a
social entity which has retained its essential
characteristics throughout history. An ahistoric
view point is a worthless point of departure. This
type of study can only provide insight into traditions and customs which do little to contribute
to the knowledge of the reality it studies.

The same situation has occurred in Mexico -and
still occurs- when a Neoclassical approach is used
to analyze *campesino* economy. In studies of profit
maximization and optimization of behavior the *campesino* is an entity alienated from "economic rationality" who works on anti-economic plots of land.
This point of view has increased prejudice towards
the *campesino* issue and is essentially a sterile

---

(2) Robert Redfield, PEASANT SOCIETIES AND CULTURE.
University of Chicago Press, Chicago, 1956, p. 86.
Redfield went beyond this formal notion, but not
much further when he equated *campesinos* interests
with a "cultural condition", interacting with
other "aspects" or "dimensions" of the society to
which *campesinos* belong.

206 The Struggle for Rural Mexico

way of trying to come to any theoretical or practical conclusions on the rural crisis and its solutions.

Conventional research was seriously affected
when it eventually had to admit the failure of its
inherent expectations. "Up to World War II, it was
still possible to believe -as both Marxists and Neoclassical economists did- that capitalist expansion
would develop the Third World. It might do so in an
outrageous exploitative way, but the result would
still be development. Since World War II, it has become clear to a number of serious thinkers that this
is not the case. Most of them have been Marxists,
but there are representatives of the established
wisdom, like John Hicks and Hyla Minti." (3) This
concern has even reached the economic centers of
world power. Recent analyses by the World Bank,
which are the basis for its Strategy for Basic Needs,
start out with the conclusion that success of the
strategies adopted since World War II corresponds
to the increasing poverty and hunger in two thirds
of the world.

What is clearly obvious in all this discussion
is the central issue of concern over the radical
failure of long-nurtured predictions that the *campesinos* would fade away. The fact is that they do
exist and their numbers increase daily: two thirds
of humanity, the "Vast Majority" as Harrington calls
it, demands an explanation of its existence and of
its possibilities for development. The matter is of
genuine widespread concern. Shortly before the
dramatic withdrawal of U.S. troops from Vietnam,
the Secretary of Defense, Robert McNamara gave a
strange speech in Montreal. He said that poverty in
under-developed countries (poverty which is essentially that of the *campesinos*), has been the main
source of violence -past, present and future- in
the post World War II period. "In future years", he
added, "violence will flare up in the nations in
the southern hemisphere." This interpretation runs
parallel to the awareness that productivity is not
helping reduce shortages, nor is it solving the problem of development. "Peasant suspiciousness towards 'progress' is no longer unfounded nor un-

(3) Michael Harrington, THE VAST MAJORITY, Simon
and Shuster, New York, p. 129.

warrented. They have seen how this progress has been
imposed by the global history of corporate capitalism and they have seen the power of this history
even over those who are looking for an alternative.
This suspiciousness cannot of itself form the basis
for an alternative political development. The pre-
condition for this alternative is that peasants develop self-awareness. If they manage to do this,
then they as a class would have a way of attempting
to change their class experience and characteristics." (4) While conventional wisdom maintained its
sterile race against time, obstinately entrenching
past economic and institutional inertia even further,
new streams of thought began to appear in Mexico,
regarding the drawing up of new political options.
The academic debate on the nature of *campesino* economy tended to become a political issue, the direct
concern of those groups and classes who seek social
change.

The hypothesis of articulating modes of production as a characteristic feature of all social formation was one of the positions which came to the
forefront of the discussion. The *campesino* issue
was included in the "simple mercantile mode of production," which was articulated and subordinated to
the capitalist one. This approach also assumes that
in order to exist, capital needs to penetrate non-
capitalist realities, a key for its expansion. This
view underlines the conventional notion of *campesino*
extinction as a result of assimilation into the proletariat, following the classical sequence. It points
out that "from the point of independent revolutionary organizations it is crucial to settle accounts
with the agrarian past. Marxist interpretation of
the agrarian problem takes on great relevance in
Mexico, for it means -as far as the ideological
struggle is concerned- the precise differentiation
of the theoretical and political space of the
bourgeosie and of the petit bourgeosie from the
specific space of the proletariat. Summing up, the
great weight of populist agrarianism bequeathed
from the 1910 Mexican Revolution and from the Cardenist reforms, must be clearly distinguished from
proletarian positions, so as not to overwhelm the

(4) John Berger, "Towards understanding peasant
experience", in RACE AND CLASS, Vol. XIX, No. 4,
Spring, 1978, p. 358.

independent popular movement only beginning to develop in Mexico. A proletarian view is needed not
only of bourgeosie characteristics and domination
mechanisms, but also of other popular non-proletarian classes and strata (mainly the *campesino*
class) which frequently become an exceptionally
legitimate basis of bourgeois power." This approach
defines the *campesinado* "as a social class different
from the proletariat," from an "alienated, external
interpretation, of what the *campesinado* is" that
points out "the petit bourgeosie character of *campesino* production which is evident from the simple
mercantile condition of its mode of production and
its property links with the land." This position
suggests that "the petit bourgeosie side (of the
campesino) has exhausted its revolutionary potential
and that now it is time for the proletarian side to
reveal itself." All this corresponds to the idea
that the *campesino* is "an exploited petit bourgeois." The context within which this evolution
would be possible implies a capitalist framework
with tendencies to proletarize and impoverish the
campesino on the one hand, and to refunctionalize
him on the other. (5)

This line of reasoning, which sees the *campesino* as a non-proletarian class with an "extra-
capitalist" existence (although subordinated to
capital), has entered the debate at several points.
For some, the tendency to "proletarize" *campesinos*
in conventional terms, will continue; certain
authors have used statistics to show the progress
of this tendency throughout the century and con-
clude that only a few *campesinos* are left. Proletarians (defined as salaried workers in the conventional sense) now predominate in rural areas.
Others foresee that for a long period yet to come
there will be a need to refunctionalize *campesinos*. They will continue as members of a non-capi-
talist mode of production, in order to satisfy
the needs of capitalist development and reproduction. Finally there are others who accept all this,
except the fact that capital can neither proletarize nor reorientate *campesinos* and therefore has no

(5) Roger Bartra, "Una extinción imposible en mar-
cha permanente", 1978 (Xerox).

option but to eliminate them. Since this assumption
is made within a world framework, it suggests that
the only way campesinos can avoid this fate (or
rather the lack of one) would be through the creation of a strong political organization on an international level, which would enable them to confront
the forces which at this level try to destroy them.

Other streams of thought mistrusted the hypothesis of the articulation of different modes of
production and denounced its structuralist and
Althusserian faults. They also questioned the idea
that vast sectors of the world population were still
alien to capitalist production even though subordinated to it. They consider campesinos not as a mode
of production but as a social class which forms part
of the capitalist society in the same terms as any
other class. They even rejected the classification
of campesinos as petit bourgeoisie, and saw them as
strictly proletarian because of their contradictions
with capital. They did point out, however, that although they were proletariat, they were different
from industrial or agrarian workers because they are
subject to specific mechanisms of exploitation, different from those of other workers. Bearing in mind
this peculiarity, they claimed that campesinos could
establish alliances with workers since both are
proletarians (in contradiction with capital), but
with their own assertions due to differences in
history, present situations and future prospects.
Seen from this point of view, it is unlikely that
in the near future, a classical process of proletarianization will occur, namely that capitalism
could integrate campesinos as permanently salaried
workers. The prospect of the physical elimination
of campesinos, through genocide or through the
slower but equally efficient rural or urban "marginalization" (which goes beyond the existing conditions needed to maintain a reserve industrial army)
requires the creation of a political alternative,
fully capable of recognizing the specific campesino
situation, regarding which different possibilities
have been expressed.

Besides these approaches and positions dealing
with current and future problems, there are others
which look to the past. Kulakization, the progressive agglutination of individual plots of land
resulting from the dynamics of the "more capable and

hardworking *campesinos*" still influences the analysis of many groups. Many of them would unhesita-
tingly share the same opinions as President Plutarco
E. Calles in 1924: "My preference for the middle
class is mainly based upon my efforts to create a
class of small *campesino* land owners. I yearn to see
each *campesino* possessing a plot of land to work.
The conversion of each *campesino* into a landowner
is the best way of avoiding revolutionary and political turmoil. With this the *campesino* could establish personal and even commercial interests in
support of the present situation." As will be remembered, Calles did not consider the Mexican *ejido*
or the common cultivation of the land as "true
forms" of the economy and he claimed that the community should be a transitory stage in creating
smallholdings. Past experience has shown that explicit propositions to eliminate *ejidos* or native
communities are not advisable. Because of this,
some recent positions suggest ways of doing this
without declaring so explicitly. Thus, suggestions
are periodically made to legalize the generalized
practice of leasing *ejido* plots, create legal conditions for their voluntary alienation or promote
associating mechanisms among private *ejidatarios*,
comuneros and *minifundistas*, to allow direct intervention of the capitalist corporation in land development, so far prohibited by the Constitution,
though not in practice.

Opposed to these proposals, are agrarian claims
which denounce them as ways of trying to recons-
titute *latifundios*, a position which no one in
Mexico could easily defend. Along with the old arguments, new ones have been put forth which try to
place the debate in an international context. The
transnationalization of capital hypotheses and the
analysis of modern agribusiness operating conditions
on a world scale show what the consequences would
be for Mexico if she blindly continues along the
path laid down by the new international division of
labor.

2

THE DISPUTE OVER RESOURCES

The academic and political debate over rural affairs, is in fact covering up an intense dispute
over productive resources that is determined by
the general situation. Although it does not refer
exclusively to land and agricultural production,
its major strategic dimension is found in these
areas.

On the most obvious level, the dispute developed
around the use of so-called "oil revenue." The discussion was directed above all, at the rationality
of oil exploitation. One of the first questions relates the level of production to proven reserves,
and points out the risk of exhaustion before the
appearance of alternative sources of energy. Even
though it is a crucial problem that must be rigor-
ously examined, the fact that Mexico is, at present,
the world's fifth major oil producer -given the
level of its reserves and the frequent announce-
ments of new discoveries- had weakened the argument
in this respect.

A second question that has aroused public attention refers to the technical, social and economic
conditions under which production is taking place.
Adverse implications, as a consequence of the rapid
advance of activities in the exploration and production of oil, on the ecological system and on the
social condition of large sections of the population, have been pointed out. Although this topic
has been attracting more public attention than
ever, it tends to be considered as "the price of
modernization" and has not inhibited further activities. It has only led to suggestions for modifying
some current practices.

Intense political controversy has emerged concerning the "oil platform", that is controversy over
the specific level of production which should be
maintained. This is a many-faceted problem. The
level fixed by the present government at the beginning of 1977, was reached before its deadline, and
in 1979 the possibility of raising it was openly
scheduled. Many people believed that this was due
to external pressure, rather than national needs
and therefore opposed the measure. Others pointed
out that the strategic interest of other countries
-in short, the United States- is not related so
closely to the immediate production of petroleum
(since Mexico continues to be a marginal supplier
for the U.S.) as to the development of exploitation
capacity. The main point, according to this argument, is that Mexico should "be ready" to increase
its production rapidly. Although a policy of
"closed wells" would be maintained, it would be in
a position to respond to unexpectedly high demands
in times of crisis. Official statements have denied
the possibility of Mexico's replacing Middle East
supplies but the question remains open. On March 18,
1980, when the President of Mexico announced a
moderate increase in the "oil platform", the Director of *Petróleos Mexicanos* warned that it would be
possible to continue increasing production capacity,
but that such a policy is precisely what many consider to be unwise or irrational for the best interests of the country. Closely related to this is the
question of the use of oil revenues. In fact, a
large part of the argument about a conservative
exploitation policy did not originate from concern
over reserves, but from anticipation and fears over
the "absorption capacity" of the Mexican economy
and society for this revenue. While there was great
internal pressure to generate resources that would
permit development plans to go ahead and particularly to attend to those most in need, warnings
were formulated about the inflationary effects that
an uncontrolled increase of oil revenue could have.
Within the present context and its political correlation of prevalent forces, fears of a "Venezueli-
zation", or an "Iranization" of the country expressed, for many, the idea that oil revenues would
tend to stimulate still further concentration and
centralization of economic and political power.

In this context, the association between oil and rural areas appears to be very direct. The current government pointed out, right from the start, that its two major priorities were food and energy. There is a tendency to accept the recommendation made by the ex-Minister of Petroleum of Saudi Arabia while passing through Mexico: "It is necessary to transform oil wealth into agricultural prosperity before it's too late." On announcing a moderate increase in the "petroleum platform" on March 18, 1980 the President recognized the limited achievements of his government in the priority area of food, as compared with the great advances in energy production, and announced an ambitious program for food self-sufficiency in Mexico: the *Sistema Alimentario Mexicano* (Mexican Food System) a model that establishes production and consumption goals and promotes a *campesino*-based strategy. (See Appendix).

It is necessary, however, to place the question in a wider context. At the beginning of 1979, President Carter enthusiastically picked up the proposal of an American congressman who suggested an exchange of corn for oil in trade with Mexico. While the proposal stirred up angry adverse reactions in Mexico and the President felt obliged to reject it explicitly in his next Report on the State of the Nation, the fact is that Mexico is exporting oil, while the need to import food has increased. As has already been indicated, seven million tons of food, almost half of which is corn, will have to be acquired abroad to satisfy 1980 demands. The agricultural and cattle-raising trade balance, traditionally favorable, has been deteriorating rapidly. Although the direct exchange of corn for oil appears to be little more than a simplification that makes no sense, the implications derived from this are certainly not.

In 1978, when a National Plan for Industrial Development was made public, a forecast was included which since then has been the object of analysis and concern. According to tendencies observed and under the assumption that there would be no substantial change in them, the Plan pointed out that in 1990 the country would be dedicating two-thirds of its oil revenue to food imports. Another econometric

model carried the projection forward to the year
2000. According to this estimate, by such time Mexico would have to dedicate all of its oil revenue to
food imports. This implies, that the country would
have been running desperately to keep in the same
place.

Within this context, it is assumed that growing
amounts of resources will have to be channelled into
agricultural and cattle raising development to increase food production. Thus at the forefront of the
discussion is the need to define the main protagonist
of the task. It is not just a matter of attracting
public resources, although these constitute a coveted
prize, but rather an attempt to establish whose position will be strengthened by such resources and the
programs and measures associated with them, for when
they get to the rural areas they will find themselves
in the middle of a dispute that has been gaining in-
tensity. Credit, subsidies, infrastructure and all
the other elements that integrate the "auxiliary
services package" can only be controlled and applied
through control of the land and of the productive
processes where they materialize. This is, finally,
the crux of the conflict.

As has been discussed throughout this book,
campesinos have managed to retain for themselves the
formal usufruct of most of the available agricultural land in the country and a large part of the
pastures. They may be *ejidatarios, comuneros, colonos, nacionaleros,* or private *minifundistas,* but
they are all *campesinos,* and the usufruct that they
possess is rarely disputed openly in formal legal
terms. As has also been said, however, this does not
mean that they find themselves in a position to
define how production should be oriented or the conditions under which the productive process should
develop. This orientation and these conditions have
gradually gained ground in terms of the logic
imposed by multinational agribusiness, either directly or through intermediaries: national agribusiness, farmers, *rancheros, caciques...* or State
enterprises.

The conflict has developed in a variety of ways,
although its inherent violence is generalized with
a tendency towards intensification. Invasions of
land are daily occurrences. Those led by *campesinos*

to recuperate land taken from them receive greater
news coverage, although cattle raisers and other
agents seem to invade land more frequently. The
latter use the agrarian backlog (hectares redistributed only on paper) or the legal indefinition that
prevails in extensive areas as an excuse while often
resorting to force, either private or public. These
generally brutal actions develop along with many
other, sometimes very subtle forms. This does not
mean however, that they cease to be the symptomatic
expression of a deep conflict, an authentic dispute
for the nation -as an outstanding analyst called it-
that at any moment oversteps, or threatens to over-
step the limits of the political context within
which an attempt is made to overcome contradictions.

SELF-SUFFICIENCY AND COMPARATIVE ADVANTAGES

The dispute over resources is revealed in a strategic manner through the general orientation of
production.

   One dimension of the problem has been aired
under the theoretical -and ideological- cover of
the comparative advantage thesis. With the application of conventional profit criteria, it seemed natural for many years that the country should concentrate on producing those articles that had "comparative advantages" -natural or economic- in order
to obtain benefits from international trade: it
would export products that could be sold "expensi-
vely" and would import "cheaply" those which it
produced less "efficiently." In this way, the need
to import was considered acceptable, just as it
was to employ the best productive resources in export crops, as long as the commercial agricultural
and cattle-raising balance continued to be favorable.
Even when imports reached massive levels, it was
observed that rural areas would be able to "pay"
for them, because their production still generated
a favorable net balance of foreign exchange.

   In the seventies, the technical debate over the
comparative advantage thesis was revived. Besides
refuting the logic of the argument, using as a
point of departure the theoretical advances that
authors such as Arghiri Emmanuel had developed,

an examination of the international experience was presented to expose the mythical character of the theory, which prevented the forces which really determine the direction and benefits of international trade from being seen clearly.

Above or aside from these technical aspects, however, political arguments were brought to the forefront. The prospect of increasing grain imports on an impoverished world market, made it clear that, despite economic convenience, it was vital to avoid the worst of all dependencies, that of the stomach. The 1972 world food crisis confronted more than forty countries with the problem of starvation, and scarcity knocked at the door of the industrialized world itself, even though the latter seemed to have long since overcome such difficulties. Whether it was convenient or not to sell "expensive" articles on world markets and buy "cheap" ones, the fact was that it was not possible to get the products required at any price. All this served as a warning signal. At the end of that year, absolute priority was granted to the goal of self-sufficiency in national food production.

This, however remained on paper, as good intentions, yet another item on the long list that Mexico has drawn up throughout the years. During the rest of the decade, the goal became further removed until it seemed unattainable. Analyses which tried to explain why this had happened stressed, the "deviation" from government programs: many of them maintained previous orientations through inertia and were unable to adapt to the new circumstances, but this was only part of the story. The main question was different: who were to be the protagonists of the new orientation of the productive effort?

The logic of agricultural and cattle-raising operations, national or multinational, was -and is- tied to profitability criteria. While the policy of controlled prices for basic foodstuffs is maintained -and there is nothing to lead one to think that it can or should be abandoned, although efforts to "free it" have gradually been observed- economic logic will separate basic crops from "modern" agriculture. For reasons already indicated

multinational agribusiness has been barred from the
production of corn and other basic foodstuffs. Its
real choice, like that of many national economic
agents -such as the cattle raisers- is not among
various crops but between producing commercial products (such as meat and milk) or not participating
in agricultural and cattle-raising production at
all. In this way, the policy of self-sufficiency
that was generally accepted at formal levels has
unacceptable implications for the structures of
domination: it means giving *campesinos* the main
responsibility for satisfying national productive
needs.

THE ORGANIZATION OF PRODUCERS

Organizing *campesinos* has become a central aspect in
the discussion of the rural crisis, although the
manner in which this is done depends on the objectives. For those who insist on a "neutral" perception of the problem, only the question of productivity is discussed: to attain the required results,
campesinos have to be organized in such a way as to
raise productive efficiency, to improve income and
to reach the physical goals of production. For
others, it is a matter of organizing *campesinos'*
productive activity in such a way that, given the
restrictions which have prevailed in the judicial-
political context, agribusiness can act within this
boundary with greater flexibility and profitability.
For others, organizing *campesinos* is not the central
issue as much as creating the conditions in which
their own productive and social organization will
give way to their liberation.

An important sector of opinion, both inside and
outside government, has been oriented to promoting
associative schemes. The overall logic of its proposals suggests that public or private agribusiness,
without giving up profitable lines of business,
would extend its activities to basic production,
displacing traditional agents of lesser economic and
political power, currently necessary intermediaries
in the operation with *campesino* producers. The
operation could be predictably profitable, assuming
that there would be important official subsidies
and that diverse costs, risks and uncertainties of

the activity would again be assumed by the *campesi-no*. From another angle, the associative scheme would seek to respect formally the current agricultural structures -the *ejido*, the community, the legally permitted dimension of smallholdings- although in practice it would inevitably damage them. This mechanism, in fact, would imply freeing the expansion of the scale of operations from legal and other restraints. Although the scheme has obvious liberal overtones, it means abandoning the original dream of small producers, expanding at the cost of their neighbors, in order to pass directly to modern forms of capitalist agricultural operations. The purpose, in some cases, has been to create large and highly productive units or farms and, in others, to generalize the agricultural contract system, passing over the tenure system which still continues to be politically untouchable, and preventing in this way its performance as an obstacle to expansion.

Another school of though, not substantially different from the previous one, also emphasizes collectivization programs. Through diverse models of collective production organization, it tries to convince *campesinos* to adopt patterns of organization and division of labor that would allow them to raise productivity and adjust more adequately to global needs. Diverse mechanisms to overcome the traditional limits on collectivization have been proposed: expulsion of the labor force, as a consequence of increased productivity which generates internal and inevitable conflicts. Likewise, progressive forms of collectivism, that give greater flexibility to the process, have been suggested. Other proposed mechanisms, without clearly showing how this can be done, have tried to prevent collectivization from being converted into another control instrument which subjects peasants to public and private agencies through direct contact with collectivized units.

Finally, another school of thought stresses the regulation of relations between *campesinos* and the rest of society under the assumption that what has been discussed is essentially the relation between labor and capital.

On one hand, the unionization of temporary or
permanent wage laborers is suggested, a move that
up to now has not been possible. The problem is
partly associated with the difficulties of collective contracting, given the lack of consistency
between those who own or have title to the land and
agribusiness, the *cacique*, or State enterprises,
which manage it. Furthermore, most rural wage
laborers only find seasonal work of an occasional
nature on farms where there is no possibility of
collective organization. While the unionization
efforts in productive units persist, they have
engendered other lines of action that stem from
campesino organizations, which would adopt the form
of unions when members establish a relation with
capital under wage labor conditions.

On the other hand, given that wages are not the
general form of relation between capital and labor
in agricultural and cattle-raising production, it
has been suggested that the regulating effort be
directed to the organization and strengthening of
"collective mercantile contracts." Through these,
the power of collective organization could confront
capital under more equal conditions. In order to
adapt to the specific characteristics of *campesino*
production, instead of wage-negotiated contracts,
like those of industrial workers -in which capital
directly contracts labor force, the object of the
negotiated contract would be the materialization of
productive efforts. Contracts would include provisions on resources that would be supplied by the
campesinos -land, labor force, means of production,
etc.- and those supplied by the economic agent
-public or private- taking part in the contract.
The terms of appropriation of value and surplus
value amongst the participants would be the object
of negotiation, in the conventional terms of a
collective contract.

Closely related to these propositions is that
which refers to the acknowledgement and respect for
campesino productive organizations. Assuming that a
self-governing, democratic and integrated structure
tends to predominate, it is suggested that rural
development must not consist of the substitution of
these forms of organization for others, promoted
by government and its agencies or by private ones,

which by disarticulating them, create conditions for the control and subjection of *campesinos* through organizations set up from above and outside.

To recognize, respect and support organizations that *campesinos* themselves have developed means to take as a point of departure those schemes associated with the authentic participation of *campesinos* in group decisions. With advances towards superior forms of organization, conceived of and developed by *campesinos*, they would be in a position to acquire complete control over resources and activities, in order to modify their relation with other agents effectively, and undertake more ambitious projects. This implies, of course, establishing deeply rooted relations between productive and political *campesino* organizations, as well as pinning their development, strengthening and independence, on alliances with other social classes that share their interests and projects.

3

THE PRESENT SITUATION: IMPASSE, CROSSROADS, OPPORTUNITY

The struggle for rural Mexico has been long, bloody, and difficult. It is far from over, and it is not an exaggeration to say that not only the *campesinos'* destiny is at stake but also that of the entire nation.

Historical experience indicates that capitalist development in agriculture has taken place in a sort of social vacuum. The *campesinos* have been violently and radically expelled from their lands, for their place to be occupied by other agents. The operation of <u>clearing of estates</u>* that in England transformed the peasants into available labor force for vigorous industrial development or the extermination war that was waged against the Indian occupants of North America, are not chance or peculiar incidents which can be explained in terms of determined circumstances or specific periods of those nations. They constitute the basis of the model that, with obvious variations, has characterized capitalist expansion in agriculture: and in this model -as history shows and authors of the most diverse theoretical and ideological positions warn- *campesinos* have no place except as demolition material for constructing the society to which they should incorporate themselves, ceasing to be what they are.

If the genocide of the first century of colonial domination in New Spain had been consummated, perhaps it would have resulted in a form of productive integration similar to that of the above model. A million *campesinos*, however, survived, *campesinos*

---

* In English in the original.

222 The Struggle for Rural Mexico

that from then on refused to be extinguished and could not be absorbed in any other form by the society to which they belonged. Today, after having suffered all kinds of aggression and forms of exploitation, and having known moments of splendor and hope, Mexican *campesinos* form a population of more than thirty million.

Moreover, when they make contact with the rest of the country's population, they easily recognize their brothers, children and grandchildren, who still carry the spirit of *campesino* society and culture.

In the villages of Mexico, a new consciousness has been forming over the years. It is clear that *campesinos* still find themselves trapped in their own prejudices and in those that urban life transmitted to them about the reality they live in. They have not completely abandoned their local vision of the world, although mass communication has been tearing this apart. Their wavering between the magical-empirical logic from which they come and the scientific-technological ideas to which they are directed is an expression of dangerous ties to centuries of domination. It is not easy to articulate their interpretative models of the world with those prevailing, so that from this interaction a new and more complex one emerges. Within the tangle of conflicts in which their life unfolds, however, a new historical impulse seems to be working its way forward.

Campesinos are driven by a concrete dilemma. While they observe how the economic and social structure in which they have lived until now is falling to pieces, they find themselves obliged to try their luck in a world still foreign to them, and they find that this world does not offer them an option for survival and development. Although it unceasingly presents itself before them as the promised land, it becomes an unattainable goal: there is no economic, social or political space into which they can be admitted. It does not leave them any other alternative than to construct their own option.

The passiveness they show is in many ways misleading. "It hides latent violence that threatens

to explode in the phrases that, with letters in
white lime, cover the walls of one of the poorest
ejidos to the east of Morelos (the birthplace of
Zapatismo): The silent *campesino* will never be
heard!." (1) They have already begun to break their
silence and their voice tends to turn into a cry.
Accustomed to violence -their eternal companion-
they know that once turned loose, it becomes uncontrollable. Although the impatience or despera-
tion of some is difficult to appease, most still
believe it is necessary to explore roads different
from those of total violence, or at least to take
the time and effort to try.

The most important possible strategy is alliances. The workers have changed. In the years of
revolutionary momentum, red batallions from the
Casa del Obrero Mundial contributed to the defeat of Villa and were willing to fight against
the armies of Zapata. In spite of the success of
their alliance with the *campesinos* in the '30s, the
workers, tied to other forces, shared the fruits of
progress that radically excluded the *campesinos*
during the following decades. Even today those who
approach them offering solidarity, often persist in
the conviction that the alliance between workers
and *campesinos* has to be established under the
principle of inequality: the former has to direct
the latter, since they do not believe the *campesinos*
are capable of representing or directing themselves
or of conceiving -along with other groups- a common
project of liberation. In spite of all this, new
attitudes have developed among the city workers and
intellectuals who have identified with them. Little
by little, reality is conquering prejudice. Workers
are rethinking their alliance with the *campesinos*.

These are not unfounded rumours, but neither are
they the expression of a project, which is very far
from having been drawn up. Such serious absence
actually constitutes the greatest danger at the
moment. "The other side" has a project underway.
Perhaps they would not be able to put it in writing
or give it an appropriate conceptual structure, but
it is a logic that belongs to the real world and

_____

(1) Clarissa Hardy, OP. CIT., p. 194.

that the structures of domination try to further.

In spite of the difficulties described throughout this book and of what has been called "a blind
alley," and despite inflation, unemployment, and
the depth of the present crisis, Mexico is far from
being a bankrupt nation. She possesses a variety of
options. Some of them, however, would generate
illusive growth, would give a reassuring image of
progress and would lessen -through various pallia-
tives- the most serious problems to the point that
after a period of time the serious contradiction
which has been developing would inevitably explode,
and that would occur under serious and dangerous
conditions for the country and her inhabitants. The
economic, social and political cost of this road
seems to be of such a magnitude that the idea of
consciously pursuing it becomes indefensible. The
question is centered, consequently, on the serious
investigation of the availability of alternative and
less costly roads.

Both the options of conventional development
and those of the *campesinos* are based on various
fairly realistic assumptions: the need to increase
internal production of basic foodstuffs; the urgent
need to improve the situation of what has been
euphemistically called the "informal urban and rural
sector," and above all of the *campesinos*, the need
to eliminate or moderate the level of violence that
is being registered in the rural areas; the advisability of extending and strengthening the economic,
social and political organizational efforts in rural
environments; the impossibility or serious limitations of a policy of high prices for the producers
of basic foodstuffs as a strategy for fostering production, in view of the need to maintain control on consumer prices in a highly inflationary
context; the advisability of channelling a significant portion, greater than in the past, of available
public resources, in particular those generated by
oil, to agricultural and cattle-raising activities.

These elements, with others of lesser importance, provide food for thought as to which road to
follow. Although conventional voices of the past are
still heard supporting *neolatifundismo* at all costs,
they tend to admit that the "modern sector" will not

be able to play a prominent role in the production
of basic foodstuffs, because of price limitations
that affect the profitability of operation. An important role as a "modernizing agent" is attributed
to it, however, so that through investments or technological and administrative transfer it would
"reorganize" campesino production. In order to attain this, formulas of mercantile association between "modern" agents and campesinos are being
insisted upon.

Together with this possibility, the sudden
broadening of State responsibility is also proposed,
both in quantitative as well as qualitative terms:
the government should be directly involved in production, in some cases, and in others in strengthening its "support" programs for campesinos through
activities that would give it greater influence
over their activities and forms of organization.
The massive application of subsidies for these proposals would be dedicated specifically to "favoring
the labor factor." This implies, primarily, recognizing in a more or less explicit form that the
"support" programs, above all credit and marketing,
had not properly considered the campesinos real income; by including the latter in their economic
calculation, the authorities would try to anticipate
expressly within the "support" packages the equivalent of the campesinos salary, in order to encourage
campesino interest in production and the improvement
of their situation. The approach also means making
more evident, and therefore more liable to control,
the subordination of campesinos' labor to public
capital. It includes, likewise, the characteristic
stress of the last decades on the organization of
the producers, meaning the effort that consists in
adapting the campesinos to models of organization
more in accordance with their needs and with the logic of official or private agents who contact them.
All this, of course, would be accompanied by large
social service programs, together with an agroindustrial promotion along intensive labor guidelines.

In agrarian affairs, conventional thought
currently suggests rapidly bringing the agrarian reform to its conclusion. On one hand, urging the end
of redistribution underlining that there is no

longer land available for this process although
some areas still exist. On the other hand, it is
stated that the redistribution lag in agrarian reform should be brought to an end, with a great effort towards regularization. Strictly speaking, nobody expects to see in a couple of years what has
not been achieved in sixty. It is an impossible job
which, besides making effective a "redistribution
on paper," would require the resolution of land
conflicts -among *campesinos* or between them and
other agents- that in many cases have persisted
for decades and that do not seem "solvable" under
present legislation. To give an idea of what this
means, it can be noted that from 1940 to 1976 Presidential resolutions were issued that redistributed
52.7 million hectares among the *campesinos*; during
this period, according to official figures, the
"effective" redistribution was only of 25.6 million hectares, which implies that 27 million
hectares were "pending execution." This "lack of
execution" is explained by a variety of reasons, but
all of them involve serious conflicts between individuals and groups, with no easy solution. Under
such conditions the proposition does not suggest
the possibility of an unrealistic solution of "ar-
ranging" and "resolving" in a few months all that
is pending. Instead it means <u>freezing</u> the situation,
as was planned in 1930 by former President Calles,
who pointed out with a sense of urgency that what
should be done was to fix a peremptory term during
which all land claims were to be presented and at
the end of this time "not a word more on the subject." (Another way of focusing on the "freezing"
would be to observe the rate of redistribution,
whose annual average over the last three years represented about half that of the past sixty years.
This slowing down has been accompanied by the massive issuing, often careless and hasty, of individual certificates of protection from distribution
under the agrarian reform, such as the granting of
unconstitutional concessions to the cattle-raising
latifundistas and other agents.)

   The possibility of "wiping out" the problem of
tenure is not pointless. Insecurity, legal disorder
and irregularities in the redistribution process
are a basic source of rural conflict and are causing
serious social and economic damage. It is a funda-

mental *campesino* demand that could be supported by
many social groups. The problem lies in the terms
of its establishment. The argument that there is no
more land to redistribute contradicts, above all,
the historical memory of the *campesinos*. In 1950,
the head of the *Departamento de Asuntos Agrarios*
of the Alemán government, maintained this with
equal firmness; afterwards it was proclaimed that
more than forty million hectares were redistributed
"on paper" and seventeen million "de facto." Periodically this argument has been stressed and periodically more "redistributable" land is located. To
this we should add the *campesinos'* concrete awareness of this situation. In each village, in each
region, in each federal entity, they have found
susceptible land and have undertaken measures in
this respect. The phrase that "there is no more
land left to redistribute" means for them the rhetorical denial of a reality that they perceive
daily.

"Freezing the situation," on the other hand,
is also unacceptable for the *campesinos*. It would
not only mean admitting that the land liable to distribution they have identified is not being redistributed, but also accepting that the arbitrary
invasion of their land, by a variety of agents, is
legally sanctioned. As has already been indicated,
a good part of the existing conflicts did not originate from the taking over of the land by the *campesinos* -although they have seen themselves compelled
to resort to such illegal recuperation- but to the
constant invasion of *campesino* land, not only by
agricultural and cattle raising agents, but also by
the promoters of urban expansion, a process that
adopts many different forms.

It is possible to conceive, however, legal and
political formulas that -without falling into
unacceptable extremes for the *campesinos*- would
give way to a stage of intense regularization of
land tenure conditions. Its success and viability
would not only be associated with a social dimension (the degree to which authentic concern for the
satisfaction of the *campesino* demands is reflected),
but also with the possibility of achieving, at the
same time, productive, economic and social development that would open up a way for the relief of the

existing contradictions. In fact, it is necessary
to recognize that very many land tenure problems
will no be "resolved" if a parallel economic formula satisfying the basic demands of the *campesinos*
cannot be found. In specific areas and conditions
redistribution -which has to be carried out at any
rate- can cause a deterioration of the situation if
better ways of development are not opened up at the
same time. It must also be recognized that the conventional patterns of development mentioned earlier
can be an effective complement to these legal and
political formulas, in order to diminish the level
of the existing conflict, give way to the most
urgent demand of the *campesinos* and achieve important productive and economic advances. They would
not be a "definite and thorough solution" of the
agrarian question (is there really a solution which
can be considered as such in the short run, within
the prevailing productive horizon?), but would
appear as a rupture of the present impasse, as an
effective way of getting over the crisis and as a
means to gain the economic and political time necessary to try other deeper and more permanent solutions, which may be thought possible as a result
of the "fabulous" oil wealth.

This is the real danger: the political feasibility and the possible initial success of the barely
updated conventional route. It would yield "encouraging" results in a short time. Politically effective management of the plan would allow for moder-
ation or isolation of the deepest and most radical
renovating impulses and would raise politically
manageable hopes. It seems, furthermore, the most
obvious and expeditious road; for some, it
appears unavoidable, or at least it constitutes the
most likely perspective. With a bit of luck and a
little more political ability, by means of revitalizing diverse institutional apparatuses of the
Mexican State, it would seem possible to travel this
road in the '80s without excessive difficulties and
without losing the type of "stability" that has
characterized Mexican society over the last fifty
years.

But this is not a good road. Taking into account the facts and conditions that this book has
attempted to make clear, it would be a way of

getting close to economic, social and political
catastrophes of incalculable consequences. It could
only be travelled through a more authoritarian
exercise of power, a rigid growth of Mexican society and a profound disarticulation of the fundamental organizational structures, under conditions
of serious economic and social lags for the majority
of the population, and the content of these phrases
is not intended as sensationalism: they are intended
as a warning under present conditions.

One of the essential blindspots of this project is the present state of the agricultural and
livestock operation and its tendencies. As a new
incarnation, agribusiness has been replacing the
developmentalist lines of Government undertaken
since 1940, and has been integrated, in strict
alliance with the political and economic centers of
decision, on a national as well as an international
level. Among the outstanding characteristics of
this project there is a deepening of the conventional process of modernization, a growing subordination
of the productive apparatus of the rural areas to
agroindustrial demand, the change in cultivation
patterns and urban eating habits, and in particular
the exclusion of large sectors of the population
from the possibility of acquiring effective demand.
The scheme synthesized in the previous paragraphs
seems to omit this fundamental fact. By not explicitly including it in the reflection, it is impossible to perceive that in its development the plan
would tend to strengthen the national and multinational agribusiness project, although it expressly
seeks other results. In fact, it would tend largely
to favor it. Thus, the advances that have been
difficult to see would be negated in practice and
the crisis would deepen. The logics of the subsidy
would be incapable of confronting the logics of
economy. Public action would not be an option or a
break in the behavior of agribusiness, but one of
its main supports, as has been occurring in this
period. The contradictions would hopelessly tend to
become unmanageable. If the inherent dangers of
the profound crisis (2), present at the interna-

(2) Enrique Ruíz García has been making a precise
and scrupulous account of the crisis, contributing
elements that allow us to characterize it, anticipate its consequences and conceive ways of confront-

tional level as well as the national, are added to
this, the prospect becomes intolerable.

Mexico, however, has another option. It is,
without a doubt, as beset with difficulties as the
previous one, but of a different nature. It has
the substantive limitation of not having achieved
precision in its specific definitions, in order to
integrate in a concrete organic force the obligations that form it and that have emerged from many
spheres. However, its possibilities are undeniable.
It takes up the most profound and vigorous lines of
the history of the country, the historical possibilities of the project are enriched and its limits
enhanced.

This other option has a common denominator
with those set up by other groups of workers. Without giving up a long-term radical perspective, it
proposes to promote structural transformations from
now on, that lead to the root of the problems, within the perspective of a capitalist society as the
expression of a strategy of accumulation of forces.
This line of reasoning does not include the hope
that a series of linked reforms would -by accumu-
lation- produce the changes needed. At the same
time, it firmly rejects the idea that overcoming
existing contradictions will be a more or less
automatic result of their becoming more acute, that
is, the situation in which they become unbearable:
according to this, it would only be possible "to
accelerate" the process, through bold isolated actions that propitiate conditions for a "power
assault" without modifying its sign. The new approach, on the other hand, considers it vital that
the process be taken over in order to unleash appropriate changes before its own inertia makes it
unmanageable or before contradictions can be overcome only at unacceptable costs. Taking over the
process is not interpreted here as a need to construct an independent social and political organization, capable of doing so: it also includes, as

_____

ing it. See, among others, his essays in UNO MAS
UNO in 1979 and 1980, particularly April and May,
1980.

a relevant feature of this organization, its capacity to influence the present as a strategy for
preparing the future.

What does this *campesino* option mean finally?
Land, once again. *Campesinos* already know that
having it is not enough, but they also know that
nothing is worse than losing it. They will fight to
conquer and reconquer it a thousand times and will
do so socially, collectively, or as a community,
with the force of a group that has refused to exchange its organic solidarity for the illusive step
leading to homogenized individualism. It is land
once more, but the drive to search for it is what
establishes -day after day- a greater distance with
respect to the anarchist tradition and the liberal
trap. Land belongs to those who work it, but now
this work is not individual but collective. Pressures are continually felt to individualize *campesinos* and limit them to their *ejidal*, communal or
private land. *Campesinos* even reproduce individualism among themselves as self-defense, as the
ultimate expression of their desire to survive. At
the same time, however, the very fabric of solidarity is taken up once again in the villages and
the *campesinos* rediscover, together with the technicians, that the enormous efficiency and poten-
tiality of smallholdings can only be unfurled within the integration of the group, when the force of
the collective organization is combined with the
vitality of individual creative initiative. *Campesinos* are demanding that social agrarian reform be
set in motion in order to bring the anarchist-liberal reform to its historical conclusion. They
are now beginning to know that not only land should
belong to those who work it.

Campesinos want freedom through land. What is
most obvious is that repression and violence must
stop. They have been discovering however, that the
logic of the coercive oppression exercised over
them, is symptomatic of weakness, rather than
strength. They see that the growing inability of
the dominating structures to maintain economic control over resources, through political means, im-
pels them to use violence. As they cannot and do
not always want to answer violence with violence,
the *campesinos* have begun to fabricate their own

political freedom: to create organizations and
areas of negotiation that will enable them to resist
the domination they are subjected to, accumulating
strength and setting up radical projects of transformation.

Together with political freedom, *campesinos*
demand economic freedom but not that of liberal demand
the failure of which they have already witnessed.
Economic freedom for *campesinos* means gradually
overcoming and eventually eliminating the regulations and organic norms of the economic relations
which maintain and through which they are exploited.
What has to be rejected is the "direct producer"
myth, together with that of the purely mercantile
or financial nature of their economic relations in
order to accept them completely as production relations in which labor and capital come into contact,
i.e., in which private and public capital is the
form of economic relationship. If they are to be
recognized as proletarian workers, *campesinos* demand
that their relations be established upon that base,
and that they be submitted to the regulations and
negotiating systems that have historically permitted
labor to achieve progress at the expense of capital.
In this way, they would be able to suggest the modification of the nature of tense relations and the
substitution of agents, in order to make room for
those that would be able to establish relations
with them based on solidarity and not on exploitation. (3)

The consolidation and development of the
campesino group are conditions of this economic freedom in as much as it conforms to its own patterns,
traditions and organic capacities. *Campesinos* know
that "producer organization" is required but they
reject that it implies irrationally modifying their
own organizations in order to make them fit into

_____

(3) There should be no mistake in this. If the relationship between the union and the *campesino* group
is established on the basis of gains for the former,
it will be reconverted, simply into another intermediary in the chain of agribusiness (or of capital
as a whole). The worker-boss will destroy all possibility of an effective alliance.

"bureaucratic pigeonholes," public or private.
These have to adapt to the form of organization
that the *campesinos* have constructed, and this must
constitute the point of departure for the authentic
development thrust. Instead of integrating themselves into formal organizations that have converted
them and would continue converting them into modified instruments of domination. *Campesinos* demand
complete respect for the forms that historically
have yielded positive results for them and in which
participation and self-government for effective
control of resources can be fact and non fiction.
Their organizations will truly be of a *campesino*
nature, and productive, when they represent the
channelling of efforts towards their own land, and
have a unionist nature when establishing relations
with other agents under the form of wage labor. In
this way, the *campesino* organization would be able
to adopt the form most suited to the mechanism of
exploitation to which it is exposed, so that the
unionization of agricultural workers would be more
of a product of the *campesino* world, in touch with
its realities and not an unreal extrapolation of the
urban industrial world.

In the new interplay of freedoms *campesinos*
have to fight basically for that of their alliances
and class solidarities. On a short-term basis, it
has become a condition for the progress of their
immediate claims. On a medium and long-term basis,
the deep alliances, of authentic organic content,
are essential for conceiving and carrying ahead a
liberation project which becomes the renewed historical construction of Mexico as a Nation.

One of the features of this option, which is
barely beginning to be seen, is the conscious inclusion of the *campesinos* in the historical project.
Various elements have contributed to the creation of
this consciousness. On one hand, the fact that
campesinos were radically excluded from the long-
standing model had to make itself seen by means of
machete-blows in the midst of rhetoric that systematically maintained that they were within, and had
so maintained for a long time. On the other hand,
recognition of the real historical role of the *campesinos*, in the past, present and, above all, in
the future has been a conquest of enormous impor-

tance, derived to a great extent from the action of
campesinos themselves that also had to break deeply
rooted theoretical and political prejudices. Finally, there is the growing conviction that all authentic determination to get away from the logic of
multinational agribusiness and its national partners
found within the nation -to its disgrace- has inevitably to go through the *campesinos* themselves, who
at present constitute the only force capable of
opposing it efficiently.

Step by step, with all the trials, errors and
characteristic setbacks of a process of this nature, old alliances are reconstructed, the irre-
verent characteristics of others are recognized,
the solidarity of those that found themselves
dispersed, isolated and confronted is becoming
stronger, and the foundations for the joint construction of a new social project are being laid.

Some facts remain as permanent accusation.
Mexico is the 12th country in the world in population and 13th in territory. It is found among
the first twenty countries -that is, in relation
to area and population- in terms of electric power
generation, gross national product, kilometers of
roads and highways, licensing of vehicles, tele-
phones, mining, etc. But there are certain aspects
in which the relation is out of proportion. bringing out the imbalance: it is fifth in oil reserves
and 15th in the production of food; at the same
time, it falls below 60th place in per capita
production, physicians or hospital beds per inha-
bitant, life expectancy at birth and food per
capita. Thus, in the country that occupies the
ninth place among the producers of food in the
world, half the population suffers from serious
levels of malnutrition: it is underfed. *Campesinos*
add to their serious calorie and protein deficit
a high degree of illiteracy and a mean school level
of only 1.3 years (one tenth of the U.S. mean).
Year after year, a million of them have to leave
the country and expose themselves to all kinds of
humiliations in order to earn a living. This is the
result of the intolerable agrarian delay that runs
parallel to the abusive explosion of urban development -which is also being overwhelmed in the contradictions of its hypertrophiated cities. Mexico

needs to take another road; and it has what it takes
to be able to do this: both people and resources.

The new option is not a comfortable one, nor
is it secure, perhaps not even probable. (The obstacles posed by the domination structure are infi-
nite; and to dismantle them is a task as subtle and
delicate -even when this is done with violence- as
the dismantling of an explosive device.) But what
looks like a serious uncertainty for the immediate
future, what seems to be an excessively optimistic
and utopian enterprise -as though it were the result of excited enthusiasm rather than of the
scientific foresight on which it is based- can count
on the certainty of the future. It was the same
certainty that was shown on December 4, 1914, when
Francisco Villa and Emiliano Zapata allied the Northern Division with the Southern Liberation Army.
The certainty that made them say:

> Zapata: *"Los campesinos le tienen mucho amor*
> *a la tierra. Todavía no lo creen cuan-*
> *do se les dice: 'esta tierra es tuya',*
> *creen que es un sueño..."* *
>
> Villa: *"Ya verán cómo el pueblo es el que*
> *manda y el que va a ver quiénes son*
> *sus amigos..."* **

---

* *Campesinos* have much love for the land. They
still don't believe it when you tell them:
'this land is yours,' they think it is a
dream..."

** "Now you will see how people are in command and
they will find out who their friends are..."

APPENDIX 1

THE RECENT EVOLUTION:
THE MEXICAN FOOD SYSTEM

On March 18, 1980 when commemorating the Mexican oil expropriation, the President of the country made the announcement of the decision to postpone Mexico's incorporation to the GATT (a matter that had been negotiated and examined publicly for almost two years), and to implement the Mexican Food System (SAM).

The relationship between these two decisions is much deeper than the circumstance of their simultaneous release. Both correspond to the effort of furthering an autonomous project of development and of taking again a historical initiative before the process of transnationalization of the economies to which the country is exposed.

The SAM gave place to an intense debate in the whole country. It has now become imperative to refer to it when examining the problems of rural development in Mexico. The announcement was made when the originals for the Spanish version of this book were already in print, and therefore it was not possible to include its analysis. For the English edition we thought it useful to add such an appendix with an analysis of the SAM from the political and ideological standpoint since we believe that here is where its genesis and perspectives lie. After a brief description of its explicit contents and of the frame of circumstances where it was produced, reference is made to some theoretical and ideological problems involved in this debate. These reflections are used as the frame of reference to give shape to a hypothesis on the basic meaning of the SAM seen under the light of the experience of its two years' existence.

The announcement of the SAM was made when it
was a well-founded proposal, although not a clear
and specific program of action. Two years have elaps-
ed since then. It is premature to make an evaluation,
especially if we take into account the scope of the
initiative. Further, account should be taken that
this was launched when the present administration was
half way through its mandate. Frameworks and structures were already configurated. In many cases, the
realization of the SAM meant merely changing the
name of programs that were being implemented, without making the necessary transformations and adap-
tations. All this may contribute to explain the
ambivalent reactions that the SAM elicited, to which
we will refer in these pages.

THE STRATEGY

The strategy announced and implemented on March, 1980
is not the result of improvisation. We discard the
possibility of it being politically, technically or
administratively so. It was not devised within the
walls of an advisory office. It was not made by the
group created around it which a conceited critic
considered as equivalent to a Ministry of State,
though it never was of more than 200 people. With
this we are not depriving the work of this specific
group of its merit. We can and we must recognize the
talent, the capacity and the passion they had towards
their job, being careful, though, of not turning them
into the rooster of Chantecler (that thought the sun
rose because of its crow).

The depletion of a development model and the implementation of a new strategy are not done overnight,
as if they were an acrobat's somersault. March, 1980
was arrived at after a long series of successes and
failures, advances and frustrations, experiences of
all sorts. In fact, the rural development model began to be considered as depeleted since the beginning of the seventies, and in 1965 analysts began
stressing the need to replace it with another. For
fifteen years, and especially during the last ten,
several attempts were made to set it aside and explore other routes. The strategic issue of self-
sufficiency, for example, was debated and solved, in
terms of a definition, as early as 1972, when top

priority was given to the National Agricultural and Animal Husbandry Program. Speaking of concrete actions there is no aspect or dimension of the new strategy that has not been proposed or attempted before, though in a different scale, dimension or context.

In this sense, the agricultural and cattle raising policy applied from 1977 to 1979 is <u>also</u> an antecedent of the SAM, although in many aspects it might seem as its antagonist. During that time, the traits and elements of the previous model were depleted to the extreme, but others were essayed or continued to be developed or incorporated to the new strategy. This is definitely among other reasons because of its <u>final</u> nature- the one which gives meaning to public action in matters of agricultural and cattle raising issues of the 1976-1982 administration.

In the public debate over these subjects, other ingredients of public action have deserved as much or more attention than the SAM. In some cases, such as the Law on Agricultural and Cattle Raising Development, it has been proposed that these are policy elements that are not only different from but also opposed to the SAM or they are assimilated to one single project, and traits of the Law are used to disqualify the SAM and give it a meaning different from the one it explicitly has. It is pointless to continue with a byzantine discussion over these issues. As a <u>factual</u> reality, besides real or attributed intentions, the SAM has occupied the central focus of public action during this period. Regardless of the meaning or importance of the Law, for example, its practical implications are to date quite limited, especially if compared with those of the SAM. Nevertheless it is clear that it might have very important effects if instead of ellaborating on the strategy proposed by the latter, another route were attempted. Such a possibility as we will discuss later, is believed to be poorly viable.

For these reasons, the analysis is concentrated on the Mexican Food System as the main expression of the agricultural and cattle raising policy of the past two years.

The SAM is a strategic proposal of development, made by the President of the Republic (Head of Government and of the State) with implications in the following fundamental spheres:

a) Orientation of production

It implies that the logic of social needs should prevail over that of national and transnational capital when configurating the patterns of production and consumption. In order to "arrive at food sufficiency, albeit minimal, for all Mexicans" and to reach self-sufficiency in national food production, (1) the SAM proposes to subordinate criteria of profitability under these priorities and to set productive targets on the basis of nutritional requirements (quantitative targets) and regional patterns of production and consumption (qualitative targets), instead of making them depend upon market indicators (effective demand).

b) Social development

The SAM proposes to give second priority to conventional issues (irrigation areas and private entrepreneurs of the countryside), and concentrate on "the impoverished *campesinos* on seasonal lands." (2) Such a shift in the definition of the main actors of productive processes not only presupposes the reallocation of public resources for agricultural and cattle raising development, whose fate and beneficiaries would have to be radically changed, but also the substantive transformation of the structures and forms of social organization of the rural world. "It is not simply a matter of increasing the country's production, but also the income of the *campesinos*." (3) To this end, the proposition is, together with the *campesinos*, assume the productive risks, subsidize technological change and support organizational processes. (4)

---

(1) López Portillo, José. "Una alimentación suficiente, objetivo prioritario," in A dar la batalla a la alimentación, México, CNC, August, 1980, pp. 1 and 2.
(2) Office of Advisors to the President of the Republic, Sistema Alimentario Mexicano, primer planteamiento de metas de consumo y estrategia de producción de alimentos básicos, México, Presidencia de la República, March 1980, p. 21.
(3) López Portillo, J. OP. CIT. p. 1
(4) Office of . . . OP. CIT. p. 22.

c) Administrative Action of the State

The SAM proposes to alter current patterns of
official action in the countryside, which are based
on sectorial (by field of activity) and institutional criteria (by agency responsible), since it defines
itself as "a special strategy within the Overall Plan
for Development: it is not a plan in addition to
others, but a procedure that gives sequence to actions so as to coordinate them." (5) It implies the
overall commitment on the part of the State, which is
not based on specific agencies nor on certain civil
servants, but rather on the whole of public administration and, in the last analysis, on the Head of the
Executive Power.

This is the SAM: a policy and political proposal
for the Mexican State. Because of its initial <u>form</u>
(of technical document and political discourse) some
have chosen to see it as a cabinet phathom or a mere
rhetoric and demagogical exercise. Such apprecia-
tions are both rhetorical and demagogical, not the
SAM though, when considering its genesis, its substantive contents and its scope instead of its mere
appearance.

First, let us consider its gestation. Immediately it might appear as an initiative of the Executive
Power, but it is not a happening nor an <u>originative</u>
gesture. The "initiative" is in reality the specific
form of a response to the whole of processes expressed in the rural crisis for many years already.
It is only possible to explain and understand this
specific form within the context of its social and
political gestation, directly linked with *campesino*
mobilization.

In a very concrete sense, the SAM is an exploit
of public awareness that should be recognized as
such, bluntly. Accept the meaning and significance of
the concrete material force of *campesinos*, translate
it into programs, establish its relationship with
the current needs of the country and with internal
and external contradictions, and shape the elements
of a rural strategy associated with the construction
of the national project, these are the tasks that
have been undertaken by the most enlightened and
advanced groups of the country for years, and which

(5) López Portillo, J., OP. CIT. p. 1

find, in this scheme, one of their most wholesome
expressions.

Nevertheless, before this newborn baby that has
not yet found its political context -popular mobi-
lization- to give full reality to its substance, a
destructive process was triggered:

-On the one hand, the domination structures
formally jeopardized by the SAM, instead of making an
open attack or critique, they used the opposite tac-
tics: taking over the scheme as if it were their own
to deprive it of its specific contents. In concrete
terms, the intention was to sterilize it: turn it
into a simple administrative entelechy... a bureaucratic or budget adjustment... a move to update or
adapt the effort undertaken... another turn of the
screw of a model that was to remain untouched. They
did so and they continue to do so... day after day...
those who believe that the world is an object that
one is to manipulate; those who understand Public
Power as the only protagonist in society; those who
understand power, from the perspective of power, as
an exercise of exclusion; those who incessantly try
to change things to make everything remain the same.

- On the other hand, "critical" formulations
have tended to do the same thing. These have been
the mechanical counterpart of the domination discourse based on ancient dogmatic attitudes. Mani-
chaean simplification or the well-known maximalism
blocked the perception of the genesis and contents
of the SAM. Abstract reductionism led to negate
campesino involvement in the conditions that determined the SAM (as the political answer of the State
before social mobilization), and this not only prevented the critical examination of the proposal itself, but it was timely adjusted to the attempts of
exclusion made daily against *campesinos*, both in
theory and in practice, in academia and in politics.

Hence the importance of giving shape to organic
answers, authentically stemming from the people,
enabling them to take in their hands a process which
is really their own. It is imperative to have a clear
conscience of the enormous difficulties of truly
implementing a proposal of this nature: realize that
it is a profound change, a pathway that intends to
make a radical shift in the patterns followed up to
now, an unprecedented possibility in this dimension,
albeit significantly based on empirical experience.

For critical examination and political action to
occur, all this requires, first and foremost, to
seriously face the problem of the characterization
of *campesinos* -which still seems to be surrounded by
dogma and prejudice.

Another dimension of the strategy defined by the
SAM which one must keep in mind to fully grasp its
meaning is the extreme situation reached by the rural
crisis in 1979: agriculture was an insurmountable
obstacle for capital's growth and for a new stage of
accumulation to take place.

It is imperative to keep in mind the qualitative
and quantitative role than Mexican agriculture plays
in capital formation, both nationally and interna-
tionally. Besides the contributions that are ordina-
rily recognized such as food, raw materias and
foreign exchange, agriculture provided the conditions for the reproduction of labor force, which are,
concretely, the ones that were finally disarticulated
by the hindmost effort to continue with the realization of the post-war model. It was no longer viable
to keep low salaries in the industrial sector on the
basis of agriculture, because of the deterioration
of production. Above all: the reproduction of *campesino* labor force, on the broad seasonal agricultural
base, could no longer take place. The fact that for
the first time the agricultural and cattle raising
trade balance was adverse or that a dangerous dependence from abroad was created is not as burden-
some as this internal contradiction whose lack of
solution may have the gravest of consequences on the
overall development of the Mexican society, even
within its own productive lines and parameters. This
is, perhaps, what is now clear to the most modern
fraction of the constellation of social forces which
constitute the Mexican State. And it could be the
key to understand the SAM.

RESULTS

It would be meaningless and superficial to evaluate
a strategy for rural development that is only a
couple of agricultural cycles old. The analysis of
what has happened in such a short period can only be
taken as a hypothesis of the probable potentialities
of the attempt. It could be useful to show the extent in which it really represents a change with respect to previous trends and, especially, with res-

pect to the model of the last four decades. Besides,
it can be used to study the validity and viability
of the undertaking: find out if truly a new road towards development is open, define to what extent is
it necessary and suitable to continue walking along
it, reaching further in that same direction, or if
it is necessary to change the orientation.

a) Shift or recovery?

The advance of production in 1980 and 1981 is
well-known. In 1981 it was really spectacular. The
overall rate, which by far exceeds that of population growth, does not reflect sufficiently the magnitude of this figure. Other indicators are more
efficient for this purpose. Corn production remained
within the range of 8 to 10 million tons between
1964 and 1977. In 1981 it was 15 million: a leap of
over 50% with respect to the average of the very
long previous period. The overall effort of production, as expressed in the ten main crops, was within the range of 15 to 18 million tons from 1966 to
1976. It reached 29 million -almost double- in 1981.

These data, however, are not indicative of a
shift. We could be dealing here with a recovery of
the dynamism that the fourty year old model had
during its first twenty years of life. It is worth
suspecting, for example, that the 1978 increase
(when corn production reached 12 million tons and
the ten main crops, 23) was an advance with these
characteristics.

In order to put forth the hypothesis of a shift,
it is necessary to consider the source and meaning of
production's dynamism. To what extent were the basic
patterns of the model changed?

Before making such an analysis, it would be
worth discarding the weather as the main factor to
account for the recent evolution. There was good
rain in 1981. It was both abundant and timely, and
this had a positive effect on productive results.
Nevertheless, it is not possible to attribute such a
change in the range of total production volume to
the weather only. Like everywhere else, the weather
determines fluctuations of production within a certain range, not beyond it. Every ten years we will
have about three like 1981, and an equal number as

1979. Far from contributing to uncertainty, weather changes correspond to a forecast of high probability regarding annual levels of production, within the range determined by the State and the structure of the agricultural and cattle raising situation. In 1976, when we had a year almost as good as 1981, from the standpoint of the weather, total production decreased and crops were kept within the historical ranges of the previous period. The agricultural disaster of 1979 was foreseeable and foreseen. We reject, then, the versions that attributed it to natural calamities, since it seemed the inevitable result of a line of policy and strategy that after decades of being in force, had sunken us in an agricultural crisis that reached its abyss. Today we must equally reject all versions that, on the other extreme, proclaim the superiority of the weather to account for what happened.

Having discarded the weather, the hypothesis of a shift must be centered on the analysis of the type of crops, agriculture and producers that correspond to the dynamism observed. The post-war model was associated with commercial crops, technicalized agriculture subject to the logic of profits, market indicators (predominantly those of the international market) and with private commercial producers. It would have been a shift if we were dealing with basic products of the sort of agriculture with little technology and subject to the logic of *campesino* producers, social needs and priorities.

There is no doubt as to the general reorientation of production. The increasing food deficit of the seventies, which generated the continued increase of imports (that accounted for one fourth of national basic consumption), was not only due to the stagnation of production. This was clearly associated with the persistent insertion of our economy into transnational logic. In spite of this stagnation, Mexico continued to be one of the first food producers in the world. The problem was that the productive effort was concentrated on the satisfaction of external demands and those of select strata of the population.

The transnationalization of Mexican agriculture means her specialization as a <u>purchaser of cereals</u>

-with low production of basic foodstuffs- and as
producer-exporter of meat, fruits and vegetables
(besides the production and consumption of non-
foodstuffs). These trends correspond, on the one
hand, to the phenomenon of cattle encroachment in
the country (a factor of use of land) and, on the
other, to the dynamism of fruits' and vegetables'
export cultivation at high prices (a factor of
absorbption of productive resources).

According to these trends, the crisis of the
past two decades did not affect all products equally.
In aggregate figures, cattle production maintained
moderate and high rates while agriculture stagnated
or decreased. In a product by product analysis,
there is a group that kept very high rates of growth
-well above those of the population- since 1960. It
is made up of "three animal-intensive items
(poultry breeding and pastures, hogs) which take up
most of the national production of balanced foods,
of which two inputs (sorghum and safflower, in the
form of paste) and tomato, are products with a strong
tendency towards exports." The products which showed
rates lower than those of the population are "exclusively agricultural and include basic foodstuffs for
domestic consumption, such as corn, beans, rice, and
to a certain extent, sugar." (6)

These trends had double impact: cattle proli-
ferated and substracted land from basic agricultural
production, and the dynamics of fruits and vegetables
substracted resources. Cattle activities directly or
indirectly used half of the area destined to agricultural and cattle raising production. As far as
production of fruits and vegetables is concerned,
although the area was always on the small side,
this was not the case with resources absorbed,
(high quality irrigation land, inputs, credits, subsidies, equipment, etc.) which constantly increased.

Figures por 1981 point towards a reversion of
these processes: first, the qualitative leap in
production of crops for domestic consumption which
were in a process of frank deterioration; second,

(6) Gonzalo Rodríguez, "Tendencias de la producción
agropecuaria en las dos últimas décadas," in Economía Mexicana, CIDE, No. 2, 1980, p. 68.

the loss of dynamism in "transnationalized" sectors. Since the former issue is quite evident, we shall ellaborate on the latter.

Of course, it is impossible to give figures to show that the process of cattle encroachment of the country has stopped; this process cannot change from one year to the next. Nevertheless, there are some clues of interest. The phenomenon involved, among other things, the extensive expansion of cattle on agricultural land. Its reversion would not necessarily imply the involution of cattle production, though it could mean its "reconcentration:" the recovery of agricultural land devoted to cattle raising and its use for intensive production; this would include the utilization of non-agricultural resources to increase productivity. And this is exactly what seems to be happening.

In States like Chiapas -with a high agricultural potential- during the past years the area devoted to basic crops stagnated and production showed very little dynamism, while the one devoted to cattle more than doubled, as well as the number of heads. There are no data on what happened in this aspect during the past two years, but the great increase of basic production recorded recently in these States may be attributed to the recovery of agricultural land previously used for extensive cattle production, since there was no significant widening of the agricultural frontier in these, and the increase in yields was insufficient to account for production improvement.

In predominantly cattle-producing States, especially in the North of the country, the high consumption of balanced foods with mostly chemical inputs and without a corresponding production increase, allows us to suspect of the direct or indirect use of areas previously controlled by cattle for agricultural purposes.

Another element which points towards the same direction is the clear loss of dynamism shown by the production of poultry and pasture (as well as egg production), an item which was among those of highest growth during the previous decade and which, together with that of hogs (which is also undergoing difficulties), consumed most of the balanced foods with a predominantly agricultural composition.

All the above, and many other elements (such as the decrease in cattle and beef exports, with less dynamism in the export production of fruits and vegetables, etc.), seem to support the hypothesis of the shift in issues related to the general orientation of production by type of crops.

The second element of the shift, type of agriculture, is associated with the third, type of producers. The post-war model implied being in the hands of private commercial producers, and this, among other things, required the allocation of huge public resources in order to achieve or to keep their high technicalization. It was an enclave operation. We would be dealing with a shift if public resources for agricultural and cattle raising development were concentrated with the *campesinos* in terms of the logic of social needs and priorities, so as to promote technological change in the wide front of the seasonal agriculture base.

There is no information to allow us to define with accuracy the various contributions to the productive advancement of 1981. However, there are sufficient elements of information to confirm that there was great dynamism in *campesino* production by reverting the previous trends in a radical manner, although this does not necessarily imply that private commercial production stagnated.

First, basic crops whose production was strongly increased are of a "*campesino* nature:" they are produced mainly by seasonal *campesinos*. This traditional bias was maintained during the advance. Although no doubt, private commercial producers also contributed to the increase, there is clear evidence that it is fundamentally attributable to the contribution of *campesinos* to basic items.

Second, the significant increase in rural employment, of which there is abundant empirical evidence (the lack of unskilled labor in the construction industry is not the least important of these) is clearly due to the expansion of *campesino* production. On the one hand, private commercial production absorbs large volumes of labor and, in general, it showed very little dynamism. On the other hand, if the increase in basic production had been basically due to private commercial production, inevitably

there would have been a fall in rural employment
due to the conditions on which private entrepreneurs
produce these crops.

Third, the large amounts of public resources
devoted to support basic production were mostly destined to seasonal *campesinos*. Some elements of the
"package" were evidently utilized by private commercial producers, either because of their general and
standard nature (such as guarantee prices) or because their allocation was "diverted" (credit). However, regardless of the biases in the application of
resources which occured in practice and which one
cannot estimate, several objective elements confirm
the existence of a shift in their fate: items that
were traditionally destined to support private commercial agriculture and that were only utilized by
it, were reduced; huge resources were channeled to
items that are exclusive of *campesino* producers;
application was concentrated in predominantly *campesino* areas, etc.

No doubt, academic juggling will be made to
prove otherwise. For example, it will be seen that
the highest <u>percentual</u> increases in corn production
were recorded in areas where private commercial producers prevail over *campesinos*, while in some of the
"*campesino* States" increases were not as high and
there were even decreases. Such a reflection does not
consider the various departing points, nor the probability of *campesino* expansion to those "commercial
States" which could account for the decline in their
physical yields observed in 1981, rather than the
utilization of marginal land by private commercial
producers.

Although available information makes us take
any evaluation with reservations, we believe that
what we have stated so far is sufficient to seriously support the hypothesis that there was a significant shift in basic patterns of agricultural and
cattle raising production which allowed for the
abandonment of the model of the past four decades to
<u>start</u> an effort oriented in another direction.

b) <u>Is it necessary to keep the new direction?</u>

The question is especially relevant at this
moment in time, where there are more than enough

symptoms to prove that a restoring effort is being
undertaken. Many voices have joined the celebration
of results in 1981 to prevent the continuation and
intensification of the effort that rendered them
possible. Few openly doubt about the target of self-
sufficiency: public consciousness prevents it. More
often than not it is sustained that we have almost
reached it, that therefore it is not necessary to
stress it and that we must insist again in comparative advantages. Criticism against orientations
that are supposedly alien to market indicators a-
bound, and the new orientation is attacked with the
well-known arguments of economic profitability in
production.

Hence, it is worth stressing that to maintain
the same route is not only necessary, but imperative.

From the standpoint of Mexico's relations with
other countries, food production self-sufficiency
has clearly become the objective condition for national independence and for any attempt to carry out
an autonomous project of development. Food will
continue to be a political instrument of domination;
its price will increase, there will be critical scar-
cities -particularly when the effects of the dynamics
of resource conservation in U.S. production become
more accentuated- the weakness of the oil market and
of other traditional Mexican export markets will
continue to impose severe restrictions on economic
affairs with other countries. These are, together
with many other, elements of prevision that require
to concentrate the maximum effort on targets of
self-sufficiency, knowing that it is the only way
possible to reach it and to maintain it.

Internally, the first item in the agenda of
change is to correct unequalities. In reaching this
objective which has the most diverse implications on
the overall development of the Mexican society, there
is no individual factor of any kind that could be
compared to the increase of campesino income. Although it is possible to quantify the fact, there
are sufficient empirical and analytical indicators
to bluntly state that the new strategy did have a
significant impact on this. Besides the data and
phenomena which certify the increase in rural employment (main source of increase of campesino income...

and the healthiest), other data point towards the same direction.

- It appears that temporary or permanent migration outside *campesino* fields has lost dynamism, and there have even been trends of return.

- The number and magnitude of *campesino* "emergency mobilizations" (which increased until the end of 1979 and the beginning of 1980, and were clearly responses to the deterioration of production and living conditions) decreased, as well as the number of repressive actions reported by the daily press.

- A study of income distribution showed a 20 to 60 points decrease in Gini's coefficient applicable to the rural population, which would be indicative of a surprising improvement in income equalization.

- There are many indicators of increase in effective demand for basic products in areas that are predominantly *campesino*, etc.

c) <u>Is it viable to keep the same direction</u>?

Arguments presented on the first part of this Appendix lead us to affirm that the viability of the undertaking depends basically on the maintenance and strengthening of the political co-relation of forces that made the shift possible, as well as the Mexican State's capacity to respond to inside and outside pressures which militate against it and against social and national interests. It is not possible to ellaborate here further on the analysis, which documents its viability, but let me, at least, express one conclusion: this is the only way to carry out an autonomous project of democratic construction in accordance with Constitutional objectives.

With the assumption of the political viability of the attempt -based on the strengthening of *campesino* organizations and their alliances with other groups of workers- it is necessary to examine its economic viability.

On this regard, one must keep in mind that from this year on there will be restrictions on public finance which in practice will prevent -beyond any political will of support to the *campesinos*- the

maintenance of the pace of increase in public resources' allocation for agricultural and cattle
raising production recorded in 1981, and will even
tend (probably in 1982) to reduce the absolute
amount in real terms. Very likely, the net transfer
of resources will be decreased, particularly the
amount of subsidies to the countryside (as well as
to the rest of the economy).

Such a perspective -which seems inevitable- is
a factor in favor of furthering the strategy initiated, not against it, and this for several reasons.

Carrying the strategy further, on its own explicit terms, presupposes entrusting the task increasingly to producers themselves and to respect
their organizations, supporting them directly so
that they may advance in technological changes and
modify the economic relations they have with other
agents, which constitute, at present, the main obstacle for their development. It might be that for
the strategy to be initiated, a massive injection
of resources was needed following more or less conventional procedures and through the existing institutional channels. In order to advance further, however, it is imperative to alter these patterns.
Public action will only be more vigorous and efficient on this regard if it is quantitatively reduced and qualitatively changed. There must be more
of a normative and regulatory intervention, more
resources of productive support, and less direct
operation by State apparatuses, less bureaucratic
control, less overall subsidies. It is necessary, in
particular, to combat against the tendency seen in
certain spaces of the new strategy towards turning
it into an instrument of public control of production and producers, and heading towards the bureaucratization of society.

Ellaborating on the strategy means, first and
foremost, to liberate the autonomous energy of producers -sample of which was given in 1981 in spite of
the restrictions they faced- by adjusting public
action to needs and conditions, instead of looking
for their transformation from the top and from the
outside, under the compulsion of economic and political power. To support producers on the basis of
respect towards their organizations is much more
effective and less costly in terms of public re-

sources, than to try to impose upon them a form of organization or of productive behavior that is alien to them, regardless of how good it might seem in writing or through experience. Obviously, the effort here should be of support and respect towards their development, in order for them to have access to higher forms or organization and functioning, not to remain the way they are. But such an access should be decided by them and should be made according to their own patterns, not imposed against their realities as the project of a "higher" instance. And this is less costly.

To abandon the strategy and return to any of the previous versions, or to attempt its continuation without changing its operating mechanisms in the sense indicated above -i.e. without ellaborating on it nor carrying it further in its same direction- would account for such a pressure on public finance that it would be impossible to attempt such possibilities. In some cases, the viability of application would depend of an increase in "welfare expenses" or those of "control" that the foreseeable allocation of public resources could not pay for. In others, the magnitude of investments and current expenses of the public sector that should be channeled would also reach insustainable levels.

In any case, both economically and politically, ellaborating on the strategy undertaken seems the most viable possibility ahead of us.

The SAM is, definitively, a firm and clear demonstration of Mexico's State and society capacity to respond to a rural crisis that is only comparable to that of the turn of the century, because of its depth.

It is a response which reflects on today's priorities the *campesino* background and historical reality, transforming it into a modern productive dynamics.

The core of the sort of changes we need today is to correct the structure of unequality that characterizes Mexico's society. The strategy which we associate with the name of the SAM may be the main pillar of support for an undertaking of this nature.

One of the main challenges we face in view of
the processes of inflation and devaluation is the
increase in labor productivity which, in order to
have the desired effect, must be achieved on a wide
productive front. If according to conventional
patterns, it bases itself on high technology enclaves, its results will be defeating the purpose.
Along this line of advance, the strategy set in motion with the SAM uncovered the capacity of the social base to absorb technological changes which increase labor productivity, and which therefore
fulfill their function and have their effect on the
whole of economy and society.

Unreserved, the 1981 harvest has to be credit-
ed to the account of the SAM. It is not a mere productive result. It contradicts the trends of what we
have called the agricultural or rural crisis. It implies a substantial increase in rural employment and
in *campesino* income. It definitely alleviates the
balance of payments. It relieves ports and transport
facilities. It lessens dependence from abroad. There
is no measure or individual value factor equivalent
to it for the correction of inequalities, the fight
against inflation and the revaluing of our productive apparatus.

There are more than enough grains of salt. As
many as triumphant attitudes. Because of its nature and scope, the SAM is not achieved nor depleted
in a couple of years. It has only set itself in motion. It weaknesses and inefficiencies, the devia-
tions and obstacles that it has undoubtedly had are
the reflection of the short-term limitations and
obstacles placed by the structures it affects along
its path. The remedy is to ellaborate on the strategy,
not to change the route. Present restrictions may
have positive consequences: a SAM with less resources
but more adequately distributed, an institutional
apparatus more interested in supporting than in
making or controlling, an operational system based
on the autonomous energy of producers rather than on
bureaucratic procedures... in the coming years it
may be a more efficient and profound strategy.

The SAM proposed to orient productive efforts
towards the attainment of national self-sufficiency
in food production. But this is not, we insist,
what makes its difference and constitutes its merit,

though undoubtedly its success is that it clearly and adequately reflects such a significant policy orientation. The SAM's nature is its manifest commitment with the *campesinos*, to which it gives the leading role in the realization of the task. Such a commitment is an enormous and complex task which requires, among many other things, the ability to change power in order for the transformation of productive and social reality to become the central theme for the democratic construction of our society.

APPENDIX 2

DATA ON THE MEXICAN COUNTRYSIDE

TABLE I
POPULATIONS OF MEXICO, 1521-1978

YEAR	INHABITANTS	YEAR	INHABITANTS
1521	9 120 000	1980	9 577 279
1793	4 483 680	1892	11 502 583
1803	5 764 731	1900	13 607 259
1810	6 122 354	1910	15 160 369
1820	6 204 000	1920	14 334 780
1830	7 996 000	1930	16 552 722
1842	7 016 300	1940	19 653 552
1852	7 661 919	1950	25 791 017
1861	8 212 579	1960	34 923 129

Source: *Anuario Estadístico de los Estados Unidos Mexicano*
1975-1976, S.P.P., 1979; Preliminary figures of tʰ
Population Census, 1980. S.P.P.

ABLE 2

OMPOSITION OF THE MEXICAN POPULATION
Total Population Percentages)

EAR	TOTAL POPULATION	MEN %	WOMEN %	ECONOMICALLY ACTIVE POPULATION %	ECONOMICALLY INACTIVE POPULATION %	RURAL POPULATION %	URBAN POPULATION %
930	16 552 722	49.0	51.0	31.2	68.8	66.5	33.5
940	19 653 552	49.3	50.7	29.8	70.2	64.9	35.1
950	25 791 017	49.2	50.8	32.3	33.1	57.4	42.6
960	34 923 129	49.8	50.2	32.4	41.3	49.3	50.7
970	48 225 238	49.9	50.1	26.8	33.4	37.9	62.1
980	67 383 000	49.4	50.6	35.1	28.2	--	--

ource: General Population Censuses, D.G.E., S.I.C.
        Preliminary figures of the Population Census, 1980. S.P.P.

TABLE 3

AVERAGE FAMILY INCOME: BY SOURCE AND LEVEL OF INCOME, 1975
(pesos per month)

MONTHLY FAMILY INCOME	NUMBER OF FAMILIES	PERCENTAGE OF FAMILIES	AVERAGE FAMILY INCOME	WAGES AND SALARIES a/	FROM PRIVATE NON-AGRICULTURAL ENTERPRISES
Total	10 208 925	100.0	3 260.37	2 072.83	510.68
0	16 547	0.2	*	*	*
1 - 500	1 533 407	15.0	215.98	58.01	33.55
501 - 700	578 756	5.7	606.03	248.11	79.09
701 - 950	794 472	7.8	828.68	388.50	120.43
951 - 1250	889 555	8.7	1 099.01	611.38	221.84
1251 - 1700	918 944	9.0	1 479.17	996.30	210.88
1701 - 2200	1 063 504	10.4	1 967.04	1 412.91	255.84
2201 - 3000	1 249 808	12.2	2 610.93	1 902.71	354.56
3001 - 4000	865 596	8.5	3 519.67	2 564.56	469.92
4001 - 5200	695 026	6.8	4 584.26	3 503.94	629.71
5201 - 7000	625 835	6.1	6 024.41	4 777.12	551.61
7001 - 9200	345 941	3.4	7 987.63	6 206.31	1 199.20
9201 - 12250	282 537	2.8	10 531.41	6 942.30	1 920.21
12251 and over	348 997	3.4	24 385.46	10 304.67	5 063.80

* Insufficient sample information to estimate average.

a) The reduced participation of wages and salaries in low-level family income
   can be explained by the fact that a greater number of family heads work for
   themselves and do not have a fixed salary in the business or enterprise; the
   income of these families are computed as income from private enterprise. Most
   of them are small merchants, retail salesman, small farmers, or in small
   service concerns.

Source: *La Población de México, su ocupación y sus Niveles de Bienestar,*
   S.P.P., 1979.

I N C O M E   S O U R C E

FROM AGRICULTURAL AND CATTLE ENTERPRISES	FROM OPERATIONS IN FICED AND ROTATING CAPITAL	FROM OPERATIONS IN CAPITAL GOODS	FROM TRANSFER PAYMENTS	CONTINGENCIES
280.95	183.46	11.89	170.36	30.21
*	*	*	*	*
99.26	1.28	0.67	23.22	0.01
227.38	2.58	0.0	48.47	0.41
264.68	4.66	0.0	50.02	0.41
174.89	6.48	2.38	81.91	0.16
161.30	6.00	0.05	103.43	1.24
159.60	19.75	2.59	115.93	0.44
214.51	15.80	3.76	117.48	2.12
325.72	21.85	1.35	131.93	4.36
369.68	18.29	4.95	149.03	8.68
384.48	49.96	25.65	223.55	12.05
256.15	119.32	38.47	167.12	1.08
347.38	253.11	27.13	1 005.19	36.09
1 908.94	4 693.50	198.07	1 427.83	789.38

TABLE 4

GENERATION OF AGRICULTURAL VALUE BY CROP AND AREA - 1970-1980
(percentages)

Product	Sesame	Alfalfa	Cotton	Rice	Oats	Fodder oats
1/ % of occupied area	1.63	1.24	2.55	1.04	0.39	0.69
2/ % share in value	0.95	3.66	6.75	1.34	0.17	0.62

Product	Peas	Dry hot pepper	Green hot pepper	Strawberries	Beans	Chickpeas
1/ % of occupied area	0.11	0.17	0.31	0.04	10.40	0.93
2/ % share in value	0.15	0.62	1.38	0.42	5.01	0.37

Product	Fodder corn	Watermelons	Sorghum	Fodder sorghum	Soybean	Tobacco
1/ % of occupied area	0.13	0.17	7.96	0.12	1.58	0.28
2/ % share in value	0.27	0.53	7.02	0.21	1.81	0.95

Product	Palm kernel	Peaches	Henequen	Lime	Mango	Apples
1/ % of occupied area	0.06	0.16	1.14	0.02	0.24	0.22
2/ % share in value	0.04	0.74	0.55	0.06	1.22	0.93

1/   Area in hectares
2/   Value in thousands of pesos

Source: *Dirección General de Economía Agrícola; Serie estadística*, SARH.

Peanuts	Safflower	Barley	Fodder barley	Onions	
0.36	1.92	1.68	0.07	0.15	
0.34	1.72	0.82	0.06	0.50	
Chickpeas	Broad beans	Tomato	Linseed	Corn	
0.49	0.33	0.42	0.08	45.29	
0.66	0.13	3.90	0.06	21.13	
Wheat	Avocado	Cocoa	Coffee	Plums	
4.71	0.24	0.46	2.42	0.02	
4.78	1.94	0.82	5.57	0.06	
Oranges	Banana	Grapes	Melon	Potatoes	Pineapple
1.03	0.45	0.18	0.12	0.38	0.07
1.67	1.53	0.98	0.51	1.63	0.42

262   The Struggle for Rural Mexico

TABLE 5

CHARACTERISTICS AND USE OF THE SOIL IN MEXICO, 1970.
(In percentages)

REGION	Agricultural total Crops			Agri-cultural Total
	Seasonal use land	Irrigated	Perennial	
Arid and Semiarid	15.2	6.3	2.0	3.5 23.5
Temperate	19.0	3.9	2.5	3.7 25.9
Dry Tropical	13.7	3.9	3.0	3.0 20.6
Humid Tropical	13.5	0.6	15.8	4.4 29.9
Total	61.4	14.7	23.3	14.6 100

* Refered to forest, agriculture and cattle sectors.

Source: *Programa de Desarrollo Agropecuario y Forestal*,
   Consejo Nacional de Ciencia y Tecnología, México, 1979.

Total economic area *

Pasture	Forests	Productive Uncultivated Land	Bound to be Exploited
34.5	8.7	2.7	1.4
4.2	3.6	0.1	0.2
6.0	5.6	0.9	1.2
3.2	10.7	0.3	0.9
47.9	28.6	4.0	3.7

TABLE 6

LIVESTOCK
Species relative share
(Percentages)

YEAR	BOVINE	EQUINE	PORCINE	OVINE	CAPRINE	ASININE	MULES	NUMBER OF HEADS (In Thousands)
1965	39.1	9.0	16.5	12.5	13.8	5.3	3.5	58165357
1966	38.8	9.1	16.4	12.2	13.6	4.8	4.9	60440725
1967	38.9	9.1	16.4	11.8	13.5	5.1	4.9	61133583
1968	38.6	9.2	16.1	12.5	13.0	5.2	5.0	61585117
1969	37.3	9.2	16.7	12.3	14.0	5.2	5.0	62323598
1970	39.1	9.1	16.1	12.0	13.5	5.0	4.9	65195448
1971	39.5	9.0	16.1	11.9	13.4	5.0	4.9	66458250
1972	40.2	9.0	16.0	12.0	12.7	4.9	4.8	67196003
1973	40.0	8.9	16.2	11.9	13.2	4.7	4.8	68656178
1974	39.1	9.6	16.4	11.8	12.9	4.9	4.9	66101638
1975	40.5	9.2	16.5	11.8	12.3	4.7	4.7	70000394
1976	41.2	9.1	17.0	11.2	11.9	4.6	4.6	70125945
1977	41.4	9.1	17.3	11.1	11.6	4.6	4.5	70523280

Source: *Manual de Estadísticas Básicas (Sector Agropecuario y Forestal)*
          S.P.P., 1978.

TABLE 7

TRADE BALANCE: AGRICULTURE, CATTLE RAISING AND FORESTRY
(selected products) 1950-1980 (thousands of pesos)

Year	Exports	Imports	Balance
1960	4 857 383	889 736	3 967 647
1965	7 921 533	1 024 449	6 897 084
1970	8 033 244	1 562 247	6 470 997
1971	8 003 084	2 120 811	5 882 273
1972	9 653 358	2 656 311	6 997 047
1973	13 210 621	3 902 660	9 307 961
1974	10 403 930	10 452 347	- 48 417
1975	8 550 434	10 117 861	- 1 567 427
1976	15 831 231	5 664 578	10 166 653
1977	27 755 057	11 030 041	16 725 016
1978	33 922 729	13 413 046	20 509 683
1979	37 422 461	19 646 440	17 776 021
1980	33 351 163	45 141 727	-11 790 564

Source: Annual Report. Banco de México.

TABLE 8

LAND REDISTRIBUTION: REAL AND NOMINAL
1916-1980

PRESIDENT	PERIOD	NO. OF ENDOWED EJIDOS	REDISTRIBUTION BY PRESIDENTIAL RESOLUTION IN HECTARES
Venustiano Carranza	1916-1920	326	167 935
Alvaro Obregón	1921-1924	748	1 133 813
Plutarco Elías Calles	1925-1928	1 622	2 972 876
Emilio Portes Gil	1929-1930	1 350	1 707 757
Pascual Ortiz Rubio	1931-1932	540	944 538
Abelardo L. Rodríguez	1933-1934	1 581	790 694
Lázaro Cárdenas	1935-1940	11 334	17 906 430
Manuel Avila Camacho	1941-1946	3 074	5 044 450
Miguel Alemán	1947-1952	2 245	4 844 123
Adolfo Ruiz Cortines	1953-1958	1 745	4 936 665
Adolfo López Mateos	1959-1964	2 375	11 361 270
Gustavo Díaz Ordaz	1965-1970	3 912	14 139 574
Luis Echeverría Alvarez	1971-1976	2 274	16 814 350
José López Portillo	1977-1979	590	1 799 939

Source: Zaragoza, José Luis y Ruth Macías. *El Desarrollo
Agrario y su Marco Jurídico*. Centro Nacional de Investigaciones Agrarias. México 1980.

REAL REDISTRIBUTION IN HECTARES	NO. OF BENEFICIARIES BY PRESIDENTIAL RESOLUTION	NO. OF BENEFICIARIES BY REAL REDISTRIBUTION	ANNUAL AVERAGE OF REAL REDISTRIBUTION IN HECTARES	AVERAGE REAL RE-DISTRIB. BY EJIDATARIO
381 926	46 398	77 203	76 385	4.9
1 730 686	134 798	164 128	432 671	10.5
3 186 294	297 428	302 539	796 573	10.5
2 438 511	171 577	187 269	1 219 255	13.0
1 225 752	64 573	57 994	612 876	21.1
2 060 228	68 556	158 393	1 030 114	13.0
20 145 910	811 157	764 888	3 357 651	26.3
5 970 398	157 836	122 941	995 066	48.5
5 439 528	97 391	108 625	906 588	50.1
5 771 721	231 888	226 292	961 953	25.5
9 308 149	304 498	289 356	1 551 358	32.2
23 055 724	216 695	374 520	3 842 620	61.6
12 017 050	284 870	218 918	2 002 841	54.9
1 468 892	26 667	42 795	489 630	34.3

TABLE 9

COMPOSITION OF SERVICES ON LAND
(in thousands of hectares)

YEAR	HARVESTED AREA	AREA WITH TECHNICAL ASSISTANCE	AREA OF LAND UNDER SEASONAL USE	IRRIGATED AREA	FERTILIZED IRRIGATED AREA	MECHANIZED IRRIGATED AREA
1965	12 751	-	10 772	1 979		1 833
1966	13 680	-	11 793	1 886	1 341	1 091
1967	12 542	-	10 376	2 165	1 168	1 068
1968	12 778	-	10 651	2 127	1 278	1 050
1969	12 110	-	9 926	2 183	1 405	1 142
1970	12 462	-	10 480	1 983	1 320	1 209
1971	12 845	-	10 630	2 215	1 545	1 258
1972	12 132	-	9 984	2 147	1 418	1 234
1973	13 052	1 088	10 891	2 160	1 267	1 427
1974	12 245	1 354	9 877	2 367	1 493	1 602
1975	12 720	3 129	10 358	2 362	1 440	2 026
1976	12 016	2 764	9 516	2 492	1 625	1 900
1977	13 124	3 469	10 339	2 784	1 592	2 041
1978	16 554	5 578	11 376	4 818	1 874	1 793
1979	14 873	6 602	9 971	4 902	-	2 138
1980	16 805	8 743	11 729	5 076	-	2 167
1981	18 173	9 195	12 721	5 452	-	2 934

Source: *Manual de Estadísticas Básicas (Sector Agropecuario y Forestal)*
           S.P.P. 1978-1981 Anexo Estadístico histórico J.L.P. del V Infor-
           me de Gobierno 1981.
           - No data available.

TABLE 10

AREA IRRIGATED WITH GOVERNMENT INFRASTRUCTURE
1926-1980*(hectares)

YEAR	ACCUMULATED AREA	ANNUAL AREA
1926-1946	827 425	
1947	947 732	120 307
1948	1 052 063	104 331
1949	1 134 538	82 475
1950	1 198 297	63 759
1951	1 252 964	54 667
1952	1 452 937	199 973
1953	1 595 920	142 983
1954	1 747 976	152 056
1955	1 888 071	140 095
1956	2 048 925	160 854
1957	2 133 429	84 504
1958	2 211 237	77 808
1959	2 236 838	25 601
1960	2 278 074	41 236
1961	2 320 800	42 726
1962	2 357 403	36 603
1963	2 418 581	61 178
1964	2 456 095	37 514
1965	2 492 085	35 990
1966	2 553 219	61 134
1967	2 610 416	57 197
1968	2 707 207	96 791
1969	2 795 135	87 928
1970	2 849 300	54 165
1971	2 932 766	83 466
1972	3 065 327	132 561
1973	3 171 447	106 120
1974	3 293 438	121 991
1975	3 467 236	173 798
1976	3 581 343	114 107
1977	3 746 902	165 559
1978	3 895 129	148 227
1979	4 149 189	254 060
1980 p	4 254 695	105 106

* Rehabilitated areas are not included.
p Preliminary data.
Source: *Secretaría de Agricultura y Recursos Hidráulicos,*
     Informe de Labores.

TABLE 11

GEOGRAPHIC DISTRIBUTION OF OFFICIAL CREDIT TO THE AGRICULTURAL
SECTOR: BY TYPE OF CREDIT

(Amount in Million of Pesos)

	Short Term	Long Term	Total	%
Aguascalientes	13.3	19.3	33.6	1.1
Baja Calif. Norte	164.7	5.0	169.7	5.9
Baja Calif. Sur	9.4	7.2	16.6	5.7
Campeche	24.1	11.1	32.2	1.1
Coahuila	153.2	29.2	182.4	6.3
Colima	24.5	9.7	34.1	1.2
Chiapas	98.2	26.0	124.2	4.3
Chihuahua	80.5	9.2	89.7	3.1
Durango	163.4	27.6	191.0	6.6
Guanajuato	64.7	29.7	94.4	3.3
Guerrero	19.2	2.1	21.3	0.7
Hidalgo	8.6	1.1	9.7	0.3
Jalisco	62.1	11.3	73.4	2.5
México	9.2	5.4	14.6	0.5
Michoacán	209.9	45.5	255.4	8.8
Morelos	41.0	3.5	44.5	1.5
Nayarit	59.8	7.4	67.2	2.3
Nuevo León	6.7	2.3	9.0	0.3
Oaxaca	74.3	24.3	98.6	3.4
Puebla	31.9	9.1	41.0	1.3
Querétaro	8.7	4.3	13.0	0.4
Quintana Roo	9.8	2.7	12.5	0.4
San Luis Potosí	16.4	10.7	27.1	0.9
Sinaloa	378.5	29.2	407.7	14.1
Sonora	206.4	42.4	248.8	8.6
Tabasco	7.8	29.2	37.0	1.2
Tamaulipas	91.3	13.4	104.7	3.6
Tlaxcala	6.1	2.8	8.9	0.3
Veracruz	38.8	19.1	57.9	2.0
Yucatán	209.7	96.8	306.4	10.6
Zacatecas	24.9	34.6	59.5	2.1
Totals	2 317.1	571.2	2 888.6	100.0

Source: Manual de Estadísticas Básicas (Sector Agropecuario y
          Forestal) S.P.P. 1978.

Short Term	Long Term	Total	%
101.6	30.7	132.3	0.7
910.4	46.5	956.9	5.4
195.3	11.0	206.3	1.1
212.2	5.1	217.3	1.2
860.8	98.5	959.3	5.4
129.0	6.2	135.2	0.7
645.8	54.7	700.5	4.0
754.1	135.5	887.6	5.0
1 059 1	92.2	1 151.3	6.4
678.0	223.2	901.2	5.0
404.2	4.7	408.9	2.3
17.0	15.1	32.1	0.2
732.3	110.5	842.8	4.7
731.2	33.3	764.5	4.2
857.3	84.2	941.5	5.3
203.3	31.3	234.6	1.3
344.8	82.7	427.5	2.4
184.4	36.6	221.0	1.2
362.0	45.4	407.4	2.3
212.9	29.5	242.4	1.3
93.7	36.5	130.2	0.7
91.3	48.1	139.4	0.8
194.4	140.0	334.4	1.8
1 001.8	211.8	1 213.6	6.8
1 952.5	238.3	2 190.8	12.3
62.1	20.6	82.7	0.5
1 277.2	-	1 277.2	7.1
66.7	8.3	75.0	0.4
758.0	41.5	799.5	4.5
92.8	179.1	271.9	1.5
488.8	65.8	554.6	3.1
15 675.0	2 164.9	17 839.9	100.0

APPENDIX 3

INSTITUTIONS OR ACADEMIC CENTERS RELATED TO RURAL ISSUES

Centro de Capacitación para Programas de Desarrollo Agrícola en Areas de Puebla, Pue.

Centro de Ecodesarrollo

Centro de Investigación de Desarrollo Ovino

Centro de Investigaciones Agrícolas de la Mesa Central

Centro de Investigaciones de la Península de Yucatán

Centro de Investigaciones Agrícolas del Noroeste

Centro de Investigaciones Agrícolas del Noreste

Centro de Investigaciones Agrícolas de Sinaloa

Centro de Investigaciones Agrícolas del Sureste

Centro de Investigaciones Agrícolas de Tamaulipas

Centro de Investigaciones para el Desarrollo Rural

Centro Internacional de Mejoramiento de Maíz y Trigo

Consejo Nacional de Ciencia y Tecnología

Centro Nacional de Productividad

Colegio de Postgraduados en Chapingo

Colegio Superior de Agricultura Tropical

Comité Promotor de Investigaciones para el Desarrollo Rural

El Colegio de México

Escuela de Agricultura de la Universidad de Guadalajara

Escuela de Agricultura de la Universidad de Guerrero

Escuela de Agricultura de la Universidad de Michoacán

Escuela de Agricultura de la Universidad de Nuevo León

Escuela de Agricultura de la Universidad de Sonora

Escuela de Roque, Guanajuato

Escuela de Agricultura del Instituto Tecnológico y de Estudios Superiores de Monterrey

Escuela Nacional de Antropología

Escuela Particular de Agricultura de Ciudad Juárez

Escuela Superior de Agricultura, Culiacán, Sin.

Escuela Superior de Agricultura Antonio Narro, Saltillo, Coahuila

Escuela Superior de Agricultura "Hermanos Escobar"

Escuela Superior de Agricultura y Zootecnia, Gómez Palacio, Dgo.

Fondo de Cultura Campesina

Instituto de Investigaciones sobre Recursos Bióticos

Instituto Mexicano de Estudios Sociales

Instituto Mexicano de Investigaciones Tecnológicas

Instituto Mexicano de Recursos Renovables

Instituto Mexicano del Café

Instituto Nacional de Investigaciones Agrícolas

Instituto Nacional de Investigaciones Forestales

Instituto Nacional de Investigaciones Pecuarias

Instituto Nacional Indigenista

Instituto Nacional para el Desarrollo de la Comunidad Rural y de la Vivienda

Instituto para el Mejoramiento de la Producción de Azúcar

Instituto Politécnico Nacional

Instituto Tecnológico y de Estudios Superiores de Occidente

Universidad Autónoma Agraria "Antonio Narro"

Universidad Autónoma de Chapingo

Universidad Autónoma Metropolitana

Universidad Iberoamericana

Universidad Nacional Autónoma de México

APPENDIX 4

GLOSSARY

Agiotista.- Moneylender.

Agrarista.- Agrarian activist .

Almud.- A dry measure, about 0.8 of a liter -- of land, about half acre.

Amo.- Master, head (of householf or family), owner, boss.

Amparo.- Legal recourse against actions of authorities considered to be unjust. An 'amparo' stays the legal process until the propriety of an action can be considered by a judge. In agrarian matters 'amparos' are usually invoked against presidential grants of land.

Avecindados.- Those who cultivate land under different systems of land tenure according to agreements with the community, individually or collectively, but are not covered by any legal definition.

Avío.- Short term credit for cultivation. It only covers direct production costs, and this usually only partially.

Banco de Crédito Rural.- Rural Credit Bank.

Banco Nacional de Crédito Agrícola.- National Agricultural Credit Bank.

Braceros.- Mexican peasants migrating as temporary agricultural workers to the United States.

Cacicazgo.- A form of domination in which economic, social and political power is concentrated in only one person, family or group.

Cacique.- Generic term, colloquially used to refer to the local agent who represents and operates the dominating structures. In the text it is suggested that he is an economic agent, an intermediary between the campesinos and capital. He carries out different social and political functions which are reproduced by capital and at the same time strengthen it.

Callismo.- President Plutarco Elías Calles' doctrine.

Campesino.- A peasant, whose productive activity is subordinated to capital and inserted in its logic, within a labour organization that functions under its own internal logics, intimately related to the requirements of working the land. Generally the peasantry maintains strong community structures with informal organizations based on solidarity relation-ships. They also tend to diversify their productive and service activities. Generally they directly hire their labour force for a salary. (They are not considered salaried workers here, due to the fact that their own contribution has a decisive impact in the annual logic of their reproduction.) They are considered as constituting a specific social class within the capitalist society. They are of proletarian nature but analytically distinguishable from industrial or agricultural workers, because of the specificity of the exploitative mechanisms they are subjected to, and also because of the nature of the social contradictions that define their existence.

Casco.- The main living quarters of an 'hacienda'.

Casilla.- Place to live, shared by peons, as a complement to their salary.

Casta.- Caste — a system of rigid social stratification characterized by hereditary statues, endogamy, and social barriers sanctioned by custom, law or/and religion.

Centavos.- Cents.

Central Campesina Independiente (CCI).- Independent Peasant Central.

Centro Internacional de Mejoramiento del Maíz y el Trigo (CIMMYT).- International Centre for the Improvement of Corn and Wheat Production.

Código Agrario.- Agrarian Code.

Colectivados.- Peasants organized in a collective manner, according to different modalities and purposes.

Colonia.- A system of domination established by the Spanish crown in America, including the territory currently occupied by Mexico. The 'colonial' period in the history of Mexico runs from the beginning of the XVI century until 1810. The 'colonia agrícola' is a specific regime of land tenure encouraged mainly during the 1940s. It was part of the land colonization programmes. It was an alternative to the 'ejido' and the small private holdings, although quite similar to the latter. It is regulated by an ad hoc constitutional law.

Colono.- Owner of a piece of land in a 'colonia agrícola' (see supra).

Comisariado de Bienes Comunales.- The authority in an Indian community, formally elected by the 'comuneros' according to terms stipulated by law. His role and status depend on his relationship with the non-legally recognized but actual authorities of the community. He is therefore a manifestation of the intromission of external forces within the community.

Comisariado Ejidal.- The maximum authority of an 'ejido', formally elected by 'ejidatarios' according to terms stipulated by law. Frequently he carries out functions which differ from those legally assigned to him. His class origin and his political role depend on the co-relation of forces within a local, regional or national perspective.

Comisión Agraria Mixta.- Mixed Agrarian Commission.

Comisión Nacional de la Industria del Maíz para Consumo Humano.- National Commission of the Corn Industry for Human Consumption.

Comisión Nacional del Maíz.- National Corn Commission.

Comisión para el Incremento y Distribución de Semillas Mejoradas.- Commission for the Increase and Distribution of Improved Seeds.

Comisiones Nacionales de Irrigaciones y Caminos.- National Commissions for Irrigation and Roads.

Comité Regulador de los Mercados de Subsistencia.- Committee for the Regulation of Subsistence Markets.

Compañía deslindadora.- Companies formed during the last part of the XIX century which obtained concessions for defining the limits of agricultural lands.

Compañía Nacional de Subsistencias Populares (CONASUPO).- National Company for Popular Subsistence.

Comuna.- Usually a rural community organized on a communal basis.

Comunero.- Member of an Indian community, which constitutes a specific modality of land possession, legally recognized, on which a socio-economic structure habitually exists. This structure has traditional production characteristics.

Confederación Nacional Agraria.- National Agrarian Confederation.

Confederación Nacional Campesina.- National Peasant Confederation.

Confederación Nacional de la Pequeña Propiedad.- National Confederation of Small Holders.

Congreso Permanente Agrario.- Permanent Agrarian Congress.

Consejo Agrarista Mexicano.- Mexican Agrarian Council.

Consejo Nacional Cardenista.- National Council based on Cárdenas' doctrine.

Consejo Supremo de Pueblos Indígenas.- Supreme Council on Indian Communities.

Consejo de Vigilancia.- The authority of an 'ejido', formally elected by its members according to terms stipulated by law. It may represent the same interests and forces as the 'Comisariado ejidal' (see supra), or the opposite ones. In the latter case the interaction between both authorities reflects the dialectics of the contradictions within the 'ejido', which also can be seen in the very composition of the two groups.

Convención Nacional Agraria.- National Agrarian Convention.;

Cooperativa.- Cooperative.

Coordinadora Nacional Plan de Ayala.- National Coordinator for the Ayala Plan.

Coyote.- A specific type of 'cacique' or other agent who operates within the sphere of commercial intermediation.

Crédito rural.- Rural credit.

Criollo.- A person of native birth but of European descent.

Cristero.- Defender of Christ. Participant in a mes- sianic peasant movement in last part of the 1920s. The debate over the socio-political nature of the movement still persists. It was stronger in the central parts of Mexico. Many of its consequences can still be seen. Lorenzo Meyer, in his book "LA CRISTIADA" (Siglo XXI Editores, México 1979), gives an ample description of the movement and also presents a hypothesis of its origin and content, but this has not been generally accepted.

Cuartillo.- A quarter of an 'arroba' (about 6 pounds); a grain measure.

Delegación Agraria.- Official representative in each federal state of the Secretaría de la Reforma Agraria. Its basic functions are legally regulated.

Departamento de Reglamentos de Irrigación.- State office responsible for irrigation regulation.

Dirección de Asuntos Agrarios.- (State) Office of
Agrarian Affairs.

Dirección General de Economía Agrícola.- Department
of Agricultural Economics.

División del Norte.- Pancho Villa's army.

Ejidatario.- Member of an 'ejido'.

Ejido.- A specific form of land tenure, stipulated by
law, in which the individual right to the exploitation
of a specific plot of land is recognized. The right
is not equivalent to private property, since it is
restricted to direct exploitation of the plot of land.
Legally, the 'ejidatario' cannot sell, rent or mortgage
his plot of land. Inheritance is regulated by
certain legal stipulations which may prevail over the
explicit will of the 'ejidatario'. The organization
of production in the 'ejido' may take different forms
within the limits and restrictions laid down by the
law, on the basis of 'ejidatarios' decisions. It must
satisfy different formal requirements in order to
acquire legal representation.

Empresario.- Total or partial owner of a capitalist
enterprise which can be formed as an individual
family unit or as a mercantile group.

Encomienda.- Certain goods (land and people) assigned
or granted by the Spanish Kings. 'Encomenderos'.-
people in charge of...

Finca.- Rural property. Estate.

Fondo de Garantía y Fomento de la Agricultura.-
Organization which gives credit for agricultural
promotion.

Gavilla.- Gang of bandits' sheaf of grain.

Golondrina.- (Swallow) This term is used to describe
through an analogy with swallows, those 'campesinos'
who migrate regularly in search of agricultural
employment, both within and outside the country.
Although this kind of behaviour is characteristic of

most 'campesinos' and not just of a specific group,
in this text the term has been used to refer to those
who have severed their links with the land and their
place of origin. Since this destroys the original
analogy from which the term first arose, it is suggested that another analogy be used to point out the
vagrant and rootless nature of this social group.

Hacendado.- 'Hacienda' owner.

Hacienda.- A large agricultural property. It has its
origin during the colonial period and adopts its
definitive characteristics in the last part of the
XIX century. Although the term was still used after
the 1910 Revolution to denote large landed properties,
its characteristics disappeared after 1910 when its
economic roots and political context changed radically.

Hacienda pulquera.- 'Hacienda' where the main product
was 'pulque'.

Henequen de luna.- Practice of stealing 'henequén'
from one's own plot in order to sell it to intermediaries, thus avoiding the control of the official bank
which had given credit for the crop. It is known as
"moon lighting" because it is done at night.

Influyente.- Person who uses his political or economic
power in order to promote his own interests through
forceful pressure on authorities, which is often
illegal.

Instituto Mexicano del Café (INMECAFE).- Mexican Coffee
Board (Government Agency).

Instituto Nacional de Investigaciones Agrícolas.-
National Institute for Agricultural Research.

Jornal.- A monetary payment (sometimes in kind) for a
day's work on the land.

Jornaleros.- Temporary or permanent agricultural
labourers.

Labrador.- Someone who directly works the land.

Latifundista.- Latifundist; large land-owner.

Ley de la Reforma Agraria.- Agrarian Reform Law.

Ley de Ejidos.- The 'Ejido' Law.

Ley de Riegos.- The Irrigation Law.

Liga Nacional Campesina.- National Peasant League.

Luneros.- People who have to work on Mondays (lunes = Monday).

Mecate.- Hemp rope or cord.

Medieros.- 'Campesinos' who cultivate other people's land and must give the owner half of the harvest obtained.

Mestizos.- People of mixed Caucasian and Indian ancestry.

Minifundista.- Peasant who owns or cultivates a small plot of land, generally less than five hectares. He can only use his own or his family's labour force on the exploitation.

Movimiento de Liberación Nacional.- National Liberation Movement.

Movimiento de los 400 Pueblos.- Movement of the 400 Villages.

Movimiento Nacional Plan de Ayala.- National Movement 'Plan de Ayala'.

Mozo.- Man servant; stable boy; young man.

Mulato.- A person of mixed Caucasian and Negro ancestry.

Municipio Libre.- Political and administrative area, which forms the basis of the legal structure of federal power in Mexico. The "freedom" of the 'Municipio' (its relative autonomy) is a matter that is deeply inserted within the social struggle of the Mexican people.

Nacionaleros.- 'Campesinos' who occupy and cultivate national lands.

Neolatifundistas.- Rural entrepreneurs who have control (commercial or financial) over a cultivated area, the size of which exceeds the legal maximum allowed.

Nixtamal.- Fermented maize in a mixture of water and lime — a prior stage for the production of the 'masa' (corn flour) for 'tortillas'.

Obreros agrícolas.- Salaried agricultural workers.

Oficina de Estudios Especiales.- Office of Special Studies.

Oficina de la Pequeña Propiedad.- Office dealing with small holders' issues.

Pacto Constitucional.- The Constitution of the Republic.

Pacto de Ocampo.- Agreement celebrated in 1975 between the leaders of the main national peasant organizations for the joint defense of their interests.

Panal.- Hollowed out stem of the 'maguey' cactus where 'pulque' is further fermented.

Partido Nacional Agrarista.- National Agrarian Party.

Partido Nacional Revolucionario.- National Revolutionary Party. Precursor of the official political party.

Partido Revolucionario Institucional (PRI).- Revolutionary Institutional Party. The official political party.

Peón.- During Porfirio Díaz' dictatorship (late XIX and early XX centuries), workers on the 'haciendas' were referred to as peons.

Peón acasillado.- A yearly-contracted works, who brought his family to live on the 'hacienda'.

Peón de tarea.- Piece work 'peon'.

Petróleos Mexicanos (PEMEX).- Government enterprise responsible for oil exploitation in Mexican territory.

Piojal or *Pegujal*.- Small piece of land, no larger than a quarter of a hectare, given, for their own use to peons who had gained the confidence of the 'hacendado'.

Plan de Veracruz.- The Veracruz Plan.

Plan Nacional de Desarrollo Industrial.- National Plan for Industrial Development.

Plan Sexenal.- Six year plan.

Prestanombres.- Name lenders.

Productora Nacional de Semillas.- National Seed Producer; State agency.

Propios.- Semi-urban lands.

Pulque.- The fermented juice of the 'agave' cactus.

Ranchero.- Owner of a ranch. By extension the term is applied to farmers and cattle raisers and to their administrative staff, as well as to the rural middle class.

Rancho.- A small or medium-sized private property hiring salaried workers and operating on a profit-making basis.

Raya.- Weekly salary.

Real.- Former Mexican currency worth ten cents.

Recampesinización.- A process in which peasants return to rural areas and to farming.

Refaccionario.- Long-term credit for productive investments.

Reglamento de la Colonia.- Legal regulations for rural settlements.

Rentista. - A person who makes his living through renting his land to others. Frequently the peasant 'rentista' actually makes most of his living through offering his labour for sale, once his land has been alienated. The rent he receives is only an additional income or represents a requirement for cultivating his own land.

República Restaurada. - Expression used by some historians to refer to the period of government which started after the defeat of Maximillian by the Mexican armies.

Secretaría de Agricultura. - Ministry of Agriculture.

Secretaría de Agricultura y Recursos Hidráulicos. - Ministry of Agriculture and Water Resources.

Secretaría de Gobernación. - Ministry of the Interior Affairs.

Secretaría de Programación y Presupuesto. - Ministry of Planning and Budget.

Secretaría de Recursos Hidráulicos. - Ministry of Water Resources.

Sistema de Encargos. - The putting-out system.

Tabacos Mexicanos (TABAMEX). - Government agency responsible for tobacco production.

Terrateniente. - Owner of large land properties providing at the same time an income and a political and economic position in society.

Tienda de Raya. - Term which reveals the nature of the 'hacienda' stores during Porfirio Díaz' period: since the peon's salary (his 'raya', see supra) was used to pay real or fictitious debts with the 'hacendado', the peon was forced to request credit for the goods he needed in order to survive.

Tlachiquero. - 'Peon' in charge of 'pulque' production.

Tlapexquera. - Type of jail to punish a 'peon acasilla-do' who tried to abandon his job.

Tlaxilole.- A share of 'pulque' given to 'peones' as a complement to their salaries.

Tortillas.- A type of corn pancake.

Tortillería.- Place where 'tortillas' are produced and sold.

Unión General de Obreros y Campesinos de México.- General Union of Mexican Workers and Peasants.

Vara.- Variable unit of length, about 2.8 ft.

Villistas.- Villa's followers.

Zapatistas.- Zapata's followers.

APPENDIX 5

SUGGESTED BIBLIOGRAPHY
(IN SPANISH)

1.- Statistical Information:

As pointed out in the Foreword, the statistical
information available on rural Mexico is notably
deficient. This will only be corrected through the
Agricultural and Livestock Census, planned for 1981.

An excellent critical analysis of the situation
can be found in Yates P.L. "Apéndice Estadístico", El
Campo Mexicano, (E.E.C., 1978)*

The "Secretaría de Programación y Presupuesto",
periodically publishes the currently available basic
statistical information. The following publications are
available for studying rural matters:

Manual de Estadísticas Básicas (Sector Agropecuario
y Forestal);

Manuales de Información Básica de la Nación (Cómo
es México y la Población de México, su Ocupación y sus
Niveles de Bienestar);

Anuario Estadístico de los Estados Unidos Mexicanos;

Agenda Estadística, 1979;

Encuesta Nacional de Ingresos y Gastos de los Ho-
gares, 1977;

Niveles de Fecundidad en México, 1960 - 1974;

* The abbreviations of publishers are explained at the
end of this Appendix.

Proyecciones de Población en México, 1970 - 2000;

Cartas (geographical, geological, use of soils, potential use of soils, touristic, etc.)

The Secretaría also publishes a monthly "Gaceta Informativa" with up to date data on its publications, to obtain it, (as well as back numbers), write to the following address:

Balderas 71 - 4o. piso
México 6, D. F.
Tel. 510-32-91

or

Ave. Artículo 123 No. 88
México 1, D. F.
Tel. 551-87-80

The Dirección General de Economía Agrícola of the Secretaría de Agricultura y Recursos Hidráulicos (Leibnitz 20 - 10o. piso, México 5, D.F.) publishes a weekly _Boletín Interno_, as well as a monthly magazine _Econotecnia Agrícola_, with valuable statistical information and monographic studies.

The Secretaría also has plenty of information available acquired during the design of the Plan Nacional Hidráulico. It also has the sampling survey results and other studies made by different departments of the Secretaría.

Recently it published an _Anuario Estadístico_ which contains the information used as a basis for the "Plan Nacional Agropecuario de 1980".

The Secretaría Técnica of the Gabinete Agropecuario has compiled information on rural Mexico, part of which has been published in a bulletin of limited circulation. Other institutions of the agricultural and cattle raising sector in particular the "Banco Nacional de Crédito Rural" and "CONASUPO", have a valuable stock of information in this field.

Finally, Reyes Osorio S. et al Estructura Agraria y Desarrollo Agrícola en México, F.C.E., 1974, is still a fundamental reference, both for informative and analytic material.

2.- Historical Information:

For general historic insight see the collection of Problemas Agrícolas e Industriales de México, in which important studies on rural Mexico by both foreign (Chevalier, Mc Cutchen, Mc Bride, Turner, Tannebaum, Wetten, etc.) and Mexican researchers appear.

With regard to Mexican Agrarianism, the books by Jesús Silva Herzog, Emeritus Professor of the School of Economics of the Universidad Nacional Autónoma de México, are indispensable. In particular see:

La Reforma Agraria en México y en Algunos Otros Países (author's edition, 1934);

El Agrarismo Mexicano y la Reforma Agraria (FCE, 1959);

El Mexicano y su Morada (CA, 1960);

Trayectoria Ideológica de la Revolución Mexicana (CA, 1963);

Inquietud sin tregua, ensayos y artículos escogidos 1937-1965 (CA, 1965).

Silva Herzog himself coordinated the Colección de folletos para la historia de la Revolución Mexicana, published by the Instituto Mexicano de Investigaciones Económicas, of which it is worth mentioning the four volumes on La Cuestión de la Tierra.

In the Colección de Fuentes para la Historia de la Revolución Mexicana, F.C.E., 1955 and following years, some original documents of the period are reproduced, of which some, such as plans, speeches, manifests, etc., are directly related to the agrarian issue.

Enrique Florescano published a Bibliografía del Maíz, C. 1972, which contains a rigorous scientific

compilation. The same author also published Origen y
Desarrollo de los Problemas Agrarios de México,
1500-1821, Era, 1975. Also of interest is Frank A.G.,
La Agricultura Mexicana 1521-1630 - CEPAENAH, 1976.

For studies on Zapata and Zapatismo reference
must be made to:

Magaña, G. Gral., Emiliano Zapata y el Agrarismo
en México (LER, 1975).

Womack, J., Zapata y la Revolución Mexicana (S
XXI, 1974).

A. Orive Alba's La Irrigación en México - G. 1970
gives a most interesting insight into rural history.

3.- The Indian Issue

In INI, 30 años después, revisión crítica INI,
1979, the Instituto Nacional Indigenista (Ave. Revolución 1279, México 19, D.F.), got together a number of
classical and recent texts related to the Indian issue.
The Instituto has also published a great variety of
texts on this subject. Among these, R. Pozas "Chamula"
INI, 1977, can still be considered a model for research
and analytic penetration.

4.- Agrarian Reform

The work of Reyes Osorio and Silva Herzog quoted
above, deals extensively with this subject. They
continue to be of interest but, are beginning to be out
dated.

De la Peña, M.T., Mito y Realidad de la Reforma
Agraria en México (CA, 1964);

Durán, M.A., El Agrarismo Mexicano (S XXI, 1967);

Fernández and Fernández, R., Economía Agrícola y
Reforma Agraria, (CEMLA, 1962) and

Romero Espinosa, E., La Reforma Agraria en México
(CA, 1963).

Also see:

Reyes Osorio, S. y et al, Reforma Agraria, Tres
Ensayos (CENAPRO, 1969);

Restrepo I. and Sánchez J., La Reforma Agraria en
Cuatro Regiones, (SS, 1972) and

Guetelman, M., Capitalismo y Reforma Agraria en
México (Era, 1974).

More than ten years ago Jorge Martínez Ríos
prepared a basic reference work on the subject: Tenen-
cia de la Tierra y Desarrollo Agrario en México, (Bibliografía selectiva y comentada), (IIS, 1970).

5.-   Current Situation

Some specialized magazines have collected
statistical information reports of direct research
results as well as analytical and theoretical essays.
See in particular:

Comercio Exterior;

Cuadernos Agrarios;

Narxhí - Nandhá (Revista de economía campesina):

Nueva Antropología and

Revista del México Agrario.

There are also articles on the subject in:

Demografía y Economía;

Cuadernos de Discusión;

Cuadernos Políticos;

Estrategia;

Historia y Sociedad;

Investigación Económica;

Problemas del Desarrollo;

Revista Mexicana de Sociología y

Revista Mexicana de Ciencias Políticas y Sociales

Also in the publications of the Centro de Estudios Sociológicos de El Colegio de México.

Among the books published in Mexico during the last ten years, it is worth while pointing out the following:

Astorga, L. E. and Hardy, C. Organización, Lucha y Dependencia Económica (NI, 1978);

Aguilar, C.H., La Frontera Nómada: Sonora y la Revolución Mexicana, (S XXI, 1977).

Barbosa, A.R., Empleo, Desempleo y Subempleo en el Sector Agropecuario (CIA, 1976);

Barkin, D., Desarrollo Regional y Reorganización Campesina (NI, 1978);

Bartra, A., Notas sobre la Cuestión Campesina (México 1970-1976) (EM, 1979);

Bartra, R., Estructura Agraria y Clases Sociales en México (Era, 1978);

Bartra, R., et al. Caciquismo y Poder Político en el México Rural (S XXI, 1975);

Echenique, J., Crédito y Desarrollo Agrícola en México (1940-1978) (NI, 1980);

Feder, E., El Imperialismo Fresa (EC, 1977);

Espín, J. and Leonardo P. of Economía y Sociedad en Los Altos de Jalisco (NI, 1978);

Fernández, L. and Fernández, M.T. of Colectivización Ejidal y Cambio Rural en México (UAJT, 1977);

Gómez, J.F., El Movimiento Campesino en México (EC, 1970);

Gómez O. L., Economía Campesina y Acumulación de Capital, (NI, 1980);

Huizer, G., La Lucha Campesina en México (CIA, 1979);

Jáuregui, J. et al. Tabamex: Un Caso de Integración Vertical de la Agricultura (NI, 1979);

Montañez, C. and Aburto, H., Maíz, Política Institucional y Crisis Agrícola (NI, 1970);

Navarrete, I.M. de, Bienestar Campesino y Desarrollo Económico (FCE, 1971);

Oswald, O., Serrano, J. and Luna, Laurentino, Cooperativas Ejidales y Capitalismo Dependiente (UNAM, 1979);

Oswald, O. et al. Mercado y Dependencia (NI, 1979);

Paré, L., El Proletariado Agrícola en México: ¿Campesinos sin Tierra o Proletarios Agrícolas? (S XXI, 1979);

Restrepo I. and Eckstein, S., La Agricultura Colectiva en México, (S XXI, 1975);

Restrepo I. et al. Los Problemas de la Organización Campesina (EC, 1975);

Sánchez B. G., La Región Fundamental de Economía Campesina en México (NI, 1980);

Stavenghagen, R., Las Clases Sociales en las Sociedades Agrarias (S XXI, 1971);

Stavenghagen, R., Sociología y Subdesarrollo (ENT, 1972);

Stavenhagen, R. et al. Capitalismo y Campesinado en México (SI, 1976);

Villa Issa, M., El Mercado de Trabajo y la Adopción de Tecnología Nueva de Producción Agrícola: El Caso del Plan Puebla (CPCH, 1977);

Warman, A., Los Campesinos, Hijos Predilectos del Régimen (NI, 1973);

Warman, A. ... Y Venimos a Contradecir (ECCH, 1976);

Warman, A. et al. Los Campesinos en la Tierra de Zapata (SI, 1974).

NOTES:

1. Criteria for selection. Only texts published in Spanish in Mexico have been included in this suggested bibliography. Texts based on direct research were given priority when selection from publications of the last decade was made. Books easily available in the bookstores were also given priority (with some clear exceptions), as for example the magazine Problems Agrícolas e Industriales de México and some studies by Silva Herzog only available in libraries.

2. Reference Centres. Not all research centres and government offices related to rural matters, or specialized libraries offer reference facilities for consulting their materials.

As well as large libraries (Universidad Nacional Autónoma de México, Banco de México, Secretaría de Hacienda, Archivo General de la Nación, etc.), which have large sections dedicated to rural issues, there are other sources available in the Universidad Autónoma de Chapingo (Texcoco, Méx.), in the Centro de Investigaciones Agrarias (Lázaro Cárdenas No. 28, 5o. piso, México 1, D. F.), in the Centro de Estudios Sociológicos del Colegio de México (Camino al Ajusco No. 20, México), in the office in Mexico of the Comisión Económica para la América Latina of the U.N., (Presidente Mazarik No. 29-13, México, D.F., and in the Comité Promotor de Investigaciones para el Desarrollo Rural (Nebraska No.193, México, D.F.).

3. Publisher's Abbreviations

C   CONASUPO

CA   Cuadernos Americanos

CEMLA   Centro de Estudios Monetarios Latinoamericanos

CENAPRO   Centro Nacional de Productividad

CIA	Centro de Investigaciones Agrarias
CPAENAH	Comité de Publicaciones de los Alumnos de la Escuela Nacional de Antropología e Historia
CPCH	Colegio de Postgraduados de Chapingo
EC	Editorial Campesina
ECCH	Ediciones de la Casa Chata
EEC	Ediciones El Caballito
EM	Editorial Macehual
SXXI	Siglo XII Editores
UAJT	Universidad Autónoma Juárez de Tabasco

APPENDIX 6

SUGGESTED BIBLIOGRAPHY (IN ENGLISH)

Ames, Barry, Bases of Support for Mexico's Dominant Party, in American Political Science Review, 64 (March, 1970), pp. 153-67.

Anderson, Charles W. and Glade, William P., Jr., The Political Economy of Mexico: Two Studies, Madison, University of Wisconsin Press, 1963.

Ashby, Joe C., Organized Labor and the Mexican Revolution under Lázaro Cárdenas, Chapel Hill, University of North Carolina Press, 1963.

Ashby, Joe C., Organized Labor and the Mexican Revolution under Cárdenas. Chapel Hill, University of North Carolina Press, 1967.

Beals, Ralph L.,"Anthropology in Contemporary Mexico." In Contemporary Mexico: Papers of the IV International Congress of Mexican History, edited by James W. Wilkie, Michael C. Meyer, and Edna Monzón de Wilkie, pp. 753-68, Berkeley, University of California Press, 1975.

Brandenburg, Frank. The Making of Modern Mexico, Englewood Cliffs, N.J., Prentice-Hall, 1974.

Brenner, Anita. Idols behind Altars: The Story of the Mexican Spirit. Boston, Beacon Press, 1970.

Brothers, Dwight S. and Solís M., Leopoldo, Mexican Financial Development, Austin, University of Texas Press, 1966.

Bulnes, Francisco, The Whole Truth about Mexico, New York, M. Bulnes Book Co., 1916.

Clark, Marjorie Ruth, Organized Labor in Mexico, Chapel Hill, University of North Carolina Press, 1934.

Cline, Howard F., Mexico: Revolution to Evolution, 1940-1960, London, Oxford University Press, 1962.

Cline Howard. "Mexico: A Maturing Democracy." Current History (1953), pp. 136-142.

Cline, Howard F., Mexico: A Matured Latin American Revolution, 1910-1960, in Annals of the American Academy of Political and Social Sciences, 334 (March, 1961), pp. 84-94.

Combined Mexican Working Party, The Economic Development of Mexico, Baltimore, Johns Hopkins Press, for International Bank for Reconstruction and Development, 1953.

Davis, Tom (com.), Mexico's Recent Economic Growth, Austin, University of Texas Press for Institute of Latin American Studies, 1967.

Dulles, John W.F. Yesterday in Mexico: A Chronicle of the Revolution 1919-1936. Austin, University of Texas Press, 1961.

Dovring, Folke, Land Reform and Productivity: The Mexican Case, Analysis of Census Data, Madison, University of Wisconsin, Land Tenure Center, 63 (January, 1969).

Everett, Mike, The Evolution of the Mexican Wage Structure, 1939. 63, Mexico, El Colegio de Mé- xico, February, 1969 (revised manuscript).

Fuentes, Carlos. The Death of Artemio Cruz. Translated by Sam Hilleman. New York, Noonday Press, 1966.

Glade, Williams P., Jr., The Enigma of Mexico's Dilemma, in Economic Development and Cultural Change 13 (April, 1965), pp. 366-76.

Goldsmith, Raymond W., The Financial Development of Mexico, Paris, Development Centre of the Organization for Economic Cooperation and Development, 1966.

González Casanova, Pablo, Democracy in Mexico. New York: Oxford University Press, 1970.

Guzmán, Martín Luis. Memoirs of Pancho Villa. Translated by Virginia H. Taylor. Austin, University of Texas Press, 1965.

Hale, Charles A. "The Liberal Impulse: Daniel Cosío Villegas and the Historia Moderna de México." Hispanic American Historial Review 54 (1974) pp. 479-98.

Hansen, Roger D. The Politics of Mexican Development. Baltimore, Johns Hopkins Press, 1971.

Hertford, Reed, Principal Historical and Economic Issues in Mexican Agricultural Development, mimeographed paper.

Hewes, Gordon, Mexicans in Search of the Mexican: Notes on Mexican National Character Studies, in American Journal of Economics and Sociology, 13 (January, 1954), pp. 209-23.

Hart, John M. "Agrarian Precursors of the Mexican Revolution: The Development of an Ideology." The Americans 29 (1972), pp. 131-50.

Haddox, John H. Vasconcelos of Mexico. Austin: University of Texas Press, 1967.

Johnson, Kenneth F. Mexican Democracy: A Critical View. Boston Allyn and Bacon, 1971.

Katz, Friedrich. "Labor Conditions on Haciendas in Porfirian Mexico: Some Trends and Tendencies." Hispanic American Historical Review 54 (1974), pp. 1-47.

Kitchens, John W. "Some Considerations on the Rurales of Porfirian Mexico." Journal of Inter-American Studies 9 (1967), pp. 441-55.

Lewis, Oscar. "Mexico since Cárdenas." In Social Change in Latin America Today, edited by Richard N. Adams et al., pp. 285-345. New York, Vintage Books, 1960.

Lewis, Oscar. The Children of Sanchez: Auto-biography of a Mexican Family. New York, Vintage Books, 1961.

Lewis, Oscar. Five Families. New York, Science Editions, 1962.

Lewis, Oscar, Life in a Mexican Village: Tepoztlán Restudied, University of Illinois Press, 1963.

Lewis, Oscar, Pedro Martínez: A Mexican Peasant and His Family, New York, Vintage Books, 1967.

Maddox, James G., Economic Growth and Revolution in Mexico, in Land Economics, 36 (August, 1960), pp. 266-78.

Manne, Alan S., Key Sectors of the Mexican Economy, 1960-1970, in Studies in Process Analysis, compiled by Alan S. Manne and Harry M. Markowitz, New York, John Wiley and Sons, 1963, pp. 381-400.

Meyers, William K. "Politics, Vested Rights, and Economic Growth in Porfirian Mexico." Hispanic American Historical Review 57 (1977), pp. 425-54.

Millán, Verna Carleton. Mexico Reborn. Boston, Houghton Mifflin Company, 1939.

Mosk, Sanford A., Industrial Revolution in Mexico, Berkeley and Los Angeles, University of California Press, 1954.

Mosk, Sanford A. Industrial Revolution in Mexico. Berkeley, University of California Press, 1970.

Myers, Charles N., Education and National Development in Mexico, Princeton, Princeton University, Industrial Relations Section, 1965.

Michaels, Albert L. "The Crisis of Cardenismo." Journal of Latin American Studies 2 (1970), pp. 51-79.

Nash, Manning, Economic Nationalism in Mexico, in Economic Nationalism in Old and New States, comp. by Harry G. Johnson, Chicago, University of Chicago Press, 1967, pp. 71-84.

Padgett, L. Vicent, The Mexican Political System, Boston, Houghton Mifflin Co., 1966.

Paz, Octavio, The Labyrinth of Solitude: Life and Thought in Mexico. Translated by Lysander Kemp. New York: Grove Press, 1961.

Paz, Octavio. The Other Mexico: Critique of the Pyramid, New York, Grove Press, 1972.

Pellicer de Brody, Olga. "Mexico in the 1970's and Its Relations with the United States." In Latin America and the United States, edited by Julio Cotler and Richard R. Fagen, pp. 314-33. Stanford, Stanford University Press, 1974.

Pérez López, Enrique, et al. Mexico's Recent Economic Growth: The Mexican View. Austin: University of Texas Press, 1967.

Reynolds, Clark. The Mexican Economy: Twentieth Century Structure and Growth, New Haven, Yale University Press, in print.

Richmond, Patricia McIntire, Mexico: A Case Study of One-Party Politics, Ph.D. thesis, University of California, 1965; microfilm, Library of Congress.

Ross, Stanley R. "Mexico: Cool Revolution and Col War." Current History 41 (1963), pp. 89-94, 116-17.

Ross, Stanley R., and Is the Mexican Revolution Dead? New York, Alfred A. Knopf, 1966.

Ruiz, Ramón Eduardo, Mexico: The Challenge of Poverty and Illiteracy, San Marino, Huntington Library, 1963.

Rutherford, John. Mexican Society during the Revolution: A Literary Approach. New York, Claredon Press, 1971.

Salmerón, Francisco. "Mexican Philosophers of the Twentieth Century." In Mario de la Cueva et al., Major Trends in Mexican Philosophy, pp. 246-87. Notre Dame, Notre Dame University Press, 1966.

Simpson, Eyler N., The Ejido: Mexico's Way Out, Chapel Hill, University of North Carolina Press, 1937.

Tannebaum, Frank. Mexico: The Struggle for Peace and Bread. New York: Alfred A. Knopf, 1956.

Tannebaum, Frank. Peace by Revolution: Mexico after 1910, New York, Columbia University Press, 1966.

Townsend, William Cameron. Lázaro Cárdenas: Mexican Democrat. Ann Arbor, George Wahr Publishing Company, 1952.

Turner, Frederick C. The Dynamic of Mexican Nationalism, Chapel Hill, University of North Carolina Press, 1968.

Turner, John Kenneth. Barbarous Mexico. Austin, University of Texas Press, 1969.

Vasconcelos, José. Aspects of Mexican Civilization, Chicago, University of Chicago Press, 1926.

Venezian, Eduardo L., and Gamble, William K., The Agricultural Development of Mexico: Its Structure and Growth Since 1950, New York, Frederick A. Praeger, 1969.

Vernon, Raymond. The Dilemma of Mexico's Development: The Roles of the Private and Public Sectors, Cambridge, Harvard University Press, 1963.

Vernon, Raymond (comp.), Public Policy and Private Enterprise in Mexico, Cambridge, Harvard University Press, 1964.

Wauchope, Robert (comp.), Synoptic Studies of Mexican Culture, New Orleans, Tulane University: Middle American Research Institute, 1957.

Wilkie, James W. "Alternative Views in History: Historical Statistics and Oral History." In Research in Mexican History: Topics, Methodology, Sources and a Practical Guide to Field Research, edited by Richard E. Greenleaf and Michael C. Meyer, pp. 49-62. Lincoln, University of Nebraska Press, 1973.

Wilkie, James W. The Mexican Revolution: Federal Expenditure and Social Change since 1910. Berkeley, University of California Press, 1967.

Wolf, Eric R., The Mexican Bajío in the Eighteen Century, in Synoptic Studies of Mexican Culture, comp. by Robert Wauchope, New Orleans, Tulane University, Middle American Research Institute, 1957, pp. 177-99.

Womack, John, Jr. Zapata and the Mexican Revolution. New York, Alfred A. Knopf, 1968.

Womack, John, Jr. "The Spoils of the Mexican Revolution," Foreign Affairs 48 (1970) pp. 677-87.

Whetten, Nathan L., Rural Mexico, Chicago, University of Chicago Press, 1948.

Wolf, Eric R., Peasant Wars of the Twentieth Century, New York, Harper and Row, 1969.

Index

Credit, 40, 63, 72, 85, 89, 130, 141, 145, 177, 214, 225, 246, 249; as input, 103; bank, 185; beneficiaries, 108; institutions, 127; official, 131; private institutional, 127; state, 105, 127; system, 176; *tienda de raya,* 141; union, 64; usurious, 127, 145
Criollos, 6, 7, 14, 27
Cristero movement, 34
Crop national structure, 180–85
Cuban revolution, 44

Daniels, Josephus, 60, 63
de Almada, Alicia Calles, 193
de la Huerta, 191
Delegación Agraria, 161
Departamento de Reglamentación e Irrigación, 83
Díaz Porfirio, 32, 129, 184; dictatorship, 8, 9, 16, 160; *haciendas,* 9, 41; *latifundistas,* 36; period, 185; porfirian, 29, 108, 116, 121, 129, 144
Dirección de Irrigación, 83
Dumont, 143
Durango, State of, 146, 188, 189

Economists, Keynesian, 204; Marxists, 206; neoclassical, 206
Economy, agricultural, 102, 205; *campesino,* 108; cattle-raising, 102; Mexican, 104
Education, 29, 170, 200; rural, 33
Ejidal, centers, 49; endowment, 162–63; form, 32; invasion, 123; land, 52, 110, 115, 181, 186, 189, 231; organization, 172; plot, 115; producers, 183; production, 39, 41; rent, 184; rhetoric, 70; structure, 163; sugar mill, 67; system, 109; unions, 162
Ejidatario, 20, 30, 33, 36–38, 40–41, 48, 54, 67, 71–72, 83, 85, 88, 106, 117, 121–23, 137, 174, 182–84, 187, 210, 214
Emmanuel, Arghiri, 215
Employment, 122; in *hacienda,* 8; permanent, 117; rural, 248, 250, 254; temporary, 117
Encuentros de organizaciones campesinas independientes, 91
Entrepreneur, 127, 131, 240, 249; as agricultural producer, 131; as owner, 163; capitalist, 111; rural, 131; structure of exploitation, 153
Estrada, Nabor, 124

Europe, 28
Export, 9, 14, 15, 65, 183, 190, 246; agricultural exports, 99; cattle, 248; control, 128; cultivation, 246; food, 13; livestock, 110, 128; market, 110, 181–82; products, 17, 215; production, 148; surplus, 86, 175; trade, 16
Exporter, 18, 246

Fannon, 143
Farm, 218–19; private, 83
Farmers, 8, 31, 40, 63–66, 69–70, 83, 85–86, 88, 114–18, 128, 143, 147, 176, 179, 188, 191, 203, 214; commercial, 175, 179–80, 182; income, 60, 64; inserted in logic of capital, 179; progressive, 69, 72, 201; tenant, 38
Finance, 111; public, 251, 253
Financial, activities, 131; capital, 106, 108; mechanisms, 105, 107, 183; operation, 99, 103; organizations, 109; system, 131
Financing, 82, 131; agencies, 108; company, 184; public, 85; sources, 120; system, 103
Fondo de Garantía y Fomento de la Agricultura, 85
Food, 13–17, 28, 43, 47, 60, 69, 70, 81, 82, 84, 86, 92, 213–16, 234, 243, 246, 250; basic, 224, 225; crisis, 45, 216; deficit, 245; producers, 245; self-sufficiency, 45, 86, 240, 254; supplies, 59
Foreign exchange, 14, 69, 82, 84, 92, 215, 243

Garcia Castillon, Alfonso, 123, 124
GATT, 237
Germany, 67
Golondrinas, 148, 149, 166, 167
Grain, 175; imports, 15, 216; market, 101, 108; production, 16, 17, 180
Great Depression, 77
Green Revolution, 11, 43, 57, 58, 64–67, 73, 83, 87, 99, 101, 115, 130, 177, 179, 201
Guanajuato, State of, 174, 188, 189

Hacendados, 8, 16, 27, 18 ff., 35, 55, 70, 74, 114, 138, 140–43, 191, 203; power, 33, 140; repressive means, 140
Hacienda, 6, 7, 8, 9, 16, 26, 27, 28 ff., 37, 38, 40, 43, 55, 74, 114–16, 125, 136–42, 160

Related Books from Bergin & Garvey

TRANSNATIONALS & THE THIRD WORLD: The Struggle for
  Culture
Armand Mattelart
ISBN 0-89789-030-2

SPIRITUALIST HEALERS IN MEXICO: Successes & Failures of
  Alternative Therapeutics
Kaja Finkler

THE STRUGGLE FOR RURAL MEXICO
Gustavo Esteva
ISBN 0-89879-025-6

WOMEN'S WORK: Development & the Division of Labor by Sex
Eleanor Leacock & Helen I. Safa & Contributors
ISBN 0-89789-053-3 (cl.)
      0-89789-036-1 (pap.)

DEVELOPMENT & DECLINE: The Evolution of Sociopolitical Organization
Henry J. M. Claessen, M. Estellie Smith, Pieter van de Velde & Contributors

POLITICAL ANTHROPOLOGY: An Introduction
Ted C. Lewellen
ISBN 0-89789-028-0 (cl.)
      0-89789-029-9 (pap.)

WOMEN AND COLONIZATION: Anthropological Perspectives
Mona Etienne & Eleanor Leacock